THE BATTLE OF VERDUN

THE BATTLE OF VERDUN

ALAN AXELROD

Guilford, Connecticut

An imprint of Rowman & Littlefield

Distributed by NATIONAL BOOK NETWORK

British Library Cataloguing in Publication Information Available

Library of Congress Cataloging-in-Publication Data

Names: Axelrod, Alan, 1952-
Title: The Battle of Verdun / Alan Axelrod.
Description: Guilford, Connecticut : Lyons Press, 2016. | Includes
  bibliographical references and index.
Identifiers: LCCN 2015050745 (print) | LCCN 2015050991 (ebook) | ISBN
  9781493018604 (hardback) | ISBN 9781493022106 (ebook) | ISBN 9781493022106
  (e-book)
Subjects: LCSH: Verdun, Battle of, Verdun, France, 1916.
Classification: LCC D545.V3 A94 2016 (print) | LCC D545.V3 (ebook) | DDC
  940.4/272--dc23
LC record available at http://lccn.loc.gov/2015050745

CONTENTS

PROLOGUE

THE PRESENCE OF VERDUN

The Battle of Verdun was fought a hundred years before this book was published. Most histories of World War I place its beginning at February 21, 1916, and its end at December 20 of that year, making it a battle one day shy of ten months, the longest of the war. Some recent historians suggest that it was even longer or, at least, that the fighting at Verdun was nearly continuous from August 1914 to the armistice of November 11, 1918—virtually the entire span of World War I.

In terms of body count, it was not the single deadliest battle of the war. That would be the Battle of the Somme, with more than 1.2 million casualties. Estimates of casualties at Verdun vary widely, but they probably were somewhat less than a million. Per square yard, however, no battlefield in history had a higher density of death than Verdun. It is a grotesque statistic, but it is the product of the sheer volume of high-explosive artillery ordnance dropped on the place—an estimated ton of explosive shells (about 150 individual shells) per square yard. In a very real sense, this means that not only did the battle outlast its ten-month historical duration, it exceeded the duration of the entire war. Today, despite many decades of work by ordnance disposal experts, the land in the vicinity of Verdun is still thickly sown with unexploded shells, some of which are packed with high explosives and others with chemical agents, including "poison gas." In 1918, following the armistice, sixteen million acres of France were cordoned off, including two million acres in and around Verdun, because of the presence of unexploded ordnance. In 2009, the French Interior Ministry estimated that at least twelve million unexploded shells—out of more than sixty million shells fired—still lie in the forested land rising above the city of Verdun.[1] Every few years, unlucky tourists and hapless souvenir hunters are blown up.

Verdun remains present, both as an unexpected hazard and as a grim presence in European consciousness. To most Americans, however, Verdun seems as remote as much of the rest of World War I. Indeed, the 1916 battle took place before the United States declared war on the Central Powers (Germany, Austria-Hungary, Ottoman Empire, and Bulgaria) in April 1917. Asked who won the battle, France or Germany, a reasonably dedicated history buff of any nationality would likely answer "France," which lost more men than Germany, but nevertheless forced the German army out of the Verdun sector.

Immediately after the armistice was signed in November 1918, an American journalist asked Paul von Hindenburg who won the war. The chief of the German General Staff answered, "The American infantry"—or, more precisely, "the American infantry in the Argonne."[2]

The two major American contributions to the Allied victory in World War I were the Saint-Mihiel Offensive (September 12–15, 1918) and the Meuse-Argonne Offensive (September 26–November 11, 1918). It is reasonable to argue that both of these actions were either continuations of the Battle of Verdun or two additional Battles of Verdun, the first fought on the right (east) bank of the River Meuse, the second on the left (west) bank. Strategically, the 1916 Battle of Verdun and the two 1918 offensives were fought on the same territory. As Hindenburg saw it, this larger Battle of Verdun was won neither by Germany nor France but by the United States, which brought the very war to its conclusion on this ground on November 11, 1918.

A hundred years old, the Battle of Verdun is still present—in live shells, in human memory, in the history of warfare fought on an industrial scale that may well prefigure thermonuclear Armageddon, and as part of not only the European identity but also, more surprisingly though no less true, the American identity.

Americans have a right to be proud of what their ancestral countrymen achieved at Verdun in what history labels the Saint-Mihiel and Meuse-Argonne Offensives. The French have a right to be proud that they persevered and prevailed in the horrific 1916 battle by proving capable of driving the Germans from a part of their soil. Yet that French victory has become as proverbial an example of a pyrrhic victory as those grim triumphs of King Pyrrhus himself at Heraclea in 280 BC and Asculum in 279 BC. To a well-wisher who congratulated him on his victory over the Romans, the king of Epirus replied that "one other such victory would utterly undo him."[3] By 1916, the French as well as the British had known both defeat and pyrrhic victory in the Great War. No battle in that war had more tragic cost for so little gain. Although the Germans had been pushed back, they still occupied a large portion of France, and the war would continue for two more unthinkable years. And while the Americans unquestionably turned the tide in the Allies' favor, American losses were heavy—53,402 combat deaths in less than nine months of active fighting—and the achievement was far short of what President Woodrow Wilson had predicted: a war to end all wars. Perhaps, in the end, the greatest value in the continued presence of the Battle of Verdun is as a stark assessment of the truest calculus of war, which typically ranges not from defeat to triumph but from annihilation to pyrrhic victory.

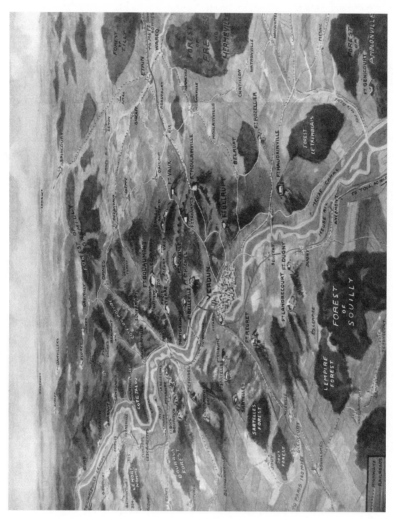

Drawn in 1916, at the time of the Battle of Verdun, this relief map provides a clear introduction to the complex hills, forests, villages, and forts that made up this sector. WIKIMEDIA

CHAPTER I

Grand Illusion

*The defense of Verdun has entered into the heart and soul of France. . . .
This battle for Verdun was a battle for moral values, fought over a
town which had acquired a wholly fictitious value in the minds of the
German and the French people alike, in the minds of the observers the
world over. Germany fought to break the spirit of France. . . . She has
not broken, but reinvigorated, the spirit of France. This, I think, is the
true meaning of the Battle of Verdun.*
                                                                    —FRANK H. SIMONDS,
               "THE BATTLE FOR VERDUN AS FRANCE SAW IT," 1916[1]

*We are all conditioned to look for Waterloo or Gettysburg or Hastings.
Faced with a bewilderingly complex battle that began in geographical obscurity, ended in confusion, and did not in any way resolve the
struggle between France and Germany, it is only natural to try to find
something there to give it meaning, and thus the origins of a horrific
struggle with millions of dead, all to no purpose whatsoever.*
               —JOHN MOSIER, *VERDUN: THE LOST HISTORY OF THE MOST
                IMPORTANT BATTLE OF WORLD WAR I, 1914–1918,* 2013[2]

NO ONE KNOWS EXACTLY HOW MANY SOLDIERS WERE KILLED IN THE
Battle of Verdun. The official French war history puts French losses at
377,321, including 162,308 killed. In his history of the war, *The World
Crisis*, Winston Churchill estimates French losses, killed and wounded,
at 469,000. Others arrived at a figure of 542,000, with 162,000 killed. The
French official history pegs Germany's losses at 336,831, including 71,504

1

killed and 17,387 taken prisoner. Churchill reckons 373,000, and other authorities put the figure at 434,000.[3] (In terms of material expended, figures may be more exact. U.S. Army historians estimate that the Germans and French fired nearly thirty million artillery rounds within the 10-by-10-mile boundary of the central battlefield.[4] This may be a global record.)

Nor is there universal agreement on when the Battle of Verdun started and ended. February 21 to December 20, 1916, is widely accepted, but historians such as John Mosier point out that there was sporadic and sometimes intense fighting on the Verdun front from August 1914—the very first month of major combat in the war—to nearly the end of September 1918, when the First U.S. Army launched the Meuse-Argonne Offensive, which was centered on Verdun. Little more than a month and a half after this Verdun end date, on November 11, 1918, the war would end in an armistice.[5]

Deciding when the battle began and ended is more a matter of historical convenience than flesh and blood. As for losses, perhaps it is more meaningful to report that, per square yard, the Verdun battlefield was marked by the highest density of dead human beings the world has ever known.[6]

That, in fact, is also the single outcome of the battle on which everyone agrees. As for the meaning of the battle, its significance, and its impact on the course of the war, interpretations range from that of historian Frank H. Simonds, who wrote in 1916 that Verdun was a "moral" victory, entering "into the heart and soul of France," reinvigorating the nation's spirit, to that of John Mosier, who described it in 2013 as "a bewilderingly complex battle that began in geographical obscurity, ended in confusion, and did not in any way resolve the struggle between France and Germany."[7]

Embalmed in the more neutral language of sober military history, Verdun can be called a French victory in that the Germans failed to break through to Paris or to recover the territory of their initial advance of August 1914, provided the noun *victory* is modified with the adjective *pyrrhic*, since, by all calculations, varied as they are, French losses exceeded German both in number and in ratio to the strength of the forces deployed. The French casualty rate was roughly 40.6 percent; the German, 30.5 percent. Both figures are catastrophic, but not equally so.

In this, Verdun can be said to represent the results of World War I as a whole. Military losses among the victorious Allies totaled 22,477,500 killed, wounded, and missing, whereas the defeated Central Powers (of which Germany was the greatest) totaled 16,403,000. These losses represented a casualty rate of 52 percent for the Allies and 65 percent for the Central Powers. Although the casualty rate was higher for the Central Powers, it was nevertheless staggering for the Allies as well. Moreover, while the Allies dictated a massively punitive peace in the 1919 Treaty of Versailles and related agreements, France, as the primary battlefield of the Western Front, suffered the greatest devastation, none of the Central Powers remotely lived up to the terms of reparation and demilitarization—under Adolf Hitler, Germany contemptuously abrogated them—and what U.S. president Woodrow Wilson called the "war to end all wars" ultimately created nothing more than an uneasy European truce lasting twenty years, give or take, and one marked by a civil war that was also a larger proxy war in Spain.

To call the entire war, like the Battle of Verdun, even a pyrrhic victory for the Allies is to be generous to the achievements of the Allies. The overwhelming impression of Western Front combat, almost all of it static, mostly stalemated trench warfare, is of slaughter on both sides. Verdun was an example of this slaughter in a particularly concentrated form. Politicians and military men in both France and Germany, however, preferred the term *attrition* to *slaughter*. This was not out of an inclination toward euphemism for the sake of euphemism, but because "attrition" is appropriate to professional and official discussions of strategy and doctrine whereas "slaughter" would be, to say the least, unseemly. In fairness, "attrition" also happens to be the more accurate word in this instance, at least in expressing the intentions of politicians and military planners. In a military context, *attrition* is the process of wearing down an enemy force by sustained action. In a more general context, *attrition* is synonymous with *abrasion* and describes a wearing away by rubbing or friction. Anyone who has used sandpaper to smooth or shape a piece of wood has exercised attrition and must also be aware that not only does the surface of the wood wear away, so does the grit of the sandpaper. Implicit in the term *attrition* is the understanding that both the object rubbed and the

3

instrument or material used to rub it will suffer attrition. The softer object will suffer more than the harder instrument or material. This same understanding is embodied in the military use of the term. Commanders who employ a strategy of attrition must expect their own forces to be worn away to some degree. The art of strategy and tactics is to ensure that your forces are stronger—harder, more durable—than those of your enemy. In World War I—and nowhere more than at Verdun—*both* sides had the same idea. Both sides were fighting a war of attrition, and both sides believed they were the more durable.

Neither side had started out with the intention of prosecuting a war of attrition. The fight everyone had planned for was to have been short, limited, and sharply offensive, not long, engulfing, and brutally defensive. Knockout attack, not attrition, was the featured dish on Europe's martial menu for 1914. Political leaders believed that economic necessity would make any *modern* war brief. The feudal realms of the past might have been capable of dedicating their economies to prolonged warfare, but modern industrial nations would not and could not finance a long war.

Military planners in Germany and France agreed. Weapons, they pointed out, were more efficient than ever: explosives more powerful, machine guns more lethally productive than single-shot arms, modern artillery now capable of spectacular velocity and accuracy. Many other entirely new weapons were on the horizon at the outbreak of war, including the combat airplane, poison gas, the flamethrower, and the tank. If economics dictated short wars, the planners believed that, as modern factories enabled mass production, modern weapons drove mass destruction, making it possible, even imperative, to kill more people faster than ever before.

Since the end of the brief, violent, and decisive Franco-Prussian War of 1870–1871, which had created the empire of Kaiser Wilhelm I and ended that of Napoleon III, generals in both combatant countries planned for the next, brief, violently decisive war. Count Alfred von Schlieffen, chief of the German General Staff, invoked the economic argument. "A strategy of attrition will not do, if the maintenance of [a field force of] millions costs billions."[8] His plan, universally known by his name, relied first and foremost on offense, but, unlike France's war plan, Plan XVII, it also included strong defensive components (of which many post–World War I military historians were long unaware).[9] Beginning in 1901, Schlieffen devised and revised versions of a war plan for the next anticipated Franco-German conflict. Because of the existing Franco-Russian alliance, he believed that Germany would have to fight on two fronts, against the French to the west and the Russians to the east. He reasoned that France, which had been building a formidable modern army since its 1870–1871 humiliation, was a more immediate tactical threat than Russia because it could mobilize far more quickly and effectively. Yes, the Russians had a vast pool of manpower on which to draw—its allies comforted themselves with references to "the Russian steamroller"—but its vast army was poorly equipped and poorly led. Schlieffen estimated it would take Russia a minimum of six weeks to mobilize effectively.

While the Schlieffen Plan was a plan of deployment—the positioning of forces in preparation for war—rather than what historians often mistakenly treat it as, an operational plan, a blueprint for movement—it created a scenario for a swift and overwhelming offensive attack against France on the Western Front and a simultaneous defensive holding action against Russia on the Eastern Front. Invading France with great force and at lightning speed would not only avoid an impossibly costly war of attrition (millions costing billions), it would neutralize the enemy on the Western Front, so that Germany could quickly shift all forces to the east for an offensive war against Russia. The key was to create the conditions that would knock France out of the war before Russia could fully and effectively mobilize. Victory over France had to be achieved within six weeks.

In contrast to the Schlieffen Plan, a long series of carefully calculated and recalculated iterations that were made beginning in 1901, the French General Staff drew up its "scheme of mobilization and concentration," Plan XVII, rapidly, in 1913. It was, however, driven by an objective that had been an obsessive French priority since the defeat of 1871, namely the recovery of territory lost to the Germans in Alsace and Lorraine. The plan was for a swift invasion of Alsace-Lorraine on either side of the

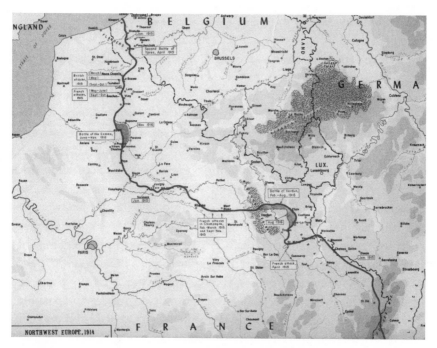

The Western Front as it appeared from January 1915 to December 1916, with the major battles indicated. UNITED STATES MILITARY ACADEMY

Metz-Thionville fortresses, which the Germans had occupied since 1871. So single-minded was the focus on this invasion that, when adopted, Plan XVII completely ignored the potential of a German advance through neutral Belgium. Only at the last minute, with the nations on the verge of combat, was Plan XVII altered to deploy troops intended to check such an advance.

Plan XVII was stark in its simplicity and relied more heavily on a combination of military and cultural mythology than sound strategy. The humiliation of 1870–1871 spurred development in France of a system of defensive fortifications along its redrawn frontier with Germany, in which Verdun was a major strongpoint. It was a logical choice, since the Latin origin of its name, *Verodunum*, means "strong fort," and it had been fortified first by the Gauls in their conflict against the forces of Rome during 58–50 BC. Yet, even as France developed its defenses—as we examine in more detail in chapter 3—French politicians as well as French generals began increasingly to scorn and abandon defensive thinking, which many blamed for the debacle of the Franco-Prussian War. By the time Plan XVII was promulgated, contempt for defense was rampant, displaced by what Colonel Louis Loyzeau de Grandmaison, who led the operations section of the French General Staff (and whom we meet at greater length in chapter 3), called the doctrine of *L'attaque à outrance*, literally, "attack to excess." [10] Not only was all-out attack better military doctrine, advocates argued, it was suited, almost mystically matched, to the French temperament, the celebrated spirit of *furia francese*: French fury.

Some military thinkers of 1913 specifically cited Georges Jacques Danton, the plump but fiery early hero of the French Revolution, who rallied earlier defenders of Verdun, those who sought to arrest a Prussian assault against the fortress town on August 20, 1792, during the War of the First Coalition. "*Il nous faut de l'audace, encore de l'audace, toujours de l'audace!*" Danton exhorted: "We must dare, dare again, always dare!" Others, however, turned to a contemporary French philosopher, Henri Bergson, who (among many other concepts) sought to define a life force or "vital impetus" he called *élan vital*. Bergson intended this concept to apply to all humanity—really, to life itself—but French patriots, politicians, and military theorists appropriated élan vital as a peculiarly Gallic dynamism, a physical-spiritual force that would prove irresistible on the field of battle. Many French commanders were persuaded that a lightning charge into German-held French territory would totally disrupt German war plans, sending the usurpers of 1870–1871 scurrying back to their homeland.

The champions of élan vital and "attack to excess" were apparently undiscouraged and unabashed by the lessons implicit in the history they cited. The phrase furia francese was associated with the Battle of Pavia, February 24, 1525, a catastrophic defeat in which 15,000 of the 23,500 troops the kingdom of France deployed against 23,000 soldiers of Spain and the Holy Roman Empire were killed, wounded, or captured. As for Danton's exhortation to "dare," it failed to prevent the Prussians from capturing Verdun in 1792. More to the point, Plan XVII was based on a gross underestimate of German troop strength—an error that would

Henri Bergson, who would be awarded the Nobel Prize in Literature in 1927, was the premier French philosopher of the late nineteenth and early twentieth centuries. His concept of *élan vital* ("vital force"), presented in his 1907 book *Creative Evolution*, became the unlikely core of ultrapatriotic French myths of invincibility in war and was used at Verdun to support such articles of military doctrine as *attaque à outrance* ("attack to excess"), which cost many French lives. WIKIMEDIA

persist throughout the war generally and during the Battle of Verdun in particular. Because French generals had nothing but contempt for their own conscripted reserve forces, they assumed that, when war came, Germany would mobilize only its first-line troops, not its reserves. Accordingly, French commanders planned to mobilize only *their* own first-line forces. It was a tragic miscalculation and meant that, from the beginning, the French would find themselves outnumbered and overwhelmed.

Driven by cultural mythology, Plan XVII lacked intellectual rigor and tactical imagination. It contemplated essentially a direct frontal assault, a bold strategy intended to allow full expression of the army's élan vital, but in fact the simplest kind of attack to defeat. The thinking that grew out of the Schlieffen Plan, in contrast, did not prescribe a frontal attack, east to west, but called for a "great wheel," a wide, turning movement counterclockwise, beginning in a *northwestward* direction, through Flanders Plain, northeast of French territory, and then downward into France from the north. Five German armies were to make this wheeling, scythe-like thrust across a huge swath of France, from the Alsace-Lorraine all the way west, nearly to the English Channel. "When you march into France, let the last man on the right brush the Channel with his sleeve," Schlieffen himself reportedly quipped.[11]

In a pattern that anticipated on a larger scale the much-praised "Hail Mary" assault of U.S.-led coalition tanks and mobile infantry against the main body of Saddam Hussein's army during the Persian Gulf War of 1990–1991, Germany's great wheel unleashed in August 1914 was meant to outflank the French army, hitting it where it was most vulnerable, mainly from the rear. Moreover, the maneuver would ensure that all the fighting was done in France, not in German territory, and would therefore destroy *French* infrastructure and menace *French* civilians. With the battle brought deep into France, French army forces would have no choice but to turn away from the German frontier. Plan XVII would not merely be defeated, it would be rendered irrelevant, élan vital and all.

Both Plan XVII and the Schlieffen Plan were prescriptions for a short, sharp, decisive war based on attack. The French plan lacked the quality of thought that had gone into the German plan, but even more important, whereas Plan XVII made no provision for defense, a defensive exigency—if not intention—was the very essence of the German strategy. By penetrating deeply and widely into French territory, the Schlieffen approach gave the Germans room to make a fighting retreat, if necessary, doing so, however, on French territory rather than into the Fatherland.

No provision for defense? Plan XVII was founded on even more destructive French military delusions. At its core was a willed and willful ignorance. "In the offensive," de Grandmaison declaimed, "imprudence is the best of assurances. . . . Let us go even to excess, and that perhaps will not be far enough." He explained that "For the attack only two things are necessary: to know where the enemy is and to decide what to do. What the enemy intends to do is of no consequence."[12] In 1909, acting in accordance with the de Grandmaison doctrine, the General Staff's liaison to the Budget Commission of the Chamber of Deputies responded to one deputy's incisive question about the army's unexpressed need to fund heavy artillery purchases with a contemptuous dismissal. "You talk to us of heavy artillery," the officer sniffed. "Thank God, we have none. The strength of the French Army is in the lightness of its guns." And as for upgrading to the modern machine guns, the inspector general of infantry rejected the idea outright, pointing out that the modern machine gun was too complicated for troops to handle, was nothing more than a ploy to impress journalists, and "would not make the slightest difference to anything."[13] In the years since 1914–1918, of course, both heavy artillery and the machine gun figure in any discussion of World War I as the conflict's most iconic—nearly sovereign—weapons.

From the appearance of Verdun and the surrounding area as they existed in 1914, no one would guess that French military doctrine had turned away from defensive considerations. Fortifications loomed everywhere across the landscape, some of them huge and impressive. These were the legacy of defeat in the war with Prussia. The takeaway lesson of that conflict seemed obvious to French military planners at the time. Means had to be found to slow an invasion while the armies were being mustered and positioned for action. No one believed that forts and fortifications could keep an invader out, but they could keep him at bay long enough

This French gun battery at the Verdun front was overrun by a German attack. The French could ill afford to lose their scarce artillery. WIKIMEDIA

to prepare an effective destructive response. And so Raymond Adolphe Séré de Rivières, a distinguished military engineer, was appointed in 1873 to a specially convened Committee of Defense to determine how and where to construct the necessary fortifications. Rivières laid out a system that ran from Dunkirk on the English Channel to Nice on the Riviera. His objective was to interdict all the principal avenues of invasion, to make such an invasion as costly as possible, and to delay penetration into the French interior long enough to mount a credible response. From the 1870s to the outbreak of World War I, France built into this system 504 forts supplemented by 278 permanent artillery emplacements. Thirty-four of these forts were in and around Verdun, guarding the vulnerable "gateway" of the Meuse River.

In chapter 4 and elsewhere, we examine and describe the Verdun fortifications in more detail. For now, it is important only to understand that they were laid out so as to create fields of interlocking fire, each fort positioned to aid in the defense of its nearest neighbors, thereby creating a cordon of artillery fire that would take a heavy toll on any invader. The

This example of the fabled "French 75," the premier field gun of World War I, was part of the *Batterie d'honneur de l'artillerie française*, which participated in the inauguration of French president François Hollande on May 15, 2012. WIKIMEDIA

principal function of a modern fort is to shelter guns and to defend external artillery emplacements. In this arrangement, the heavier the artillery, the better. Before the outbreak of the war, the French, however, had renounced the heaviest artillery. Reliance was placed on the 75-mm field gun, the justly celebrated "French 75."

Thanks to its highly advanced breech and recoil mechanisms, the French 75 was capable of very rapid and very accurate fire, but it was primarily a field weapon, with limited range, and its light ammunition was useless against hardened enemy positions. The Verdun fortresses were equipped with 75s that were housed beneath heavy steel carapaces in retractable turrets. Some forts also had significantly heavier 155-mm guns, although many of these were antiquated to the point of obsolescence. In and around Verdun on the eve of the main battle, the French claimed to have 828 pieces of artillery, but more than half of these—468 weapons—were nineteenth-century field guns incapable of an angle of fire sufficiently high to be of use over a practical range. Just 255 of the cannon at Verdun were modern 75s; of the 155-mm weapons, only 49 were equipped with modern recoil mechanisms that gave them sufficient accuracy.[14]

By way of comparison, Joffre's German counterpart, General Erich von Falkenhayn, had more than 1,220 pieces at his disposal on the Verdun front by February 1916. These included 306 modern field weapons and 542 heavy pieces, in addition to 151 Minenwerfers—mine throwers—which were mortars used against fortifications and, later, against tanks. The German heavy artillery was far heavier than anything the French possessed—or, indeed, thought they needed. The biggest were those of the "Big Bertha" class—in German, *Dicke* ("Fat") *Bertha*—gargantuan 420-mm siege howitzers. Next in size were long-barreled 15-inch (380-mm) naval guns adapted for land artillery use. Then came 305-mm mortars and more transportable 210-mm field pieces, in addition to those of 150 and 130 mm—the latter nicknamed "whizz bangs" by the Allied troops against whom they were directed. These were antipersonnel artillery pieces that fired shells at high velocity but in a flat trajectory intended to mow down troops—*whizz bang!*—without giving them time to duck.[15] Formidable appearances notwithstanding, therefore, the French were massively outgunned at Verdun. And, shortly before the main battle, the disparity would get even worse.

—

"Verdun, c'est la boulevard moral de la France," Marshal Henri Philippe Pétain wrote in his 1929 first-person history, *La Bataille de Verdun*: "Verdun is the moral boulevard of France." He meant this symbolically, in much the way that American historian Frank Simonds intended when he wrote in 1916 that Verdun had become the "heart and soul of France." Yet Pétain also wrote the literal, factual truth. The valley the fortress system of Verdun commanded—or *should* have commanded—was a high road into the French interior. Since the times of Caesar and then of Charlemagne, and ever since, Verdun had been the "strong fort" of France.

Well, "ever since" *until* Grandmaison and his followers on the General Staff directed their scorn against the means, methods, and ethos of defense. In any case, Verdun *was* something of a military backwater, a "quiet sector," from October 1914 until February 1916, the eve of the main battle. Many attributed the absence of concentrated action to what had happened here early in September 1914, during the First Battle of the Marne.

Nobody knew it at the time, but that battle—September 5–12, 1914—marked the beginning of the end for any hope that the war would be short and decisive. During most of August, the German army advanced through southern Belgium—occupying Liège on August 7 despite the town's vaunted fortification, which had been deemed impregnable—and thence, at various points, through the French frontiers, defeating a major French counteroffensive at the Battle of Lorraine (August 14–25), and forcing the French into what came to be called the Great Retreat (August 24–September 5). The five principal German armies made their great Schlieffen wheel deep into France, with General Alexander von Kluck's First Army advancing in an arc nearly tangent with the English Channel, just as Schlieffen had envisioned. Together with General Karl von Bülow's Second Army to his left, Kluck approached Paris—from either side of the capital, Kluck from the northeast and Bülow from the northwest.

As August 1914 came to a close, it appeared indeed that this would be a short war. Paris would surely fall, France would surely ask for terms, and millions would not cost Germany billions.

In the meantime, far to the east, the Fifth German Army, under Crown Prince Wilhelm, was in the process of encircling Verdun, held by elements of the French Third Army under General Maurice Sarrail—fifty-eight years old at the time but looking much older. Focused on the crisis to the west and now centered on Paris in particular, General Joseph Joffre, commander-in-chief of French forces on the Western Front—you will meet him in chapter 3—was worried that Verdun would suffer the fate that had befallen the fortress at Metz during the Franco-Prussian War.

Cut off by the Prussians in 1870, an entire army under François Achille Bazaine was neutralized, effectively locked up in its own fortified

General Joseph "Papa" Joffre. The Battle of Verdun finished him as generalissimo of French forces. WIKIMEDIA

town, useless, and impotent. If the German crown prince took Verdun, the Third French Army, Joffre feared, would suffer the same fate. He therefore ordered General Sarrail to abandon Verdun—this French boulevard both moral and literal. A free-thinking Freemason and a prominent Dreyfusard—champion of Captain Alfred Dreyfus, an Alsatian artillery officer, a Jew, falsely accused of treason by French high command in 1894—Sarrail did not think twice about simply ignoring the order. He led a stubborn, vigorous, and ultimately successful defense against the crown prince, thereby retaining Verdun as a pivot around which the French Third and Fifth Armies, the entire left wing of the army of France, was able to swing in order to support the "miracle" that was about to take place along the Marne.

For it seemed that only a miracle could save Paris from Kluck and Bülow. But the two German generals, seeing an opportunity to envelop the left flank of the retreating French armies, took their eyes off Paris and instead suddenly veered southeast, away from the French capital. For this, generations of historians have heaped scorn upon both German commanders, but the move actually made sense. After all, why take a city when you can kill an army? Nevertheless, the action did expose the right flanks of both the German First and Second Armies. On September 3, even the slow-moving, often obtuse Joffre grasped the significance of the developing situation and coordinated an attack on Kluck and Bülow with his own Sixth Army and the British Expeditionary Force (BEF) on September 6. Simultaneously, he ordered the French First through Fourth Armies, which were on the eastern frontier, to do battle against the German Fifth, Sixth, and Seventh Armies between Verdun and Toul while also spoiling an attempted envelopment of the northeastern fortress town of Nancy. None of this action in the east would have been possible had Sarrail heeded the order to abandon Verdun. Without his checking the three German armies in eastern France, the First Battle of the Marne would have been doomed, since those armies would have rushed to the aid of Kluck and Bülow.

The battle saved Paris and reprieved France, while dooming all combatants to the long war, the war of attrition, they did not want and had not expected. After the First Battle of the Marne, Verdun was also reprieved.

That is, it was not abandoned—not entirely, anyway—but absolutely no attempt was made to reinforce it or to improve its armaments, despite having just proved its utility in the "Miracle on the Marne." That it became a "quiet sector" seemed to vindicate the decision of French high command to more or less disown it. Indeed, the adherents of Grandmaison renewed their disdain for and condemnation of fortifications in general. Willfully ignoring the lesson Sarrail had provided by holding Verdun, the Grandmaison contingent insisted that modern heavy artillery rendered all fortifications obsolete—even though they themselves renounced heavy artillery. They called fortifications nothing more than "shell traps," targets marked for death and destruction. Even worse, their very existence vitiated the French spirit of bold offensive, of "L'attaque à outrance."

The First Battle of the Marne quickly began to transform the Western Front from a theater of advance, retreat, and maneuver into one of static trench warfare. To both sides, this meant shifting from a doctrine of attack and conquest to one of relentless attrition. Everywhere soldiers were digging in, hunkering down in trenches rather than charging against the enemy à outrance. Refusing to accept the full significance of this new reality, the acolytes of Grandmaison insisted that élan vital was still viable in a trench, but was impossible to exercise within the ferroconcrete walls and ceilings of a fortress. They pointed back to 1870–1871 and the ignominious defeat of Bazaine and Marshal Patrice de MacMahon, each holed up in their vaunted fortresses at Metz and Sedan, respectively. Saved by the "Miracle on the Marne," French high command, from Joffre on down, rushed to mount offensives in the hope of breaking through the rapidly congealing stalemate of trench warfare to drive back the Germans. Arguably, they possessed the manpower to do this, but—unsurprisingly—they lacked the artillery. Their answer to this deficiency was to strip the Verdun forts of all artillery pieces that were not permanently emplaced within concrete and steel. In July 1915, the order was given to Sarrail's superior, General Auguste Dubail, the magnificently mustachioed commander of France's army group of the east, which included the Verdun sector. He, in turn, commanded General Michel Henri Marie Coutanceau, who bore the title of governor of Verdun, to begin the work of transferring the guns. Dubail, who had been captured by the Germans at Metz in 1870, had little affection for fortifications and even less patience with what he deemed as insubordination. Unlike Sarrail in 1914, Coutanceau did not ignore his orders; however, he did protest the neutering of the largest fortification complex in France, the citadel that controlled access to one of the nation's principal points of entry. In response, Dubail summarily relieved him of command and installed in his place Frédéric-Georges Herr, painfully thin, absurdly monocled, sixty years old, and comfortably married to automobile heiress Anne Peugeot.

Herr made no objection when Dubail, acting under direct orders from Joffre himself, not only ordered virtually every gun that could be removed to be removed but also issued a general order that began: "Strongholds, destined to be invested, have no longer a rôle to play." On the strategic and doctrinal balance sheet, the new view summarily moved fortifications from the "asset" to the "liability" column. Forts were no longer viewed as vital means of defense but as emplacements "destined"—*inevitably doomed*—to be "invested," that is to be surrounded by the enemy such that their garrisons were sealed in, cut off and useless. In this view, what had happened in the Franco-Prussian War forty-five years earlier was "destined" to happen again. For this reason, Joffre (through Dubail) ordered that Verdun "must *under no circumstances* be defended for itself."[16] Where Verdun was concerned, the level of passivity among French high command and its field minions had reached a level that can only be described as sublime.

It took time to move forty-three heavy guns (along with 128,000 rounds of ammunition) and eleven field batteries (about 66 guns, mostly 75s), but by October 1915, Verdun—a "strong fort" since the days of Roman Gaul—was all but naked. Without guns to man, there was no need for substantial garrisons to occupy the Verdun forts. In August 1915, therefore, these were reduced, and Herr was ordered to redeploy the Verdun troops to the left bank of the River Meuse. That is, he was directed to take forces out of their fortresses and put them in *trenches* freshly dug *behind* those fortresses—such was high command's contempt for concrete and steel. Following this move out of the fortress structures, Joffre began withdrawing some of these troops from the trenches of what was now called the Fortified Region of Verdun. He wanted to use them in the offensive he planned for the Champagne.

With this understanding of the French military's renunciation of Verdun at the end of 1915, the reason historian Frank Simonds strained to spin positive and profound meaning out of the just-ended main Battle of Verdun a year later becomes clear. High command had forsaken Verdun in 1915, declaring that it, like other "strongholds destined to be invested," no longer had a role to play in modern war. Yet when Verdun was attacked in February 1916, the "defense of Verdun" suddenly "entered into the heart and soul of France"! Presumably recalling the assessment and attitude of the year before, Simonds felt obliged to note that Verdun "had acquired a *wholly fictitious value* in the minds of the German and the French people alike" (emphasis added), yet had also assumed a paramount importance embodying the very "spirit of France." [17]

If French high command denied or willfully forgot the importance of Verdun, Chief of the German General Staff Erich von Falkenhayn took pains in his 1919 memoir to point out that *he* had done no such thing.[18]

At the war's end, it was undeniable that Germany had surrendered. Whether or not this meant that the Allies had triumphed was debatable, however, given the weight of so many casualties. Still, as the nominal victors, France and the others opposed to the Central Powers not only dictated the terms of peace, they also created the context of its history. In the Allied version, victory in the war was a triumph of democracy over autocracy, and it was due, in no small part, to the French defiance of Germany at Verdun, the "heart and soul" of France and its moral boulevard.

On the German side, Falkenhayn became just one of the many scapegoats for the Central Power's humiliation at Versailles. He was widely accused of having squandered his forces piecemeal in "penny-packet" attacks, of exercising an excess of caution that ensured the futility of his troops' sacrifices, and of misspending German superiority of artillery. Why had he been unable to force a breakthrough? In his postwar memoir and elsewhere, Falkenhayn argued that his objective had never been to force a breakthrough at Verdun. What he intended to do all along at Verdun, he

Erich von Falkenhayn, controversial architect of the German assault on Verdun. It would end his reign as the most powerful man in the German army. WIKIMEDIA

claimed, was to wage a terrible campaign of attrition against the French army, to—in a phrase that became infamous after the war—"bleed France white." The phrase was a widely circulated translation. Falkenhayn himself called what he intended to bring about at Verdun an *Ausblutung*, a fatal "bleeding out" of France. In both his 1919 memoir and an article on the war he published in a military magazine[19] the same year, Falkenhayn quoted a strategic memorandum he claimed to have sent to Kaiser

Wilhelm II in December 1915. It has been known as the "Christmas Memorandum" ever since:

France has been weakened militarily and economically—almost to the limit of what it can stand—through the ongoing loss of coal fields in the northwest of the country. Russia's army has not yet been fully defeated, but its offensive ability has been so broken that it will not be able to regain anything like its old strength. Serbia's army can be considered destroyed. Italy has without a doubt recognized that it cannot count on its appetite for spoils being satisfied in the near future and would therefore probably be happy to escape from this adventure in any honorable way possible.

. . . There is only one matter—the most important one—that cannot be passed over. That is the incredible pressure that England still exerts on its allies. . . . Thus it is all the more important that all the means suitable for harming England in what is properly its own territory are simultaneously brought to ruthless application. These means are submarine warfare and laying the groundwork for a political and economic alliance not only between Germany and its allies, but also between Germany and all those states that are not yet fully constrained within England's sphere of influence. The formation of this alliance is not the topic of this exposition. Solving this task lies solely with the political leadership.

Submarine warfare, however, is a tool of war, just like any other tool. Those in charge of leading the war effort cannot avoid taking a position on this. . . .

An advance against Moscow would lead us nowhere. We do not have enough strength for any of these enterprises. As a result, Russia is not a suitable object for attack. Only France remains. . . .

There are targets lying within reach behind the French section of the Western Front for which the French leadership would need to use their very last man. Should they do this, then France would bleed to death, *for there is no retreat,* regardless if we ourselves reach the target or not. *Should they not do this, and should these targets fall into our hands, then the effect on morale in France would be enormous.*

21

For these operations, which are limited in terms of territory, Germany will not be compelled to expend itself to a degree that would leave it seriously exposed on other fronts. Germany can confidently await the relief operations that can be expected at these fronts—and, indeed, hope to have enough forces available to meet the attacks with counterstrikes. For Germany can conduct the offensive quickly or slowly, break off the offensive for a period of time or strengthen the offensive, according to its objectives.

The targets being spoken of are Belfort and Verdun. What was said above applies to both of them. All the same, Verdun is to be preferred.[20] *[Emphasis added.]*

It is a remarkable statement of war aims, linking large-scale strategy directly to targeting Verdun. The Christmas Memorandum argues that, after collapse of the great German offensive of August 1914 at the First Battle of the Marne, attrition became the only viable strategy. Logically, this would dictate that Germany shift from an offensive strategy to a defensive posture *upon French soil.* Against these entrenchments, France would be obliged to beat itself to death, in the process bleeding itself white.

And it was in fact the case that, following the "Miracle on the Marne," the German army did quite well on the defensive. All of Joffre's offensives after First Marne failed—at great cost to the French army. At Verdun, Falkenhayn explained in his memoir, he did *not* want to break through, because he did *not* want the battle to end before the French had fully bled themselves out. The longer Verdun remained stalemated, the more men France would sacrifice to it. As proof of the total intentionality of his strategic thinking in this regard, Falkenhayn cited and quoted his Christmas Memorandum to the kaiser.

But to lure Joffre to pour even more resources into holding Verdun, Falkenhayn had to abandon his own defensive posture and switch to attack mode. In so doing, he created what may be the great tragic irony at the core of the battle. By attacking and thereby prompting the *French* to go on the defensive, Falkenhayn put his own army in position to bleed *itself* white. Attrition, after all, wears down both sides. As will become clear in chapter 2, the state of weapons technology during World War I gave the edge to defenders. To the degree that he now assumed the offensive, Falkenhayn relinquished his defensive advantage, thereby rendering his army as vulnerable to being worn away as the French were.

Our acceptance of all of this—of Falkenhayn's justification of his strategy at Verdun, his understanding of how it related to German strategy in the war as a whole, the necessity to prolong the battle, and the catch-22 of having to relinquish defensive advantages in order to entice France into an Ausblutung—requires us, first and foremost, to accept the Christmas Memorandum as a historical fact. For years, historians did just that, but recent scholars have suggested that the memorandum was nothing less than a postwar fiction fabricated by Falkenhayn to explain away, or at least mitigate, his defeat at Verdun.[21]

———

In *The Guns of August*, the great Barbara Tuchman created a timeless portrait of a world bumbling and stumbling into the cataclysm of the Great War.[22] Her anatomy of this complex of tragic errors was a lesson not lost on President John F. Kennedy, whose recent reading of Tuchman's masterpiece informed his thinking during the thirteen days of the 1962 Cuban Missile Crisis and may therefore have played a critical role in saving the world from the "mutually assured destruction" of a thermonuclear war.[23]

In terms of both its seeming endlessness and the numbers involved in it—and lost in it—the Battle of Verdun ranks as one of the greatest battles in history. Likewise, and for the same reasons, World War I stands among the biggest and most terrible armed struggles in history. Yet A. J. P. Taylor, among the most distinguished of British historians, did not hesitate to call Verdun "the most senseless episode in a war not distinguished for sense anywhere."[24] In this observation, Taylor likely identified the reason why the Battle of Verdun has consistently resisted all attempts by revisionist historians to reduce its significance. In combining titanic sacrifice with tragic absurdity, Verdun embodies the very essence of the "Great War." It is the conflict's exemplary battle. As the world stumbled into a "senseless" war of unprecedented desolation, so France and Germany, despite their subsequent efforts at rationalization, stumbled into the Battle of Verdun, perhaps the most desolating episode in that most

desolate of wars. Both the battle and the war of which it was a part con-
stitute some of the most chilling and horrific events in all of humankind's
magnificent and tortured history.

Perhaps from a depth of genuine belief, or from mere delusion, or
from an emotional imperative to justify, explain, and excuse, both adversaries sought to picture Verdun as a battle fought to end all battles in the
war fought to end all wars. But Verdun was ultimately a battle ended only
by the mutual exhaustion wrought by mutual attrition and fought within
a war that did not so much end as pause for two decades before another
began. The failure of Verdun in 1916 to decide World War I and of World
War I itself to persuade the world to pursue peace offers the kinds of
lessons Tuchman found in the history of August 1914, the lessons that
guided our youthful thirty-fifth president on a course avoiding and avert-
ing what might well have been the war to end all wars.

CHAPTER 2

The Death Boom

Since war was good for business, capitalists could be expected to be more committed to the war effort. The businessmen who owned factories, mines, railways and shipping companies engaged actively with war making from the start, as did bankers and investors.
—WILLIAM PHILPOTT, *WAR OF ATTRITION*, 2014[1]

THE MEN WHO DOMINATED FRENCH HIGH COMMAND ON THE VERGE and into the opening months of World War I believed the humiliation their army suffered in the Franco-Prussian War of 1870–1871 had lessons to teach them. And indeed it did. Unfortunately, the leading voices in the French military chose precisely the wrong ones to learn.

When Marshal François Achille Bazaine was defeated at the Battle of Gravelotte, the largest battle of the Franco-Prussian War, on August 18, 1870, the French forces retreated to Metz, a heavily fortified city at the confluence of the Moselle and the Seille in Lorraine, near the point where France, Germany, and Luxembourg meet. With Marshal Patrice de MacMahon, Napoleon III personally led the Army of Châlons to rescue Bazaine and, the emperor believed, to a French victory. But before Napoleon reached besieged Metz, in which Bazaine was bottled up, the Prussians under Field Marshal Helmuth von Moltke (the Elder) intercepted his forces at Beaumont on August 30. Napoleon was forced to retreat into the highly fortified city of Sedan, in the Ardennes some six miles from the Belgian border, and a battle began here on September 1 that ended with the French emperor's surrender on the morning of the next day.

The lesson France's top generals took from a defeat at once unexpected, ignominious, and total was that, in modern warfare, fortifications are, for their defenders, traps at best and tombs at worst. Defensive tactics cannot win wars, and fortifications are all about defense. Even worse, possessing fortifications discourages a mentality of attack, and attaque à outrance, attack to the uttermost, attack to excess, became the watchword of the French army as history moved toward World War I. Citing the humiliations of Metz and Sedan, French military theorists and field commanders alike renounced and reviled fortifications.

At Gravelotte, Metz, and Sedan, it was Prussian artillery—advanced products of the great Krupp foundry at Essen—that dominated the battlefield. During the Sedan battle, Kaiser Wilhelm I raised "a telescope to see the fruits of Essen's labor." He "beheld an extraordinary spectacle—mile after mile of thrashing red trousers"—the signature feature of the French infantry uniform—"beneath the long gun line of the Second Bavarian Corps and, beyond their flashing muzzles, the deep green ridges of the Ardennes." The French withered under a "blizzard of shrapnel." Just before the artillery barrage had commenced that day, at least one French field commander glimpsed the awful future and expressed his vision of the army's coming fate in the most homely of terms: "*Nous somme dans un pot de chambre,*" General Auguste Ducrot declared, "*et nous y serons emmerdés.*" (We are in the chamber pot and about to be shit on.)[2]

Whereas the French military leaders of 1914 certainly recalled the artillery of 1870, it was on the "chamber pot" of fixed fortification that they focused. They did not want to be stuck in forts ever again, helplessly waiting "to be shit on." Yes, they had witnessed the big guns wreaking havoc on fortifications and everything surrounding them, including troops. But instead of learning from this the wisdom of emulating the ways of Krupp and developing heavy artillery for France to turn against its enemies, they simply concluded that fortifications were no match for big guns firing high-explosive shells. This did not spur them to acquire big guns but to spurn fortifications in an unthinking embrace of "attack to excess."

Yet this attitude did not absolutely harden within French military thinking until late in the decade immediately preceding the outbreak of

This high-explosive shell impact seems hardly to faze the German soldiers in a front-line trench. ABSOLUTE MEDIEN

World War I. As we saw in the previous chapter, in the years *immediately* following the Franco-Prussian War, France actually doubled down on fortification, the government appointing Raymond Adolphe Séré de Rivières to lay out a whole system of forts, from Dunkirk on the English Channel to Nice on the Riviera. At this time, planners recognized three key vulnerabilities in reliance on fortification. First, fortifications built in isolation, no matter how formidable, were inherently vulnerable. Metz and Sedan were quickly transformed from citadels into traps. The strategic value of fortifications depended on their integration into a whole *system*, a continuous line of strongpoints. Reliance on a handful of fortifications geographically remote from one another was a recipe for defeat. Second, fortifications had to be built to withstand big artillery firing high-explosive munitions. This meant putting as much of their structure as possible beneath the earth and constructing whatever was exposed out of thick ferroconcrete. Finally, military planners as well as civilian governments had to understand that the purpose of a system of fortifications was to delay an enemy invasion and advance, not stop it. Delay would exact casualties from the enemy while also buying time for defenders to mobilize, advance, and even mount a counteroffensive.

The construction of the de Rivières system began in 1873, and it was not until late in the first decade of the next century that French military thinking resolutely turned against fortifications as it seized on the "attack to excess" doctrine. This error in judgment, spectacular in itself, was aggravated by a failure to recognize that French fortifications of the early twentieth century were very different from those of 1870. The French military decisions of 1910–1915 were based on the experience of forty-year-old fortification design and doctrine that no longer existed. Yes, the fortresses of Metz and Sedan had failed under heavy fire, but it was just such fire that the new system of fortifications was designed to withstand—at least to withstand long enough to purchase the most valuable commodity a competent commander can possess: time. The French generals of 1914 acted from a nearly total absence of current data. They were, in every sense of the word, ignorant.

The France of Napoleon III was, militarily speaking, stuck in the era of Napoleon I. By 1870, however, warfare had evolved from the maneuver of grand armies in direct pursuit of territorial conquest to the positioning of armies for the most efficient infliction of attrition. Thanks to a Franco-Prussian disparity of artillery in 1870–1871—the Germans had the biggest guns—and to the genius of Helmuth von Moltke (the Elder) in positioning these disproportionate assets for greatest advantage, the attrition of the French army took place in a matter of mere weeks. Like its military thinking, French geopolitical doctrine was also grounded in an obsolete conception of empire. In 1870–1871, war, for the French, was all about territory—acquiring more while holding what you already had. For Prussia's Bismarck, war—indeed, empire itself—was about acquiring influence built not merely on military prowess or territorial extent but on national economic power. Prussia's victory in 1871 catalyzed the formation of the German Empire even as it toppled the French Empire, and it further resulted in Germany's annexation of France's Alsace-Lorraine. In empire, Bismarck saw the levers of power and influence. In the annexation,

Bismarck was far less interested in land than in what lay beneath it: coal. Coal, during the late nineteenth-century apotheosis of the steam-driven industrial age, was the indispensable fuel of a national economy, which, in turn, was the ultimate source of the nation's power and influence.

Whereas Napoleon III had been obsessed with creating an empire beyond even that of his uncle, the "original" Napoleon, Bismarck wanted to unite Germany in an empire that would give it power and influence, and he wanted from war with France only that part of the defeated nation that would fuel the fires of German industry, from which, he well understood, the greatest power and influence were now to be derived.

ARTILLERY

Under Bismarck's leadership, Germany became a major industrial power. The leverage this created was economic as well as military, as the nation's factories became world famous for producing machinery of all kinds, consumer goods, and weapons. The most celebrated producer of cannon and shoulder arms was unquestionably Friedrich Krupp AG, which, by World War I, was known as the "Anvil of the Reich."

It had begun as a foundry and smithy in the Ruhr valley town of Essen during the late sixteenth century, began specializing in crucible as well as smelted steel by the early nineteenth century, and soon branched out into making steel rollers for the mass production of eating and cooking utensils. Building on the profits of this business, Alfred Krupp began casting cannon from steel in 1847 but had to fight an uphill battle to win acceptance from the world's armies, for which bronze had always been the metal of choice when it came to artillery. He also innovated breech-loading designs in an era that knew only muzzle loaders. In the years leading up to the Franco-Prussian War, Krupp offered steel cannon to Napoleon III, who saw the value of the innovation but was checked by his own conservative high command, who refused to give up their beloved bronze. Fortunately both for Krupp and Prussia, Kaiser Wilhelm I became an early convert to Krupp's cast-steel breech loaders. Despite stubborn opposition from some in his military, including the mighty Minister of War Albrecht Theodor Emil von Roon, the kaiser ordered some five hundred pieces of heavy artillery to be supplied to Prussian forces prior to the outbreak of war. Thus the Franco-Prussian War became both a contest between old French bronze and new Prussian steel and a demonstration of the new strategic potency of artillery.

Based on the success of Krupp cannon in the 1870–1871 war and the disproportionate role artillery played in Prussia's overwhelming victory, Germany continued to build its arsenal from the company's output. This, in turn, spurred advanced development at Krupp, particularly of bigger and bigger cannon.

Nevertheless, at its outbreak in the summer of 1914, all of the belligerents, Germany included, entered World War I with a deficiency of artillery, cannon as well as ammunition. Despite Krupp's advances in heavy artillery—and despite the proven effectiveness of large guns against forts and fortifications—Germany, like France, Britain, Russia, and the United States—emphasized light field artillery over larger, heavier, hard-to-transport pieces. The leading German weapon was a 77-mm fieldpiece, and the other countries that would become involved in the war were equipped primarily with weapons of comparable caliber and firepower: Britain had the 18-pounder, Russia the 76.2 mm, and the United States a 3-inch field gun. France deployed with what was universally considered the finest fieldpiece of the time, a 75-mm gun known simply as "the French 75." Its great advantage was an innovative and highly sophisticated recoil system that was so effective at damping recoil, thereby reducing gun movement, that the weapon could be repeatedly fired before having to be relaid (re-aimed). This substantially increased the weapon's rate of fire. Nevertheless, no field weapon was capable of delivering the mass and muzzle velocity needed to pierce armor or the ferroconcrete carapace of a modern fortification. Equally important, because field cannon were designed to be used in open combat, on Napoleonic-era battlefields that allowed for extensive maneuver, they fired in a relatively flat trajectory. Weapons intended to be used against fortifications, including entrenchments, had to be capable of steep trajectories so that the projectile would fall more or less straight down on the enemy. The major armies of World War I went into the conflict armed to fight a war that, except on the Eastern Front and the first month on the Western Front, allowed for very little maneuver and was fought from trenches rather than out in the open.

An even more critical deficiency was the meager supply of ammunition among the belligerents. The need for massive ammo supplies should not have come as a surprise to the nations of Europe. During the Russo-Japanese War of 1904–1905, Russian forces fired, on average, eighty-seven thousand artillery rounds per month during the first year of that war. Eight years later, during the Second Balkan War, the Bulgarian army—far smaller than that of Russia—fired nearly a quarter-million rounds per month! Ignoring the obvious implications of this trend, France went to war in 1914 with no more than five million artillery rounds on hand. The Russians had managed to stockpile twelve million, and the Germans had a more impressive twenty million—although these had to be divided between two fronts, Western and Eastern. French high command assured its worried leaders that there would be time to catch up, because it estimated a need for no more than 100,000 rounds per month. In actuality, in 1914, the first year of the war, French forces fired nearly 900,000 rounds each month. By 1916, the year of the principal Verdun battle, this had risen to 4.5 million. The Germans were firing considerably more; although figures for 1916 are not available, it is reported that by 1918, Germany fired about eight million artillery rounds every month. At these rates, the arms industries of all the combatants found it nearly impossible to meet demand, although, for much of the war, Germany, *comparatively* better prepared, managed better than its enemies.[3]

Despite going into World War I with mostly fieldpieces, Germany did have more, better, and heavier artillery than France, Britain, and Russia. The lessons of both the Russo-Japanese War and the Balkan Wars were not entirely lost on German high command. Krupp and its smaller, less-famous competitor Skoda (established in Pilsen, in Bohemia, which was at the time part of the Austro-Hungarian Empire), rushed to fill German orders for howitzers (artillery capable of firing heavy projectiles at the high trajectories suitable for attacking fortifications and entrenchments) as well as for big, long-range guns. In 1914, the German army was equipped with 5,086 77-mm fieldpieces and only 2,280 howitzers and larger guns. But 2,280 was *seven* times the number in the 1914 French arsenal. (France had 3,840 75-mm guns and a mere 308 larger than

"Big Bertha" (*Dicke Bertha*) was the generic name for the heaviest Krupp siege guns used by Germany in World War I and at the Battle of Verdun in particular. The 50-ton cannon fired an 1,800-pound, 16.5-inch (419-mm) shell to an effective range of 7.8 miles. WIKIMEDIA

this!) Moreover, while France persisted in emphasizing manufacture and deployment of its famed 75 during much of the war, Germany almost immediately accelerated production of heavy artillery, so that its production rate soon outpaced that of the fieldpieces. By the armistice of 1918, the German artillery park consisted of 12,286 guns bigger than 77 mm, nearly twice the number (6,764) of field guns.[4]

German heavy artillery included 105-mm light howitzers, 150-mm long guns, and a heavy howitzer with a caliber of 210 mm. The army also adapted 380-mm naval guns for land artillery use. But the most impressive expression of German industrial might applied to war were the "Big Berthas." These were transported either by rail or by road. Weighing 47 tons each, they had a barrel length just over 19 feet and could launch a 419-mm, 1,807-pound shell at a muzzle velocity of 1,312 feet per second over an effective range of 7.8 miles. Krupp produced just a dozen of these, but they were extensively used at Verdun, where they created massive destruction and debilitating terror.

CHEMICAL WARFARE

It would be difficult to provide a more diabolical demonstration of industrial might in the service of war than the German artillery at Verdun. In the course of the war, France dramatically ramped up its production of artillery, ending the conflict in November 1918, with 4,968 75-mm field-pieces and 5,128 howitzers and other guns above 75 mm—most of which were 155-mm pieces. Despite its efforts, French industry never surpassed that of Germany in terms of production.[5]

But the merchants of death also explored industrial alternatives to steel and high explosives. Although the historian of firearms and artillery Ian Hogg quite accurately pictured World War I as "an artillery duel of vast proportions,"[6] it is chemical warfare—"poison gas"—that, in the popular imagination, figures as the conflict's archetypal weapon. An emblem of martial inhumanity, chemical warfare was also literally and actually a *product* of modern industry.

It was first used on April 22, 1915, against French Algerian troops holding a section of the line at Ypres, Belgium. The agent was a greenish-yellow cloud of chlorine vapor, 168 tons of it boiling up from six thousand cylinders opened by German soldiers on the rim of their trenches and carried to the Allied positions by the prevailing winds. Because it is heavier than air, the chlorine vapor was ideally suited to trench warfare, hugging the ground and seeping into shell holes and trenches alike. The cloud generated in that first attack spread over four miles of French trench, engulfing ten thousand troops. Unequipped with gas masks, half of them died within ten minutes. "The first effect of inhalation of chlorine is a burning pain in the throat and eyes, accompanied by a sensation of suffocation; pain, which may be severe, is felt in the chest, especially behind the sternum," Dr. Arthur Hurst wrote in *Medical Diseases of the War*. "Respiration becomes painful, rapid, and difficult; coughing occurs, and the irritation of the eyes results in profuse lachrymation. Retching is common and may be followed by vomiting, which gives temporary relief. The lips and mouth are parched and the tongue is covered with a thick dry fur. Severe headache rapidly follows with a feeling of great weakness in the legs; if the patient gives way to this and lies down, he is likely to inhale still more chlorine, as the heavy gas is most concentrated near the ground. In severe poisoning unconsciousness follows; nothing more is known about the cases which prove fatal on the field within the first few hours of the 'gassing,' except that the face assumes a pale greenish yellow colour."[7]

Of those who did not die, many were temporarily blinded. Two thousand of these were quickly taken as prisoners of war. If the effect of the attack horrified the victims, it also caught the attackers unprepared. They advanced into the abandoned French positions having failed to prepare reserves to exploit the breach, and so they were quickly forced to abandon the ground they had gained.

Germany's chemical genius Fritz Haber, who had given his country the means of creating a limitless supply of fertilizer as well as high explosives by inventing a process of artificially fixing atmospheric nitrogen to produce ammonia, spurred the development of the nation's sophisticated chemical warfare industry. Yet the Allies were not far behind. The British unleashed an attack at Loos, Belgium, on September 25, 1915, and the French soon followed. Both the British and the French were inexplicably much slower at developing effective countermeasures against chemical weapons. Initially, British troops were advised to do nothing more than urinate on their socks and hold them over their faces. The ammonia in the urine neutralized the chlorine. Gradually, however, both British and German troops were issued cloth masks soaked in triosulphate, which was more effective than urine at counteracting the effects of chlorine. So-called gas helmets—cloth hoods soaked in phenalheximine and equipped with goggle lenses—came next and were succeeded by the "SBR," or small box respirator. A mask covered the face, and air was supplied by a tube leading to a box (the SBR) containing a soda lime and charcoal filter. Goggles protected the eyes, and the nose was held closed with a clip. Attempting to fight in such gear was both uncomfortable and difficult, especially since the goggles cut off all peripheral vision and frequently fogged over.

The French fumbled before they finally issued the M2, a canvas face mask containing gauze pads with anti-gas chemicals. Never very effective, the M2 was eventually replaced with a more efficient, German-style mask, but not until 1917.

Even as countermeasures slowly emerged, both the Germans and the Allies commissioned new poisons from their chemical industries. In December 1915, Haber developed phosgene, carbonyl dichloride, a choking agent made all the more deadly by its odor (in low concentrations) of new-mown hay. Many a homesick farm boy, now in uniform, sniffed the aroma with pleasure, took in a deep breath, and drowned on his own liquefied mucous membranes as the phosgene turned to hydrochloric acid in his lungs.

Phosgene made its battlefield debut at Verdun on June 22, 1916. As Lieutenant Marcel Bechu, officer on the staff of the French 130th Division, recalled, the windless but lovely early summer evening was unusually quiet, which made it easy to hear "multitudinous soft whistlings, following each other without cessation, as if thousands and thousands of birds cleaving the air in dizzy flight were fleeing over our heads. . . . It was something novel and incomprehensible." At this point, a sergeant burst into the command shelter: "*Mon Géneral*," he said, "there are shells—thousands of shells—passing overhead that don't burst!"[8]

The sergeant, general, and lieutenant ventured together outside. What had started out as the scent of new-mown hay by now had congealed into what Bechu recalled as "a pungent, sickening odor of putrefaction compounded with a mustiness of stale vinegar." Strangled calls of "Gas! Gas!" arose from the trenches.[9]

The first thing Lieutenant Pierre de Mazenod noticed was how the shells, which were loaded with phosgene, descended like "thousands of beads falling upon a large carpet." Could these *all* be duds? And then the pack horses went crazy, frantic, breaking from their tethers and tearing madly through the French artillery battery. Men put on their crude French gas masks, only to find them totally useless against this new agent. Tearing the masks off, they retched, coughed, and collapsed.[10] It would come to be called "Green Cross Gas," at least by the Germans, who marked the gas shells with that symbol, and it attacked everything that lived: the leaves on the trees, which withered instantly; the war horses, which went mad before dropping dead; and the people, who drowned in a pinkish-red foam that had been their lungs. Even the flies that swarmed perpetually over and around the corpses in no-man's-land fell silent and disappeared.

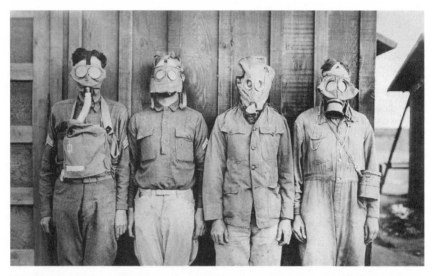

This photograph shows U.S. soldiers wearing gas masks used by the British (the two at the left), the French (third from left), and the Germans (right). Primitive though it appears, the French example shown here was a major innovation spurred by the German use of phosgene at Verdun. NATIONAL ARCHIVES

The chemical industries of Germany, France, Britain, and, later, the United States, the very same companies that, in peacetime, had developed and produced miraculous fertilizers, life-saving drugs, efficient cleansers, and a host of industrial reagents for modern manufacturing, now dedicated themselves to formulating an arsenal of novel agents of death. There was, for instance, chlorpicrin, "vomiting gas," which defeated most of the early gas-mask neutralizers. Not particularly lethal in itself, it was designed to force soldiers to tear off their masks to vomit, thereby exposing them to the other, deadlier, agents mixed with it. And then came mustard gas, ultimately the most disabling if not the deadliest of the chemical weapons. In low concentrations, it was detectable only as a scent reminiscent of lilacs in bloom. But as the concentration built up, mustard gas caused severe chemical burns wherever it made contact: skin, eyes, or the membranes of nose, throat, and lungs. Called a gas, it was actually an atomized liquid that soaked everything, lingering with high potency for weeks in shell holes, dugouts, and trenches. Days after a mustard gas attack, a soldier

36

might seek refuge from enemy machine-gun fire in a shell hole only to find himself smothering, burning, and blinded.

FLAMETHROWER

Mustard gas burned, but the merchants of death in 1914–1918 were not content with producing the mere sensation of fire. They looked back to such ancient weapons as "Greek fire," which had been developed by the Byzantine Empire late in the seventh century, and created the modern flamethrower. This weapon came in two World War I varieties. Some were fixed-mounted, with fuel tanks and propellant buried in an underground gallery or trench and connected to steel tubing and a nozzle that poked above ground, pointing toward the enemy. Others—the more common form—were portable. An infantryman carried on his back a tank of fuel (typically gasoline or gasoline blended with alcohol) and a tank of propellant (compressed air that had been chemically deoxygenated to reduce the potential for explosion). Connected to the tanks was a flexible hose feeding a gun-like tube fitted with a trigger-like lever that opened and closed a valve. This allowed the infantryman to release at will an electrically ignited stream that he could direct as needed.

Although there is evidence that the French used flamethrowers as early as 1914, the first year of the war, it was the Germans who embraced their use and produced flamethrowers in such quantity that the Allies condemned the weapons as "an inhuman projection of the German scientific mind."[11] The Germans used flamethrowers most extensively at Verdun, where, like poison gas, they were intended more to terrorize, instill panic, and create chaos than to kill. In at least one instance at Verdun, a French officer and his detachment of thirty-six men surrendered to a single German soldier the moment they saw that he was brandishing a flamethrower.

Yet it was ultimately a limited weapon. Met with the prospect of death in a relentless array of horrific novelty—annihilation by artillery barrage, tortured asphyxiation by chemical agent, and living immolation—the soldiers of Verdun continually adapted. Many died, but more adapted. In the case of the flamethrower, soldiers came to understand that the man wielding the weapon was tremendously vulnerable. Shoot him, and the chances

The Germans pioneered the use of the flamethrower at Verdun, but the French soon adopted the weapon. The *poilu* second from left carries the fuel and propellant tank on his back. MUSÉE DE L'INFANTERIE-A.A.M.I

were great that, in falling, he would unavoidably turn the flaming stream back upon his comrades. Better yet, shoot the tanks he carried, and they, he, and all around him would be engulfed in explosion and flame.

MACHINE GUN

Relatively few casualties were inflicted at Verdun—or, indeed, anywhere else on the Western Front—by the conflict's two most numerous weapons, the rifle and the bayonet. Most of the men killed or wounded at Verdun were victims of artillery barrage, and this was true throughout most of the war in Europe. The next most lethal weapon was the machine gun. The models available by 1914 could fire six hundred rounds per minute at a range of more than a thousand yards. A pair of machine gunners—one man to feed the weapon, the other to fire it—could operate from the relative safety of a trench and simply sweep away all exposed attackers. In that single word "attackers" is to be found the reason why the machine gun came in second to artillery as an agent of death. It was effective in the hands of entrenched defenders using it against soldiers who had ventured out of their entrenchments, exposing themselves in the open, to attack.

The industries of war, as they existed in 1914–1918, were capable of producing more, and more deadly, weapons of defense than of attack. While we might classify heavy artillery as a weapon of attack, it is, in fact, employed from protected, defensive positions. Artillery employed *against* enemy artillery—known as counterbattery fire—may be classified as an attack, but the problem for the French was that, deficient in heavy artillery and guns capable of long range and high trajectory, they could not readily muster effective counterbattery fire. For them, "attack" meant an infantry assault, not an artillery assault against enemy artillery. Thus, on balance, throughout the war—and nowhere more than at Verdun—the advantage always lay with the defenders.

Although heavy artillery was arguably the most impressive military expression of early twentieth-century industrial technology, the machine gun was a veritable metaphor of industrialized warfare. It was first and foremost a *machine* and then a *gun*. It automated killing, mass producing it as effectively as any factory assembly line. As a device, the machine gun was also a thoroughgoing embodiment of industrial efficiency. The first modern machine gun was invented in 1884 by Hiram Maxim, an American citizen who immigrated to England, becoming a British subject in 1900. Whereas the precursor of his weapon, the Gatling gun, was hand-cranked, Maxim's gun was truly automatic in that it used the energy of its own recoil to eject a spent cartridge, chamber the next cartridge, and fire it. The process was repeated as long as the trigger was held. Nothing, including the kinetic energy produced by its own operation, was wasted in this highly perfected industrial *machine*.

By 1914, two British-based firms, Maxim and Vickers, along with the French-based Hotchkiss et Cie (founded in France by the American gunsmith Benjamin B. Hotchkiss in 1867), were the major manufacturers of machine guns. Early in the war, Germany used the Maxim design to produce its own machine guns. Yet all of the belligerents were actually quite slow to recognize the power and importance of the weapon. And the French military, although it benefitted from the domestic presence of the

Hotchkiss firm and others, actually regarded the machine gun with some of the same disdain high command showed for both fortifications and heavy artillery. After all, rifle and bayonet could be carried by soldiers on the attack, whereas a machine gun had to be set up on a tripod, fired from cover, and served by *two* men, one to feed the ammunition, the other to aim and fire. It was a weapon of defense, not attack. The French army did place its first order of machine guns not from Hotchkiss, but from Manufacture d'Armes de Saint-Étienne, and put them into service in 1910. But, referring to the St. Étienne Mle 07, the inspector general of French infantry said it would "not make the slightest difference to anything," noting that it was complicated and therefore beyond the comprehension of the troops. In fact, it had been purchased only to impress journalists.[12] The machine gun played an important role at Verdun on both sides, but it would truly come into its own at the Battle of the Somme in the summer of 1916.

AIRCRAFT

Military aviation truly came of age at the Battle of Verdun. The Wright Brothers made their first powered flight on December 17, 1903, in a gossamer aircraft that looked like what it was: a work of exquisite handicraft. By the outbreak of war in 1914, aviation had progressed, especially in France and Germany—much less in the America of Orville and Wilbur Wright—and aircraft were quickly evolving from one-off items of handicraft into quite beautiful expressions of assembly-line industrial culture.

Historical discussions of airpower in World War I tend to emphasize the aerial duels, the dogfights, between individual pilots in the rarified air above the misery and filth of the trenches. In a war of anonymous attrition and mass slaughter, the pilots and their planes were frequently compared to knights and steeds engaged in chivalrous aerial jousts. There was certainly an element of truth in this; however, the military value of aircraft for observation and reconnaissance, not mere dogfighting, became gradually evident beginning in the very first month of the war, before the so-called war of movement congealed into static trench warfare. All sides used airplanes as well as tethered, sausage-shaped and dirigible-shaped balloons for observation. In addition, the Germans made extensive use of piloted dirigibles (zeppelins), both for observation and, later, also for bombardment—including the bombardment of Paris and London.

Before the outbreak of war and among some older commanders there was much doubt about the military value of aviation. Although most conceded that possessing high ground was always a good thing for the sake of reconnaissance and field intelligence, many questioned whether a pilot could possibly see anything of tactical value on the ground while flying at sixty miles per hour or better. Besides, how could the pilot tend to reconnaissance duties while flying and, quite possibly, also engaging in combat with enemy aircraft? There was considerable validity in the latter question, since a good many of the planes of 1914 lacked the horsepower and aerodynamics to carry anything more than a pilot. Equipping the craft with a machine gun represented too much added weight. The pilot could defend himself, if necessary, with a pistol or, if more enterprising, a rifle.

As the Western Front stalemate settled into apparent permanence, aircraft increasingly appeared to offer significant advantages, and the air arms of the Allies and Germans alike benefitted from technological innovation and improvements in unit organization. By the end of 1915, the value of aerial reconnaissance and artillery spotting could not be denied. Airplanes now served the information-gathering functions formerly performed by cavalry.

As was the case with artillery at Verdun, the Germans entered the battle from a position of greater strength. Germany brought with them the largest concentration of aircraft up to that time: 168 airplanes, a dozen tethered observation balloons, and four dirigible airships. The French, in contrast, had just two fighter escadrilles (squadrons) and four two-seater escadrilles. The typical escadrille had ten aircraft, for a total of about sixty French machines at Verdun, which meant that they were outnumbered more than two to one. French aerial observation was augmented by two, possibly three, tethered balloons.

Verdun, in 1916, would go a long way toward establishing two primary roles for airplanes: increasingly sophisticated reconnaissance and tactical bombardment, especially of rear positions. The concept of air superiority was born in the Battle of Verdun: the tactical value of driving enemy aircraft out of the airspace over a battlefield in order to command the skies for purposes of reconnaissance and tactical bombardment. Before Verdun, aerial combat had no effective doctrine. It was simply a quasi-futuristic mode of industrial-age warfare. As a result of Verdun, the concept of the air force emerged, the demand on manufacturers for more and better aircraft increased markedly, and the concept of specialized, purpose-built military planes—fighters, bombers, "observation" aircraft—rapidly evolved.

The marriage of the machine gun with airpower to produce the fighter plane was among the most advanced expressions of industrial technology in the service of war. The idea of mounting a gun on a plane was not radical, but the persistent problem was the propeller. How could the pilot direct his fire accurately without hitting his own prop? On the verge of war, designers experimented with moving the propeller to the rear of the plane, creating a "pusher" instead of a "tractor." This solved one problem, but created another. Pusher designs produced performance inherently inferior to conventional tractor designs. From 1913 through 1915, French and British manufacturers attempted to devise a synchronization gear that would reliably synchronize the gun's rate of fire with the rotation of the prop, interrupting the bullet stream so that it would flow only between the rotating blades. The results of early trials were almost universally disastrous, as rounds either damaged or destroyed the propeller or ricocheted off it unpredictably. It was not until Anthony Fokker, a Dutch aircraft designer and manufacturer who moved to Germany in 1912, designed the synchronization gear for his Eindecker (monoplane) in 1915 that the synchronized fire concept became sufficiently reliable to use in combat. Giving fighter pilots the ability to fire through the arc of the propeller without striking the blades provided German airpower with a terrific advantage at Verdun. Even so, the Fokker synchronization gear was not perfect, and the brother of Max Immelmann blamed the June 18, 1916, death of Germany's first flying ace (fifteen confirmed aerial victories) on faulty synchronization.

RAILWAY

Although air power was the most forward-looking product of the industry of death that supplied Verdun, far more important was a much older product of the Industrial Revolution. Once again, Germany was in the forefront. As early as 1842, the German Confederation proposed a scheme to build a *strategic* rail network to facilitate simultaneous military operations against France and Russia. In the Second Schleswig War (1864), by which Prussia and Austria-Hungary wrested control of Schleswig, Holstein, and Lauenburg from Denmark, the Austro-Prussian War (1866), by which Prussia gained geopolitical precedence over Austria-Hungary, and the Franco-Prussian War (1870–1871), Prussia made increasingly extensive military use of its rail system, progressively integrating it into German strategic thought.

In the years following the 1870–1871 war, a number of French commissions recommended not only strengthening eastern fortifications but also significantly extending the nation's railway network for specifically strategic purposes, essentially mirroring what Germany had done and was continuing to do. Among the specific recommendations of one special army commission was the establishment of new rail lines to Verdun and vicinity. These, along with other rail-building ideas, were not so much rejected by French high command as simply ignored. The result was that, in 1916, communications with and transport to Verdun were highly vulnerable. The main rail line running along the Meuse was severed very early in the battle when German forces took up positions on both banks of the river. An alternative line, from Paris via Ste. Ménéhould, fell under a punishing barrage from the big guns the Germans had converted from naval to land use. This left only a pair of highly tenuous lifelines between Verdun and the French interior, namely the so-called *Meusien*, a narrow-gauge railway adequate only to supplying the simple needs of the Verdun garrison in peacetime, and a rural gravel road that paralleled the Meusien for about the fifty miles between Verdun and the town of Bar-le-Duc. Fortunately, a panic-stricken French high command in 1915 ordered a crash program to widen this road to twenty-three feet (about the width of a modern American urban neighborhood lane), barely sufficient to allow two-way truck traffic. During the Battle of Verdun, this unassuming road would be dubbed the *Voie Sacrée*—the "Sacred Way"—along which one truck passed every fourteen seconds until a standard-gauge railroad was completed, often under fire, to rejoin Verdun with the larger regional rail system. In the meantime, on the German side, that nation's strategic rail network functioned most efficiently, allowing large numbers of troops to be shifted rapidly from one sector to another and ensuring that German lines were well supplied.

SUBMARINE

Verdun was, of course, an inland battle, and yet at least one oceangoing weapon, another formidable product of the turn-of-the-twentieth-century military-industrial complex, played an important part. It was the submarine.

All of the major belligerents came into World War I with naval fleets that included submarines. Among the Allies, the British Royal Navy had the most boats (seventy-four), half of which, however, were built for coastal operations only. France entered the war with fewer submarines than the U.K., but by the Armistice had seventy-five either built or nearing completion, of which fifty-five were capable of operating in the open ocean. The Russian fleet included fifty-nine submarines, most of which were already obsolescent at the outbreak of the war. Operations were confined to the Baltic. Italy operated a few coastal submarines. When the United States entered the war in 1917, it did so with forty-seven submarines, about half of which were capable of operating in the open ocean.[13]

Despite a fairly formidable underwater fleet, the Allies made far less use of submarines than did the Germans, who had 140 coastal boats and 107 oceangoing craft. Many of the most advanced German submarines were built by Krupp, the same firm that turned out most of Germany's heavy artillery. Whereas the Allied navies continually debated the proper role of the submarine, the German navy used its underwater fleet primarily to prey upon Allied commerce, U-boats managing to sink 5,554 Allied and neutral merchant ships in addition to many Allied warships. The total merchant tonnage lost was 12,191,996 GRT (gross register tonnage).[14]

Verdun pitted the industrial output of France against that of Germany. The submarine, as the Germans used it, was all about hitting the Allied economy and commerce, especially as that commerce enabled the Allies to continue to wage a war of attrition on a vast industrial scale.

A World War

Verdun was the archetypal Western Front battle, a battle of territorial stalemate, a contest of static attrition in which both sides were worn down. German submarines, however, took the war far from the trenches and fortifications of the Western Front and into the sea lanes of global commerce.

It was at Verdun that France and Germany resigned themselves to slogging out a terrible war of attrition. Facing enemies on two fronts, Germany had already planned its economy for war by setting up the legal apparatus to mobilize its science and industry under military control. The more intractable problem would be manning an army while also supplying sufficient labor for wartime production. That aside, however, German planners had already ordered stockpiling of raw materials in advance of the war. Krupp, for example, had at least one to two years' supply of such metals as nickel and copper. As for the iron with which to make steel, the company owned its own supplies of ore.

Unlike the more democratic western Allies, Germany had wartime laws that quickly put the military in charge of all government, so that civilians became subject to military bureaucracy, priorities, and management. Because the war generated tremendous revenues for Krupp and other armament industries, leading German plutocrats made an enthusiastic show of subordinating themselves to military direction. Some, like Fritz Haber, even proudly accepted special officer commissions in the army. Indeed, leading industrialists assumed administrative positions in the governing authority to ensure high rates of production and smooth relations with labor. The latter was not always easy, since socialism was on the rise in Germany. Throughout most of the war, however, all workers were generally patriotic, and most socialists suppressed their customary adversarial tendencies for the duration.

The Allies did their best to blockade imports into Germany, but there was little they could do about overland shipments entering from the east. In any case, domestic sources of coal and iron ore (beyond what Krupp already owned) were quickly developed to substitute for the reduction in imports. As German troops came to occupy Belgium and northeastern France, these areas were also exploited for their mineral wealth, as were conquests in Poland and Russia. Nevertheless, as the war dragged on, the relentless Allied blockade began to tell heavily on civilian Germany. Still, for most of 1916, the year of Verdun, German still basked in relative plenty.

In contrast to Germany, France had made little or no preparation for a long war. The country's initial mobilization efforts focused on conscripting as many young men as possible, a policy that left factories badly undermanned. By the time government administrators acted to correct the imbalance, many of the nation's most highly skilled workers had either been killed in combat or permanently disabled by it. The unplanned quality of French industrial mobilization took its toll. Fortunately, the country entered the war with a strong industrial sector, a fact that compensated somewhat for the absence of planning. French industry was also capable of highly advanced innovation—the products of which, however, often met an icy reception from military high command.

Plunged into the realities of war, the commander-in-chief, General Joffre, demanded an increase in the production of shells—from 8,000 to 100,000 per day. No doubt he needed this quantity and even more. Nevertheless, even remotely expecting French industry to ramp up production more than tenfold was unrealistic. France embarked on massive military imports in an effort to address the shortfall in domestic production. In Britain, the shortage of shells became a national scandal, and even Germany, in better shape than either France or Britain, needed imports. Given the demand from all belligerents, the industry of neutral nations—especially the United States—was in for a windfall. This put pressure on the leaders of neutral governments to guard their neutral status by ensuring that they were never perceived as taking sides. Bearing witness to the bloody futility of attrition—of which Verdun was the most stunning example—the neutrals enjoyed the tremendous boost in their prosperity but had no desire to join in the slaughter. "A world war would reach everywhere in its voracious need for manpower and material," historian William Philpott wrote. "American businessmen, Swedish merchants, Argentinian cattle ranchers, Chilean miners, Chinese labourers, Danish merchant sailors, Dutch farmers, Japanese steelworkers, Portuguese fishermen, Spanish textile workers and Swiss bankers would all be going to war."[15] The United States would enter the war in April 1917, and Japan declared war on Germany in August 1914 but participated only peripherally. The other nations in this list did manage to remain neutral while supplying the belligerents and reaping handsome profits.

THE UNITED STATES AT THE TIME OF VERDUN

The entry of the United States into World War I nearly two years after the commencement of the major phase of the Battle of Verdun would change the course of the war. Most modern historians, in fact, believe the Allies would have been defeated without American entry into combat. Nevertheless, as British historian Kathleen Burk concluded in 1985, "The major role the United States was destined to play in the First World War was that of economic powerhouse and supplier of munitions, food, and money to Britain and her allies."[16]

The news dispatches coming out of Verdun were heavily manipulated and censored on both sides, though none more heavily than those issued by French sources. "The official regulations for war correspondents are . . . severe," American correspondent Charles Inman Barnard wrote in October 1914. "All dispatches must be written in the French language and must be sent by the military post, and only after having been formally approved by the military censors." None could "be sent by wire or wireless telegraphy."[17] Yet even "as they quashed any sort of independent reportage, the Allies [France and Britain] published, through surrogates, an enormous flood of purportedly objective news and news analysis that spun the official government positions in convincing fashion."[18]

The news coming out of Verdun, from official sources on both sides, spun the Battle of Verdun as a contest with the highest of stakes, a must-win that demanded a decisive victory. Over the months of the central battle, which consumed nearly the entire year of 1916, it became apparent even to the most optimistic and the most gullible that a truly meaningful decision in this "decisive" battle would not be forthcoming. While the governments persistently officially refused to acknowledge this, let alone embody it in the battle news they released, they could not hide the extent of the daily carnage. This the revisionist World War I historian John Mosier cites as a "perfect" illustration of "what the great British historian Thomas Babington Macaulay had encapsulated in a memorable quip: that it was possible to write a history in which all the details were true, but the history itself was a falsehood."[19]

From the true "details" flowing out of Verdun, Americans were building a highly ambivalent picture. The seemingly endless clash of men and machines—both of them products of highly developed industrial civilizations—was very good for business. Demand for the instruments of death had never been greater. American financiers and industrialists had reason to hope that the "endless" battle would, in fact, *never* end. At the same time, although the concept of neutrality (as darkly defined by a blurred mixture of vague international law and even vaguer diplomatic custom) dictated that neutral nations trade equitably with all interested belligerents, neither overtly favoring nor opposing any, the flow of trade and credit from the United States to the European belligerents increasingly turned away from the Central Powers and toward the Allies. High demand, an ample supply of gold, favorable shipping, and the realities of geography made dealing with the Allies far more reliable and profitable than doing business with the Central Powers. Moreover, American financial and business interests were coming to believe that the Allies would win, which made them a far better credit risk than the Central Powers. By the time the Battle of Verdun was drawing toward its close in late 1916, U.S. firms had done some $2 billion in business with the Allies, and U.S. banks had made $2.5 billion in loans to them. In contrast, American banks had loaned by this time no more than $45 million to Germany.[20]

Yet, even as late as the end of 1916, the preponderance of *public* sentiment continued to favor American neutrality. There was no clearer demonstration of this than the reelection of Woodrow Wilson to a second White House term following a campaign propelled by the slogan "He Kept Us Out of War." Yes, Verdun was a spectacular display of military industrial might—much of it American, even in the absence of American soldiers—but its details, emerging despite the censors' spin, were of relentless slaughter, or, as military sources officially termed it, "wastage." In this hellish spectacle, Verdun, more than any other battle since August 1914, was to many Americans a great disincentive to joining what they called "the European war." At the same time, American investment, production, employment, and prosperity—in the factory and on the farm—had never been greater or more promising. Politically, the United States was neutral in 1916; morally, Americans were becoming ever more divided over the war; economically, many had already chosen sides.

CHAPTER 3

The Generals

Yes, humanity has gone mad. We must be mad to do what we are doing. What massacres! What scenes of horror and carnage! I cannot find words to express my feelings. Hell cannot be so terrible. Mankind has gone mad!

—SECOND LIEUTENANT ALFRED (FRED) JOUBAIRE,
DIARY ENTRY MADE AT VERDUN, MAY 22, 1916[1]

HE WAS A LOWLY SECOND LIEUTENANT, FRED JOUBAIRE, ASSIGNED TO the 124th Infantry Regiment, twenty-one years old, and, like so many other young men in the Great War, Joubaire earnestly recorded his experience of service and combat in a diary. Most of what he wrote was patriotic, confident, and optimistic. On May 22, 1916, after what historian Malcolm Brown aptly describes as "a long day of gallant but sacrificial fighting" near Fort Douaumont—the major Verdun citadel that French high command had blithely divested of heavy guns and most of its garrison—Joubaire wrote of the French soldiers' "irresistible élan . . . above all praise." They were, he continued, "perfectly peaceful peasants [who] proved themselves as fierce as lions, splendid warriors, heroes." Joubaire wrote of how one "cannot help loving these ordinary soldiers, these anonymous heroes, who have been sacrificing themselves daily for nearly two years, without counting the cost, without hope of glory."[2]

"How I love them!" Joubaire concluded his paragraph, only to take a sharp and sharply painful turn in beginning the next: "But for how long is it going to carry on? You wonder with anguish when and how this unprecedented struggle will end. There is no solution in sight. I wonder

50

if it will end simply for lack of fighting men." And, with that, Second Lieutenant Joubaire crossed the no-man's-land from exalted heroism to madness. "Yes," he wrote, "humanity has gone mad. We must be mad to do what we are doing."[3] Less than two weeks later, Joubaire would die in an artillery barrage against French positions at Vaux-devant-Damloup along the Meuse.

Arguably all war oscillates between heroism and madness. As many came to view World War I, however, it was the madness that prevailed, and all sentiment of heroism was merely added proof of the madness. At Verdun, it seemed to men like Joubaire, the madness of the Great War was distilled to its most toxic potency.

Doubtless that is how it felt to those who fought and saw. But even to those of us standing at a distance in time and space, left to contemplate the battle only through the printed word and a few photographs, the madness of Verdun seems, if anything, even greater.

THE GHOST AND OTHERS IN COMMAND

The principal commanders of the armies of France and Germany at Verdun are easily identified. There were General (later, Marshal) Joseph Joffre, commander-in-chief of French forces at the Western Front; General Noël Édouard, Vicomte de Curiéres de Castelnau, who organized the initial defense of Verdun; Fernand de Langle de Cary, who had failed miserably at the Second Battle of Champagne (September 25–November 6, 1915) but was nevertheless given command of the Center Army Group at Verdun, where he failed yet more miserably; and Frédéric-Georges Herr, who, having taken over Center Army Group, appeared to be presiding over a lunatic asylum when General Henri Philippe Pétain arrived at his headquarters to take over command from him.

Pétain would initiate much-needed changes in the prosecution of the Verdun battle, including the logistical organization of the Voie Sacrée, the narrow highway running from Bar-le-Duc to Verdun, to bring supplies and fresh troops.

He would also bring a new emphasis on artillery (*"Le feu tue!"*—Firepower kills!—he proclaimed), as well as his buoyant rallying cry in echo of Joan of Arc: *"On les aura!"* (We'll get 'em!). And there were other field

As commander of the Central Army Group at the outbreak of the Battle of Verdun, Fernand de Langle de Cary did little to improve the woefully neglected defenses of the Verdun sector. WIKIMEDIA

BAR-LE-DUC. — Panorama vers Notre-Dame pris de la Côte Ste-Catherine.
Visé Paris n° 3   Édition Colas

A postcard view of Bar-le-Duc, the city that served as the connection between the Verdun front and the rest of France during the 1916 battle. The main depot for reinforcements and supplies, Bar-le-Duc was linked to Verdun by *"La Voie Sacrée."* AUTHOR'S COLLECTION

commanders. Robert Nivelle and Charles Mangin were destined to vie for the title of most prodigious spiller of French blood. Nivelle succeeded Pétain as French Second Army commander and led the counteroffensives of late 1916, as relentless as they were ghastly, which drove the Germans back from their initial advances at Verdun. Under Nivelle, Mangin led the recapture of Forts Douaumont and Vaux, again at fantastic cost.

On the German side were Erich von Falkenhayn, Crown Prince Wilhelm, and Schmidt von Knobelsdorf.

Falkenhayn succeeded Helmuth von Moltke the Younger as chief of staff, the top soldier of the German army, after Germany's failure at the First Battle of the Marne (September 5–12, 1914).

And with that failure is where the Ghost makes his entrance prior to the Battle of Verdun.

As explained in chapter 1, both France and Germany intended the war that had broken out in the summer of 1914 to be a short one. "Home before the leaves have fallen from the trees," Kaiser Wilhelm II had promised his troops, and the French felt much the same way. The

Crown Prince Wilhelm (left) with General Max von Gallwitz. NATIONAL ARCHIVES

difference is that the French put their faith in the concepts of furia francese, L'attaque à outrance, and élan vital, whereas the Germans had an
actual plan. It was by no means a bad plan. Certainly, it was a comparatively detailed plan. Count Alfred von Schlieffen, chief of the Imperial
German General Staff from 1891 to 1906, had labored over it during
1901–1906, and it was tinkered with by others, most notably Moltke,
well into 1914.

The Schlieffen Plan was designed expressly to overcome—indeed, to
work around—what was known as the French "second defensive area," in
which the fortresses in and around Verdun, combined with fortified Paris
and the Marne River, would be used to make any German advance costly
and time consuming. By mostly avoiding the Verdun area and instead
advancing in a great counterclockwise wheel to the north and west, so
as to attack Paris from the west and the French army in a line from the
north, a German incursion into France could quickly threaten, perhaps
even take, the capital, flank the French army, and fight a quick war on
French, not German, territory.

Schlieffen had fought in both the Austro-Prussian War (1866) and the Franco-Prussian War (1870–1871) and so for good reason had great confidence in the speed with which German armies could move, especially when supported by a national rail network extensively developed with military utility in mind. For its part, the German high command had great confidence in Schlieffen and his plan. In fact, German officers as well as Kaiser Wilhelm II were downright worshipful toward the plan. It came to seem both invincible and foolproof.

Schlieffen had fought during the age of the great Helmuth von Moltke the Elder, a military genius whose capabilities encompassed both strategy and tactics, theory and execution. The elder Moltke died in 1891 at the age of ninety. Schlieffen, whose plan would drive the first month of Germany's 1914 war, died in January 1913, shortly before his eightieth birthday. Command of the German military fell to Helmuth von Moltke the Younger, who was both nephew and, as it turned out, pale ghost of the Elder.

The Schlieffen Plan was a tool intended to create and win a short war. Historians are divided as to whether the plan was overly ambitious and therefore doomed or whether the younger Moltke lacked sufficient resolve and command presence to ensure that his field commanders, most notably Generals Alexander von Kluck and Karl von Bülow, did not deviate from the plan. Perhaps the failure of the plan to avoid the stalemate of a war of attrition was due to a combination of both causes: complexity of strategy and a flaw in the military character of the top commander. The speed of movement, the numbers of men, and the sheer distances involved put Moltke out of touch with his field commanders. This was a problem inherent in the Schlieffen Plan. But it was also true that the younger Moltke was often described in terms that suggest comparison with Hamlet, who, of course, complained of how "the native hue of resolution" was often "sicklied o'er with the pale cast of thought," such that "enterprises of great pith and moment . . . lose the name of action." As Hamlet saw it, it was "conscience" that made "cowards of us all," and Moltke feared that overextending his forces in the West would put East Prussia in imminent danger of invasion by Russia. Perhaps he was simply too burdened by conscience to go for broke.

Whatever the precise causes of the plan's failure, Schlieffen, the man who had created it, was a ghost in 1914, an immensely powerful presence, yet one totally unable to be of practical assistance. Moltke the Elder was likewise a mighty wraith. For his nephew, his memory was a burden, a high mark he could never attain but to which he was always compared and always compared unfavorably. Reportedly, when the German army retreated from the Marne following the First Battle of the Marne (September 5–12, 1914), the younger Moltke wrote to the kaiser, "Your Majesty, we have lost the war."[4] His health, both physical and emotional, crumbled after the failure at the Marne, and he was replaced as chief of staff by Erich von Falkenhayn on October 25, 1914. Less than two years later, on June 18, 1916, Moltke died while attending the funeral of Marshal Colmar Freiherr von der Goltz, the man many believed should have been named chief of staff instead of Moltke.

FALKENHAYN'S BURDEN

H. G. Wells is probably best remembered today as the author of the science fiction classic about a Martian invasion of the earth, *War of the Worlds* (1897), but in 1917, he wrote a firsthand account of a war of the nations, endeavoring to express what the titanic conflict meant. "One of the larger singularities of the great war," he wrote, "is its failure to produce great and imposing personalities, mighty leaders, Napoleons, Caesars. . . . It is a drama without a hero."[5]

Although Wells may be counted among the armchair generals who, having no skin in the game, found it easy to criticize those who did, there is truth in what Wells wrote, which was echoed by many others over the years. The French general-in-chief, Joseph Joffre, is typically portrayed as a dullish gourmand, who could not bear to interrupt a good meal to issue the most urgent of orders. The historian John Mosier nevertheless observed that, "by comparison with [British field marshal Douglas] Haig, Joffre was a mental giant, albeit a slothful one." Yet, Mosier continues, a "particular virulence is reserved [among many historians] for Erich von Falkenhayn . . . probably because he was clearly the most successful and by far the most intelligent of the three commanding generals." This, Mosier concedes, "may sound like faint praise, given Haig and Joffre," but he goes on to cite Falkenhayn's successes prior to Verdun: at Saint-Mihiel, the seizure of Antwerp and the English Channel ports, the remarkable offensive against the Russians in May 1915, the utter neutralization of the Serbian army also in 1915, and the casualties inflicted upon the French in the Argonne.[6]

Falkenhayn went into the Battle of Verdun with a scorecard more impressive than just about any other commander in World War I—and certainly far better than the record of any of his counterparts among the Allies. He is typically characterized as a Prussian "career soldier" of the "Junker class." Now, by the time of World War I, "Junker" was a loaded term—a slur, really—especially among the Allies and such neutrals as the democratic United States. As the Germans generally used it, "Junker" was a derivation of *jung* and *Herr*—Young Lord—and denoted (by the late nineteenth century) a member of the lesser, usually rural, nobility. To non-Germans, this suggested noble birth on a grand scale amid wealth and vast feudal acreage. In the case of Falkenhayn, like that of most Junkers, it was a greatly inflated image. He was born in Burg Belchau (now Białochowo, Poland), some thirty-seven miles north of Thorn (present-day Toruń, Poland), site of the family's quite modest farm, which constituted the full extent of its land holdings. Far from wealthy, the Falkenhayns were more or less hardscrabble farmers who worked marginally fertile land in a climate that offered a parsimonious growing season. To young Erich, the most attractive feature of his immediate homeland was its association with the Teutonic Knights of the Middle Ages. They (as German history had it) defended Western civilization against the uncouth Slavic hordes, and Thorn was among their bastions—a medieval German Verdun, if you will.

Erich von Falkenhayn was hardly the first among his clan to prefer the life of a soldier to that of a farmer. The Falkenhayns had produced warriors since the twelfth century. Erich's most notable martial ancestor had served Frederick the Great as a general, for which the emperor had decorated him with the *Pour le Mérite*, a high honor Frederick had created in 1740 and which became in World War I the so-called *Blauer Max*, the "Blue Max," especially coveted among German military pilots.

Surprisingly little is known about Falkenhayn's personal life. He was born in 1861, married in 1886, and was accepted into the *Preussische*

Kriegsakademie (Prussian War College) in 1887. Admission to the Krieg-sakademie was reserved for those young officers destined to positions on the German General Staff or other high command. Yet even Falkenhayn's few admirers apparently struggled to find in him any "evidence of an intellect above the average," let alone an urge to "pursue the study of advanced military theory."[7] He did gain much practical experience, however, serving from 1896 to 1903 in the German Military Mission to China both in the run-up to the Boxer Rebellion and during the conflict. In the course of his Chinese sojourn, he was promoted from captain to major and given a role in the provisional government of Tientsin. His superiors credited him with restoring order to a dangerous and confused situation, and they did not criticize him for destroying a large section of the ancient and sacred city wall of Peking (Beijing) in order to facilitate communications, supply, and reinforcement. That act of destruction, in fact, was regarded as evidence of his efficiency, and this, combined with his stream of admirably clear reports from the front, brought the attention of no less than Kaiser Wilhelm II. On his return to Germany in 1903, Falkenhayn was given command of an infantry battalion, and three years later became chief of staff of the Sixteenth Army Corps at Metz. In this capacity, he served under General Maximilian von Prittwitz. That officer's eventual rise to full command of the Sixteenth was largely due to Falkenhayn's efficiency, which, fortunately for him, did not go unrecognized. By 1911, already a brigadier general, he was plucked for command of a prestigious Guards regiment. In 1912, he was bumped up to major general and given another posting as a chief of staff, and in 1913, after promoting him to lieutenant general, Kaiser Wilhelm II named him Prussian minister of war.

Without doubt, Falkenhayn had been quick to seize opportunity for advancement whenever it presented itself. His sudden leap to war minister, however, surprised even him. He had, perhaps, not counted on the momentum his service under Prittwitz had given him. It was a kind of preview of the institutional madness prevailing among the major militaries of Europe. Falkenhayn was rewarded because he had made Prittwitz—largely regarded as both superannuated and at best only marginally competent—look good enough to be promoted to full general and put in charge of the German Eighth Army at the outbreak of World

War I. The Eighth Army was responsible for defending East Prussia from Russian invasion, and in his capacity as its commander, Prittwitz instantly demonstrated how dangerously unfit he was for any major command. Panic stricken by the Russian army's initial advance, Prittwitz asked the General Staff for permission to retreat. Had it been allowed, Prittwitz would have been responsible for the sacrifice of all East Prussia. By this time, August 1914, Falkenhayn was little more than a month away from replacing the soon-to-fail Helmuth von Moltke the Younger as chief of the German General Staff. He was already deeply into the good graces of Kaiser Wilhelm II and had been among several top officers to encourage the German emperor's declaration of war. Falkenhayn heartily approved the removal of his former CO, Prittwitz, from Eighth Army command and his replacement by Paul von Hindenburg, who brought with him his chief of staff Erich Ludendorff. Like Moltke, Prittwitz was then put out to pasture, and, like Moltke as well, would soon die at sixty-eight: Prittwitz in 1917 and Moltke the year before.

Falkenhayn doubtless incurred the envy of the many officers senior to him over which he was jumped. What is more, his appointment as chief of the German General Staff overlapped his service as minister of war. No Allied military leader enjoyed such an extraordinary degree of power. And yet, Falkenhayn was haunted by the ghost of Schlieffen and burdened by the failure of Moltke.

It was to these figures that his unprecedented authority was ultimately subordinated. Although he did achieve much prior to Verdun, everything he did was constrained by the collapse of the Schlieffen Plan. His advocacy of the war in his counsel with the kaiser had been based on the assumption that the Schlieffen approach would mean a quick victory. The First Battle of the Marne had put the lie to that assumption. He therefore presided over the series of attempted outflanking maneuvers known to history as the "Race to the Sea" (September 17–October 19, 1914), by which the German and French armies, like wrestlers grappling in vain for a takedown hold, attempted to envelop one another's northern flank. This maneuvering moved through Picardy, Artois, and Flanders. The objective was never really to "race to the sea," but the attempts to outflank one another inexorably moved the action in that direction. In the end, the First Battle of Ypres (October 19–November 22, 1914), not the English Channel, became the finish line of the race. As a result of that battle, Falkenhayn saw no other decisive move and so halted his advance. Combined French, Belgian, and British forces brought an end to the race yet failed to put the Allies in a better position than they had been. Moreover, Allied casualties—58,155 killed and wounded—were significantly higher than those of the Germans, which stood at 46,765. Yet these sacrifices gained Falkenhayn nothing—except the realization that what the Schlieffen Plan was supposed to have made possible—*Vernichtunsstrategie*, a "strategy of annihilation"—had to be abandoned in favor of an *Ermattunsstrategie*, a "strategy of attrition".

Constrained as he was by failure—both his own and that of his predecessor—Erich von Falkenhayn, a commander whose rise was meteoric yet who lacked any reputation for genius, could offer nothing more than what a later age, the Atomic Age, would identify with the acronym "MAD," signifying mutually assured destruction. The "Race to the Sea" became a race to the end, the "end" being defined as total exhaustion of manpower and materiel. The victor in such a race was the one who never quite reached that end. The victory thus achieved would be by definition pyrrhic.

RUTHLESS INDECISION

Who could seriously consider acting on such a strategy for such an inherently self-destructive result? Second Lieutenant Joubaire believed he knew: a humanity gone mad. Falkenhayn, however, was not mad. At most, he was conflicted. He was a Prussian officer who looked very much the part: Spartan, hair close-cropped, countenance fierce—the kind of face George S. Patton Jr., a tank officer in World War I, might have approvingly called a "war face." Before assuming top command in World War I, Falkenhayn had but little direct experience of combat. The Boxer Rebellion was, after all, a small-scale insurgency, not a clash of great armies. Yet he was more than willing to get men killed in the process of killing other men. It was Falkenhayn who ordered the first large-scale use of poison gas, at the First Battle of Ypres. It was he who not only counseled the kaiser to go to war but also pressed him to authorize unrestricted submarine warfare, in which U-boats attacked passenger and cargo vessels without warning. Falkenhayn also advocated using aircraft for not only tactical bombardment in the battlefield but also strategic bombardment of cities.

The infamous Christmas Memorandum to the kaiser—discussed in chapter 1—has been held up as the supreme example of Falkenhayn's ruthless nature. Taken at face value, the memorandum is precisely that. Falkenhayn proposes to attack the Verdun sector *not* to break the stalemate of trench warfare, not to break through to the French interior, and above all not to achieve a quick victory. He proposes a prolonged battle in which France would bleed itself white. Yet the historical fact is that the actual Christmas Memorandum manuscript has never been found. It "exists" only as "transcribed" in a postwar memoir by Falkenhayn himself. For this reason, a number of historians believe it to be a fiction that Falkenhayn made up after the fact to redefine—relabel, rebrand, spin— his *failure* to break through at Verdun as his *intention* all along. In other words, the Christmas Memorandum was the work of a man trying to portray himself as purely and absolutely ruthless.

Falkenhayn's critics grant him a ruthless streak, but they argue that he was far from "purely" or "absolutely" ruthless. The gas attack at Ypres created terror in the French lines, ripping a gaping hole in the Allied trenches. Arguably, Falkenhayn and his field commanders were as shocked by this as the French themselves and were therefore unprepared to properly exploit the breach. Falkenhayn's critics argue that the failure to follow through on the results of the gas assault was not due to shock but to fear. Falkenhayn, they charge, was afraid to go for broke. He was, they argue, one of those commanders more anxious to avoid defeat than to risk all in order to achieve victory. Similarly, when Erich Ludendorff inflicted a catastrophic defeat on the Russians at the Battle of Tannenberg (August 26–30, 1914), it was Falkenhayn, Germany's top commander, who reined in Ludendorff, thereby reducing the magnitude of his victory from annihilation to crippling neutralization. To justify Falkenhayn's caution in this case, many historians point out that the Schlieffen Plan tended to divide the German high command into two camps. On the one hand were the so-called Easterners, who favored decisively defeating the Russians while holding off the French and British in the west. On the other were the Westerners, who regarded the Schlieffen Plan with a higher degree of orthodoxy and believed it was both necessary and more feasible to defeat France and Britain first while defending against invasion by the immense but inadequately equipped, poorly organized, and ineptly led Russians. To be sure, Falkenhayn was a confirmed Westerner. Adherence to the Schlieffen Plan called for a minimal allocation of resources to the Eastern Front until the war was won on the Western Front. In restricting Ludendorff, it can be reasonably argued that Falkenhayn was merely acting in what he genuinely believed were the interests of a rapid victory in the West.

But this argument does not decisively exonerate Falkenhayn on a charge of being cautious to the point of self-defeat. History's "great captains" have always been risk takers, not for the mere sake of taking risk but in order to seize opportunities when they presented themselves. This requires flexibility with regard to plans. A great general would not have allowed himself to be held in thrall to a ghost, even a ghost as formidable as that of Alfred von Schlieffen, but would have exploited advantage and opportunity, even if they had not been contemplated in the sacred plan. Perhaps the flaw in Erich von Falkenhayn was less a tendency to be overly cautious, to hedge bets in ways that significantly reduced the upside of winning, than it was a failure of imagination that trapped him in the remains of a failed plan. To be ruthless yet unimaginative is not a definition of madness, but it did produce a strategy in which both sides were doomed to lose, and thus victory was defined as not losing quite everything. Whatever this may be, it is hardly sane.

"PRACTICALLY ALL THE ART OF MODERN WAR"

On October 29, 1914, some two months after the First Battle of the Marne, the London *Times* correspondent in France dispatched a "character sketch" of Falkenhayn's French counterpart, Joseph Jacques Césaire Joffre. Presumably it was meant to be flattering. It does not, however, read this way.

"War," Joffre told the correspondent, "now consists of a series of parallel movements. The armies turn about each other, like boxers in the preliminary stages, pivoting clumsily to catch each other at a disadvantage. That's practically all the art of modern war. The rest is ding-dong battle resistance, marching and counter-marching."[8] These words of the French general-in-chief—the man blamed for allowing the Germans to penetrate deeply into France in August 1914 and credited with foiling them at the Marne the next month—are sentiments of martial futility rather than of keen strategy, closer, certainly to madness than to élan vital.

Joffre, the correspondent comments, "is rarely seen on horseback," Instead, he "spends hours daily in a motor-car." His obesity—the man's appetite was legendary—may have put the saddle off limits. Or it may just have been that modern war had not only ushered in "ding-dong battle" but also killed the heroic romance of the mounted general and instead promoted motor transport ("He wears out two chauffeurs daily"). Indeed, as the *Times* correspondent saw it, Joffre rarely ventured to the front but instead spent "long hours in an unpretentious room with a telephone to his ear."[9]

The French general was not only skilled at riding in the backseat of an automobile and talking on the telephone, his "chief characteristic is calmness" and "confidence in himself." He is "modest, unassuming," an "adaptor organizer rather than a strategist." In what the correspondent described as a "war of silence and anonymity," Joffre's "genius" shines. "It is German-made scientific war as opposed to the artistic. General Joffre has become the master of a new system which he has not invented."[10]

Try as he might to render praise unto the commander the French liked to call "Papa" Joffre, the *Times* man sketches a portrait of a bewildered, discouraged, slow, unglamorous military bureaucrat, at home in a chauffeured car or an office with a phone, best suited not to a war of heroism but one of anonymity, resigned to fighting a war according to a "system" he did not invent.

He was, in fact, always something of an outsider. Born not in Paris or Lyon, but in remote Rivesaltes, in the *département* of Pyrénées Orientales, he graduated from the École Polytechnique with a degree in military engineering rather than preparation to lead a combat arm such as cavalry or infantry. In contrast to the conservative right-wing Catholicism that pervaded army high command, Joffre was a Freemason who made no secret of his disdain for the French national religion. He did gain considerable active military experience early in his career. During the Franco-Prussian War, he served in the defense of the siege of Paris as a junior engineering officer (September 19, 1870–January 26, 1871). By the time of the Sino-French War, he had been promoted to captain and fought in Formosa (March–June 1885). He went on to see action in Indochina and West Africa. Joffre taught as an instructor at the artillery school, then served under Joseph Simon Galliéni as fortifications officer on the island of Madagascar from 1900 to 1905.

Despite religious, political, and social friction with many of his fellow officers, he was promoted in 1905 to general of division. Three years later, he was a corps commander, and in 1910, amid a purge of senior officers who advocated reliance on defensive tactics, this engineer suddenly scorned his own engineering bread and butter by denouncing fortification and heavy artillery and embracing, blindly and unquestioningly, the ethos of unconditional attack. That year, such advocacy earned him promotion to the Supreme War Council. The great Galliéni, his former CO, now recommended Joffre's appointment as chief of the General Staff (Grande Quartier General) in 1911. It was in this capacity that Joffre, with the rest of the General Staff, developed Plan XVII, the blueprint for war with Germany. A simple plan, it simply threw all available resources into a headlong attack across the Franco-German border. Neither Joffre nor his staff anticipated the great northwesterly wheel of the Schlieffen Plan, which flanked the French and would not so much defeat Plan XVII as render it irrelevant.

We should not, however, dismiss the one quality in Joffre that the *Times* correspondent identified concretely, namely his calm. Joffre had complete charge of the French war effort for the first thirty months of World War I. The qualities of calm and a resolute refusal to panic, which had impressed his superiors in earlier days and helped gain him rapid promotion, proved tremendously valuable. Plan XVII invited disaster, it is true, but Joffre's steadfast command during the disastrous Battle of the Frontiers (August 14–25, 1914) and the headlong French retreat that followed (August 26–September 4) saved the French army from the total annihilation that his deficiency of strategic thought invited.

It took precious time for Joffre to fully recognize the threat presented by the German right wing, led by Generals Alexander von Kluck and Karl von Bülow, but when he did figure this out, Joffre launched the vigorous counterattack at the Marne during September 5–12 that saved Paris and, ultimately, France itself. It also launched what Joffre described as the "series of parallel movements," the turning of "the armies . . . about each other, like boxers in the preliminary stages," that were the attempts of the French and the Germans to outflank each other during the so-called Race to the Sea of September–November 1914. This frustration prompted Joffre to launch nearly suicidal offensives in Champagne (December 20, 1914–March 1915) and Artois (January 1–March 30, 1915). Arguably, Falkenhayn showed considerable acumen in allowing Joffre to sacrifice his men in these ill-conceived assaults. At first appalled, Joffre aborted both offensives, only to reinitiate them at Artois (May 16–June 30, September 25–October 30) and Champagne (September 25–November 6) with results that were, once again, self-destructive. Joffre explained his strategy as one of "nibbling away" at the enemy to produce his version of attrition, which he called *grignotage*—"erosion." The trouble was that nibbling took time, which Falkenhayn used to hammer away at the soldiers who were doing the nibbling. Little wonder that Joffre's detractors likened grignotage to "trying to bite through a steel door with badly fitting false teeth."[11]

FALKENHAYN V. JOFFRE

It was against the background of his single great victory at the Marne—a victory both preceded and followed by defeat in a self-defeating strategy of grignotage—that Joffre was forced to confront Falkenhayn's attack on Verdun. If the infamous Christmas Memorandum to Kaiser Wilhelm II is to be believed, Falkenhayn wanted to force Joffre to repeat at Verdun the ruinous, even quasi-suicidal, offensives of Artois and Champagne. But he hoped to entice Joffre to repeat them on an even larger scale.

Pro-Allied historians unquestioningly accepted the authenticity of the Christmas Memorandum. That is, they accepted as Falkenhayn's true belief that the French understood they could not afford to lose Verdun. They also accepted Falkenhayn's proposition that, if the French chose to fight for Verdun, they would incur such heavy losses that they would have no choice but to quit the war. Falkenhayn believed this would be the case; however, he bolstered his reasoning to the kaiser (again, assuming the authenticity of the Christmas Memorandum) by arguing that if they chose not to fight for it, the French people would be so appalled that they would force the government to quit the war in any case. Falkenhayn denied that his chief objective was to actually break through at Verdun. If he somehow did manage this, so much the better. But his true intention, he claims to have told the kaiser, was simply to tempt the French to beat themselves to death in a vain effort to repel German advances or mount a counteroffensive against German defensive positions. However, to make his case airtight, Falkenhayn argued that if Germany did not attack at Verdun, the possibility existed that Joffre would actually mount a destructive offensive through that position. This, in fact, was the original premise of France's Plan XVII. But the truth was that if Falkenhayn simply held his positions in the Verdun sector, he would almost completely envelop any attempted French penetration of what was a large German bulge—or salient—into the French lines. French attackers would be caught in one tremendous and deadly artillery crossfire.

In the Christmas Memorandum, Falkenhayn sought to convince (depending on whether we believe its authenticity or not) either the kaiser or history that he was a master strategist and psychologist, artfully playing Joffre by means of a spectacular gambit. In truth, a much stronger case can be made for having chosen simply to maintain or even build up German defensive positions within the boundaries of the salient as it existed in the Verdun sector in February 1916. Attack here instead of luring them to defend Verdun, and French forces would have been bled white much more quickly and at far less cost to the Germans.

There is another hole in Falkenhayn's strategic logic, wide and deep. As we have already seen, to assume Joffre would defend Verdun at all costs was to grossly misread Joffre. Since 1914, he had consistently shown remarkably little interest in holding Verdun. From very early in the war, he had regarded Verdun as nothing more than a pool of men and materiel on which to draw for use elsewhere. During the First Battle of the Marne (September 5–12, 1914), he had gone so far as to inform those commanding the Verdun sector that they would essentially have to fend for themselves. With that, he withdrew much of the French Third Army from

Verdun and vicinity, leaving the fortresses and the territory wide open to German attack. That no attack came is evidence of how little interest Falkenhayn had in Verdun early in the war. The difference between the positions of these two commanders was that, to Falkenhayn, Verdun must have appeared like low-hanging fruit. Given the strength and scope of the German salient bulging into France here, it must have seemed to Falkenhayn that he could attack Verdun any time he chose. There was no urgency. Joffre, in contrast, should have been thoroughly alarmed that this backdoor to the French interior was wide open and largely undefended.

That Joffre exhibited not the least alarm can be explained by two things. First, as already discussed, the French army, going into the war, was dominated by an irrational disdain for all fortification. (Unfortunately for the armies of France, this sentiment was not shared by German high command.) Second, absence of alarm was precisely what Joffre was celebrated for. As the London *Times* correspondent had noted in his profile in October 1914, General Joffre was not famed as a strategist. He was, however, positively renowned—and, by the French people, much loved—for his self-confidence, an air that is best described by the French word *sangfroid*, literally, "cold blood." Modern historians often mock this trait, typically linking it to another legendary hallmark of the French commander, a gargantuan appetite that seemingly took precedence over the prosecution of the war itself. Historian Paul Jankowski points out that, when Germany attacked Verdun in February 1916, "Falkenhayn, who ate little and drank moderately, would leave the table early and work late into the night." Whereas Falkenhayn was, accordingly, "sleek" in appearance, Joffre was "corpulent" and "complained bitterly one Good Friday when meat disappeared from the lunch menu at Chantilly" (French general headquarters). Indeed, the French people, who called him "Papa Joffre" or "le grand-père" (Grandfather), showed their affection for their marshal by sending him food of all kind—treats, sweets, and delicacies—in addition to cigars, despite wartime rationing and shortages. Although by early 1916 Falkenhayn had compiled a far more impressive military record than Joffre, he received demonstrations of affection from neither his staff nor the German people. Maybe a good general, maybe not, but he was certainly unlovable.

THE SUBORDINATES RISE UP

Throughout the late summer, autumn, and winter of 1914 and for nearly the first three-quarters of 1915, both the army and the politicians either cheered or indifferently acquiesced to Joffre's policy of progressively stripping the "Fortified Region of Verdun" (a designation that came to sound increasingly ironic) of its fortification, firepower, and manpower. It was not until late August 1915, when Joffre siphoned off a large number of infantrymen from the Verdun area for use in a new—doomed, as it turned out—offensive in Champagne that the general's subordinates in the field began to raise their voices in both alarm and protest.

At the time, the Fortified Region of Verdun was commanded by General Frédéric Herr. Herr pointed out that he now had fewer than eighty thousand men and a small fraction of his original allotment of a thousand artillery pieces to cover the Verdun region's seventy-five-mile perimeter. This gave him a defensive density of just two men per three meters. He protested to General Joffre that defending Verdun with lines so thin was impossible, especially in the almost complete absence of artillery. Joffre was unmoved.

Joffre knew that his word was final within the army. What he did not count on was that one of his officers, Lieutenant Colonel Émile Driant, would go clear around him. Driant commanded the Brigade of Chasseurs Alpin, the most elite unit posted to Verdun. His politics were diametrically opposed to those of Joffre. Driant was a right-wing Catholic nationalist, whereas Joffre described himself as a "Republican officer," a secular antimonarchist who did all he could to break the hold of conservative Catholicism over the army officer corps. It was on account of his politics that Driant, a distinguished soldier and writer on subjects of war, had no prospect of rising above the rank of colonel. He was free, however, to participate in the civil government, and he did so, achieving election to the Chamber of Deputies as a representative from Nancy in 1910. He now used his political connections and his high public profile to spread within the Chamber the alarm concerning Verdun. He told his fellow legislators that Verdun was vulnerable to *"attaque brusque"*—surprise attack—and they not only agreed with him but, in turn, carried the warning to the cabinet. Among those who heeded it was Joseph Galliéni. He had been

Lieutenant Colonel Émile Driant. WIKIMEDIA

elevated to the post of minister of war after serving as military governor of Paris and earning renown for commandeering Paris taxis to rush troops from the city to attack the German west flank at the First Battle of the Marne.

Driant got just what he wanted: a military-political scandal. But then he ran up against Joffre's celebrated sangfroid. With masterfully calm indignation, Papa threatened to resign, and that, it turned out, was enough

General Noël Édouard Marie Joseph, Vicomte de Cuières de Castelnau, who did his best to organize the initial defense of Verdun.
STAATSBIBLIOTHEK, BERLIN

to throw cold water on the boiling controversy. Still, Driant and Herr persisted in their protests until at last, in January 1916, Joffre relented to the extent of sending his second-in-command, General Édouard de Castelnau, to inspect the Verdun region. Castelnau was a commander disinclined to cross Joffre, so it was no surprise that, in his opinion, the first line of defense was just fine. Nevertheless, he did allow that the second and third lines were in very poor shape.

At last, Joffre began to get the message. For him, the tipping point came about two weeks after he received Castelnau's evaluation when, by dumb luck, French intelligence intercepted an exhortation to the German Fifth Army written by its commander, Crown Prince Wilhelm, son of the kaiser. "My friends," it began, "we have to take Verdun. It must be all over by the end of February, and then the Kaiser will hold a grand review on the Place d'Armes of Verdun and peace will be signed."[12]

Well, there it was.

Number one, the German army was going to attack Verdun. Number two, the German kaiser believed that victory at Verdun would bring the surrender of France. Joffre immediately dispatched an engineer regiment to build earthworks and organize new defensive lines. He countermanded his own order to pull out two more divisions from Verdun, and then he found two additional divisions, combined them into a new corps, and dispatched it to the Verdun region. Joffre now frantically scrounged all the heavy artillery he could find and ordered it positioned to defend Verdun.

FALKENHAYN DECIDES

The principal Battle of Verdun would last a day short of ten months, involve 2,390,000 soldiers, and kill some 300,000 of them. Yet not only was the French commander, Joseph Joffre, long reluctant to defend Verdun, the German commander, Erich von Falkenhayn, was long undecided whether to bother attacking it. During the initial invasion, in 1914, his Fifth Army commander, Crown Prince Wilhelm, passed through the region but declined to attack it directly. Instead, he and his subordinates skirted it, ultimately threatening it from three sides in a salient that would exist until the end of 1916. Between 1914 and 1916, various subordinates pushed Falkenhayn to attack Verdun from the margins of the salient. Time and again, he duly considered an offensive but, each time, reneged on mounting anything definitive.

During this long period, Crown Prince Wilhelm's chief of staff, a general named Schmidt von Knobelsdorf—to this day, he remains a

Ostensibly second in command under Crown Prince Wilhelm, CO of the German Fifth Army, General Schmidt von Knobelsdorf made most of the decisions governing German conduct of the Battle of Verdun. STAATSBIBLIOTHEK, BERLIN

shadowy figure in history—remained the most persistent advocate of attacking Verdun.

He apparently believed it was of significant strategic importance. Yet no one else seems to have thought this. Verdun was hardly *the* weak spot of the French front. And, while it was certainly a viable point of entry into the French interior, it was not *the* gateway—as some later described it—nor was it the quickest way to Paris. Still, Knobelsdorf persisted. And persisted.

Obscure though Knobelsdorf was, he benefitted from the unique organization of the German army at this time. Crown Prince Wilhelm had been trained as a soldier, but it was undeniable that he held command of the Fifth Army less by virtue of his military prowess than by virtue of his royal birth. The German military organization was cynically structured to accommodate just such commanders. Although subordinate to Wilhelm, Knobelsdorf, as his chief of staff, actually made virtually all of the strategic decisions attributed to the crown prince. He may or may not have secured Wilhelm's approval to take the idea of mounting an offensive against Verdun directly to Falkenhayn. Either way, it is generally believed that Knobelsdorf planted the idea of such an attack in Falkenhayn's head.

In the Christmas Memorandum to Kaiser Wilhelm II, Falkenhayn never even mentions Knobelsdorf. Taken at face value, it would appear that, for whatever reason, Falkenhayn suddenly awakened to the strategic value of Verdun—a strategic value founded almost exclusively on his assertion that the French would defend it at all costs and thereby bleed themselves white in the effort. But there is sufficient reasonable doubt to suggest that the Christmas Memorandum was a postwar fabrication. Even if this possibility did not exist, a number of those who knew Falkenhayn recalled that he never really thought of Verdun as a strategic objective in and of itself. Nor did he believe it was a trap to force the French army to self-destruction. Most of his contemporaries believed that Falkenhayn saw in an attack on Verdun nothing more or less than a means of restoring the possibility of movement in a stalemated war. Count von Schulenberg, who eventually replaced Knobelsdorf as Fifth Army chief of staff, believed that Falkenhayn attacked Verdun so that Joffre would have to weaken his fronts to the north of Verdun, in Aisne or Champagne. This would prompt the British to transfer troops for an offensive in Artois. These shifts, in turn, would give Falkenhayn an opportunity to throw his well-rested reserves into an attack against the weakened French positions at Aisne or Champagne and to counterattack the British at Artois. Potentially, one or both of these moves would result in a desperately needed breakthrough. In short, Verdun was not an end in itself but a means to an end. It was but one move on a vast chessboard.

The sheer complexity of this chess game tends to argue against it as a valid interpretation of Falkenhayn's motives at Verdun. He had never before exhibited such subtlety of strategic thought. On the other hand, no armies had ever before in the entire history of war been so thoroughly deadlocked. Every historian who studies the Battle of Verdun remarks on the excess of caution with which Falkenhayn deployed his forces. If—and it is a big *if*—he actually did intend to force France to bleed itself white, he did so in such a parsimonious, piecemeal fashion that he doomed his own army to a horrific bloodletting. Virtually all historians condemn Falkenhayn accordingly. They say he suffered from indecision and a deficiency of courage. Others argue that he was just plain incompetent. If, however, Count von Schulenberg's interpretation is correct, he was doing at Verdun what he had done farther north. He was husbanding his reserves to exploit possible breakthroughs.

In the end, there are only three ways to explain Falkenhayn's refusal to commit wholeheartedly to the attack on Verdun. He was either deficient in boldness and courage, ultimately incompetent, or he had a larger plan, a greater vision, in which Verdun was a means to an end rather than an end in itself.

BEYOND UNDERSTANDING

Barring the unlikely discovery of some hitherto unknown diary or secret communication, we can never hope to know the mind of either Joseph Joffre or Erich von Falkenhayn. That we cannot know their minds only amplifies our sense that, at Verdun, humanity was indeed mad.

One thing history has been reluctant to afford the two principal commanders of Verdun is empathy. Both Joffre and Falkenhayn have been portrayed as at best marginally competent and at worst craven, heartless, and all too comfortable sacrificing human lives as if they were—to use that pervasive metaphor of bleeding—so many corpuscles. Perhaps it would be more productive to accord these *actual* men the same measure of understanding we give to the *fictional* heroes of Greek tragedy. Those figures strut and fret their hour on the stage in blindness. They have been thrust into situations we—and the gods—can see, but they cannot. We appreciate this, and we empathize with them as hapless exemplars of the human condition we all share. The commanders of 1916 were thrust into war on a vast industrial scale, a war that pitted flesh against iron, nerve against explosive force, air breathers against toxic gases. The enormous size of the forces involved outstripped the technology available to communicate with and coordinate them. The technology that had produced the weapons excelled when it came to weapons of defense—machine guns, heavy artillery—but was relatively deficient in creating the means of offense, the weapons of attack. This in itself ensured stalemate, a condition that led neither to victory nor peace. The span 1914–1918—and, most of all, the moment that was 1916—saw the creation of warfare that was beyond the vision of those who instigated, waged, and commanded it.

CHAPTER 4

First Blood

You cannot know what man is capable of doing to his fellow man:
after five days my shoes are greasy with human brains, I crush tho-
raxes, I encounter entrails.[1]

—QUOTATION INSCRIBED ON A HISTORICAL MARKER
AT LES ÉPARGES, HIGH GROUND CONTESTED IN
THE VERDUN SECTOR FOR MONTHS BEFORE THE
BATTLE OF FEBRUARY–DECEMBER 1916

WHAT HISTORIANS HAVE TRADITIONALLY CALLED *THE* BATTLE OF VER-
dun, which began on February 21 and ended on December 20, 1916,
has often been described as a metaphor for the entirety of World War
I. And why not? The February–December battle combined all the most
horrific aspects of the so-called Great War. The engagement there was
one no one seemed really to want; the French high command had virtually written off Verdun, and the German army had, in the initial phase of
the war, refused to attack Verdun directly. In much the same way, World
War I itself had come about less through acts of volition than fecklessly,
by reason of entangling treaties and alliances combined with failures of
diplomacy on all sides. The character of the main Verdun battle—static
slaughter, a bloodletting without clear strategic purpose, an exercise in
attrition that wasted both sides almost equally—was characteristic of the
entire war. As doomed French second lieutenant Alfred Joubaire saw in
Verdun evidence of the madness of humanity, so most of the world came
to see the whole of the war in this way.

And so Verdun seems an abundantly apt World War I metaphor. A metaphor, of course, is not reality in the sense of *the thing itself*. Rather, it is an intellectual and verbal tool we use to more effectively grapple with *the thing itself*. Metaphor is a heuristic, an expedient for solving a problem that uses a practical methodology rather than a perfect one. Intellectually, a heuristic is not a perfect understanding, but one that is good enough, shorthand for understanding. Do you want to understand World War I? Just look closely at this single terrible battle. Absorb it. Feel it. Then go ahead and imagine the entire war was like it.

When we speak of metaphor, we typically mean using one thing to describe another thing. "All the world's a stage," Shakespeare wrote in *As You Like It*. "World" and "stage" are indisputably two different things. To use "stage" as a heuristic route to arrive at an understanding of "the world" is clearly an instance of metaphor. "Verdun" and "World War I" are not distinct from one another, however. "Verdun" is actually part of "World War I," not different from it. Verdun is therefore a special kind of metaphor called a synecdoche, a part of a thing that stands for the whole of that thing, just as "the Pentagon" is a synecdoche for the American military bureaucracy or "bread and butter" is a synecdoche for a person's livelihood.

All metaphors, including synecdoches, are used to make graspable the difficult to grasp. In the case of Verdun and World War I, the synecdoche makes the difficult to grasp not so much more graspable as more bearable. As it turns out, the battle commonly known as Verdun, with a duration one day short of ten months—nearly 25 percent of the war's span—can be seen as actually having lasted almost the entire war. Viewing Verdun as a metaphor for World War I tends to minimize both the battle and the war. As Verdun was an even worse form of collective madness than Second Lieutenant Joubaire envisioned, so was World War I.

Why was Verdun worse than Joubaire thought it? Because the fighting there did not begin on February 21, 1916, but in September 1914, and it did not end on December 20, 1916, but on September 26, 1918, when the AEF—the American Expeditionary Force—finally broke through, seized, and held the long-contested Verdun-sector territory as World War I neared its armistice.

Why was the war worse? Because the armistice, prelude to the Treaty of Versailles and the many agreements related to it, did not ensure that the Great War would be the "war to end all wars," as Woodrow Wilson had hoped, but instead created conditions of surrender for Germany and the other Central Powers that yielded a peace doomed to be no more than a two-decade truce. Verdun, like the war of which it was a part, was worse than anyone had imagined.

As for the "battles" of Verdun before *the* Battle of Verdun, there were at least four: the German advance through the area in August 1914, the German offensive on the right bank of the Meuse in September 1914, the French offensives chiefly on the left bank of the Meuse in 1914–1915, and the French offensives chiefly on the right bank of the Meuse beginning in the spring of 1915. After the principal battle of February 21–December 20, 1916, the French launched a new offensive late in 1917 and then, in conjunction with the American Expeditionary Forces (AEF), there were two separate offensives in August and September 1918.

AUGUST–SEPTEMBER 1914

Although there had been fortifications in Verdun since Roman times, by the outbreak of World War I, in 1914, the actual city of Verdun was an inconsiderable town of slightly fewer than thirteen thousand inhabitants just twenty-five miles from the border with Germany. The military sector named for the town encompassed a far-flung system of thirty-four forts (of which nine were, technically speaking, mere *ouvrages*, "works,"—fortified structures smaller and simpler than full-fledged forts). The forts did mount some artillery, but their true function was to protect the more extensive artillery batteries located behind them. Forts also provided shelter for observers and infantry. Most of the forts were distributed throughout an approximately four-square-mile territory, near the southeastern corner of which was the city of Verdun. Although located at the heart of a military complex and historically a fortified strongpoint, the town itself was about as poorly situated for tactical purposes as possible. It was surrounded on three sides by high ground, which, far from being a defensive advantage, made the town vulnerable to attack. In civil terms, little

Verdun was economically insignificant. Its sole industry was farming—and meager farming at that.

The town did serve the engineer Séré di Rivière—mastermind behind the boom in French fortification building that began in 1873, shortly after the Franco-Prussian War—as one of two anchors for counterattacking a likely route of German invasion. The other anchor Séré di Rivière envisioned was Paris itself. As the French military historian Gabriel Bichet noted in 1969, French high command was initially inclined to call the First Battle of the Marne the "Battle of Paris-Verdun" instead. In part, this label was a stirring piece of propaganda, and, in part, it was high command's nod to the foresight of Séré di Rivière. Given the French success at the First Battle of the Marne, it suddenly also seemed a good idea to actually follow the engineer's more than forty-year-old lead by securing an anchor at Verdun. This would furnish pivot points at Paris and Verdun that would allow an army to position itself to outflank a Germany breakthrough—or so it seemed. In 1915, the French would even attempt to seize Vauquois and Les Éparges, the most prominent high-ground positions (buttes) enveloping Verdun.[2]

Following a plan more than four decades old, the French had neglected to secure that high ground at the outbreak of the war. They were more concerned with counterattacking the massive German thrust into the French interior. French high command was stunned by Germany's execution of the Schlieffen Plan in the first full month of the war, August 1914, with its great wheeling movement that swooped down on the French armies and on the French capital from the north and the west. Compared to France's simpleminded Plan XVII, the Schlieffen Plan was highly innovative. Yet its principal feature, the "great wheel," should not have been unexpected. French and British intelligence were well aware of the long-standing German penchant for creating strategies of envelopment as opposed to head-on attack. Indeed, the preference for the one over the other had even been openly articulated as official doctrinal policy in 1888.[3] For that matter, envelopment—preferably *double* envelopment—had been the strategic gold standard among the world's generals ever since Hannibal destroyed the Roman legions at Cannae, in Apulia, Italy, in 215 BC during the Second Punic War.

Innovative? At bottom, German strategy was rooted in ancient military thinking.

In August and September 1914, Crown Prince Wilhelm marched his Fifth Army through the Verdun sector but bypassed Verdun itself and most of the sector's forts. Thanks to French high command's prewar disdain for fortification, Wilhelm could have simply taken both Verdun and many of the forts. But he did not see these objectives as sufficiently important in and of themselves to merit an attack, no matter how easy. Instead, he began to envelop Verdun and the forts nearby, creating what would be a long-standing salient.

In most general histories of World War I, so much attention is paid to the drama of the First Battle of the Marne that the operations of the Crown Prince's Fifth Army in the Verdun sector are typically ignored. By September 6, elements of the Fifth Army had taken positions south of the village of Verdun on *both* banks of the Meuse River. The southernmost German position—which was also the westernmost—was at the town of Revigny, between Verdun, located to the northeast, and the Marne River, about twelve miles southwest. General Maurice Sarrail led the French Third Army in response to this advance by attacking the right (southern) flank of the German Fifth Army. The Germans responded with counterattacks aimed at turning the flank of the French Third Army. Coming to the aid of the German Fifth Army was the German Fourth, under General Viktor Albrecht, Herzog von Württemburg, which pressed the French from the northeast. As the French Third Army fell back under this onslaught, a gap opened at Revigny. On September 7, elements of the combined German Fourth and Fifth Armies were on the verge of breaking through the gap when French high command quickly shifted an entire army corps from Commercy, located some thirty miles east of Revigny. In this way, the line was held, albeit at the cost of stripping bare the fortified towns of Nancy and Toul. If these had fallen to an opportunistic German attack, the entire forty-mile line from Verdun southeast to Toul would have collapsed, and a German breakthrough could easily have turned the tide at the First Battle of the Marne, which was then ongoing. What saved the day for the French was the sudden, unexpected German disengagement from a battle they seemed to be winning. Even more surprising, the disengagement was followed by a German retreat to the north, as the First Battle of the Marne went against Alexander von Kluck's German First Army and Karl von Bülow's Second.

Not that the French were in the clear. The Verdun sector had thirty-four forts and ouvrages. Erected along the forty miles of high ground that formed the right bank of the Meuse between Verdun and Toul were six of those forts, of which Fort de Troyon was the most important. General Hermann von Strantz, commanding V Corps of the German Fifth Army, saw Troyon as relatively isolated from the other forts and therefore especially vulnerable. He reasoned that if he could break through here, he would have a relatively clear route of advance to the town of Saint-Mihiel, some six miles south of Troyon. Here, his corps could cross the Meuse and attack French positions from the rear, effectively catching them in the jaws of a pincer between V Corps and other Fifth Army elements. While rolling up French positions in this area, Von Strantz would also cut off Verdun from the south, thereby completing the envelopment of Verdun and the forts closest to it.

East of Verdun and running between the Meuse and the Moselle rivers in a broad north–south arc is a region of Lorraine the French government today denominates as one of the nation's *zones naturelles d'intérêt écologique, faunistique et florestique*. It bears a soft, archaic name: the Woëvre. Despite the exotic sound of the word, its basic meaning is simply *wet*, nothing more and nothing less, and it is an apt description of a low-lying plain of land watered by lakes and swamps and punctuated by small, flat-topped heights, or buttes; the French refer collectively to these as the *côtes de Meuse*. Boggy and rugged, the Woëvre had all the appearance of ground utterly unsuited to use as a battlefield and, historically, it was not used as such. For this reason, in 1914, the French high command largely ignored the Woëvre. Although it fell within the sector assigned to the French Second Army, that army's commander, General Noël-Édouard de Castelnau, had no qualms about stripping it of men in order to supply reinforcements to General Sarrail at Revigny. General von Strantz knew as little about the Woëvre as any other French general did, but he saw that this portion of the boggy plain between Verdun and Saint-Mihiel was all but undefended, and so, on September 8, elements of his corps, along with

Austrian artillery units, advanced across it. Quickly positioning his howitzers—light German ones and much heavier Austrian weapons—Von Strantz unleashed a hellish barrage against Fort Troyon.

Troyon was garrisoned by about 450 men under the command of a captain so obscure that his first name is rarely encountered in the literature. It happens to be François, but he is almost exclusively referred to as Captain (or Capitaine) Heym. Among the first wave of forts built by Séré di Rivière following the Franco-Prussian War, Fort Troyon had been designed to withstand artillery fire of vintage 1870 and was never upgraded to withstand more modern high-explosive shells. In theory, therefore, the modern howitzers Von Strantz commanded should have been more than sufficient to pulverize the installation.

Pulverize? What, exactly, did it mean to be "pulverized" by modern high-trajectory mortar shells packing a powerful trinitrophenol explosive the French called melinite? It was an explosive so powerful—four times more powerful than the high explosives created in the 1870s, when the early Rivière forts were built—that soldiers dubbed them "torpedo shells." Although much smaller than a naval torpedo, each shell could deliver the explosive force of one. If you were in a fort that suffered a direct hit by a torpedo shell, the shockwave itself was sufficient to kill you—by bursting vital organs, causing massive internal hemorrhages, or delivering a brain-killing concussion. If you were sheltered deep in the bowels of the fort, in one of its cavernous earth-fast "bombproofs," you might be buried alive or you might suffocate—slowly from lack of oxygen or more quickly due to inhalation of the toxic products of melinite detonation. Assuming you were not quickly blown to bits, crushed under debris, or asphyxiated or poisoned, the relentless impacts and detonations of a typical barrage would surely take a psychological toll. The term "shell shock," coined during World War I, was typically used to describe a cluster of psychosomatic symptoms including varying degrees of panic, generalized anxiety, the "jitters," or helplessness, and difficulty reasoning, speaking, sleeping, and sometimes even walking. If there seemed to be a single telltale sign of shell shock, it was the look of "shock," an otherworldly facial expression of frozen fear, a haunting, dazed look that British troops called "the thousand-yard stare." All of this was terrible. In fact, the psychosomatic effects of sustained shelling, especially among men stationed in a fort under attack, were often much, much worse. Men simply went mad and were impossible to control, contain, or even restrain.

For the attackers, achieving General von Strantz's objective did not necessarily require the destruction of Fort Troyon—just its surrender. The commander of the howitzer batteries therefore ordered a pause in the barrage on September 9, after a single day of shelling, to offer the French garrison an opportunity to surrender.

Although Captain Heym was not privy to grand strategy at the level of high command, he understood that his surrender would open to the Germans a route straight through a virtually undefended slice of the Woëvre. Such a breakthrough would allow the Germans to flank the French position, which would almost certainly lead to French defeat on the Marne and, quite probably, the breach of Paris itself. At this point, in what we might call the First Battle of Verdun—a battle fought before the battle that is "officially" designated by history—there was true, unalloyed heroism. The threat to Paris, already fighting for its life at the First Battle of the Marne, was very real and certainly imminent. To the surrender demand, Heym therefore replied, "Never! I shall blow it up sooner." Turning to the German emissaries, he snapped: "Get out, I've seen enough of you. *A bientôt, à Metz.*" In this way, Heym extended his defiance at Verdun to a confident promise that France would retake the fortress city captured in the 1870 war and held by the Germans since then.[4] At the very least, Heym's response invites comparison with the celebrated reply that Brigadier General Anthony McAuliffe, acting commanding officer of the U.S. 101st Airborne Division when it was surrounded at Bastogne in 1944, issued to a Nazi surrender demand: "Nuts!" And, given the vulnerability of the French flank at the ongoing Marne battle, it would not be amiss to compare Heym's stand-fast determination to Colonel Joshua Lawrence Chamberlain's resolve to hold the flank of the Union army at Little Round Top during the Battle of Gettysburg.

The shelling of Fort Troyon resumed as soon as the German representatives returned to their lines. After nightfall, the barrage ended, and the Germans assaulted with infantry. One of the enduring myths of World War I is that the Germans habitually attacked with the massed ferocity of the nomadic Eastern European–Central Asian tribe whose name the Allies (and especially the Americans) applied to them as a slur: the Huns. In fact, German combat doctrine favored envelopment, a strategy of strangling rather than charging the enemy. German attacks—especially early in the war, under the leadership of Helmuth von Moltke—therefore typically took the form of cautious probes by relatively small numbers in search of the enemy's weak spots. The assault on Fort Troyon that night was one of these operations, and when the attackers realized that the French garrison meant to fight, they withdrew. The howitzers opened up again on the next day, mainly from the Austrian artillery units advancing alongside General von Strantz. Although their fire was only marginally accurate, the relentless howitzers (on September 12 alone, there were ten sustained barrages) reduced the above-ground portions of the fort to rubble. From within that rubble, with a garrison of just 450 men, Captain Heym held out long enough for the arrival of a substantial French relief force. At this point, September 12, the First Battle of the Marne went decisively against the Germans, and Moltke ordered a general retreat. At the time of disengagement from Fort Troyon, the heavy Austrian howitzers had scored 200 direct hits on the fort, and the lighter German weapons 2,800. Despite the obsolescent engineering of the old fort, only five of Heym's men had been killed. Twenty-three were wounded.

And so the "first" battle of Verdun ended, Paris was saved, and the Verdun sector lived to fight many another day. The rallying cry most often associated with the "main" Battle of Verdun—the ten-month ordeal of 1916—was "Ils ne passeront pas!" (*They shall not pass!*). Often misattributed to General Henri Philippe Pétain when he commanded the French Central Army Group at Verdun, it was actually spoken by his successor in that command, General Robert Nivelle, whom history by and large condemns as a heedless butcher who threw away tens of thousands of French lives in one futile counterattack after another.

If anything, however, the true spirit of "Ils ne passeront pas!" was demonstrated not by a sanguine general but by a gritty captain. François Heym was barely recognized as the hero he indeed was, largely because he died defending the Woëvre hamlet of Marchéville, just weeks after his remarkable stand at Fort Troyon.

General Robert Nivelle was a master artillerist and an exponent of attaque à outrance—a rare combination. WIKIMEDIA

SEPTEMBER 18, 1914–SEPTEMBER 25, 1915

Helmuth von Moltke's order for a general retreat on September 12 was the last command he issued before his replacement by Erich von Falkenhayn as chief of the German General Staff. Among Falkenhayn's first important commands was a September 18 order to renew the effort to envelop—not attack directly—Verdun. Although the operation was to focus on the right bank of the Meuse, east of Verdun, Falkenhayn's envelopment strategy also involved action in the Argonne Forest, on the left bank, adjacent to the west side of Verdun. Just as the French had neglected to provide for the defense of the Woëvre, on the assumption that the rugged wetland made for an unlikely battlefield, so they took comfort in the assumption that the densely forested Argonne would make very hard going for a modern army, which not only had to move artillery but to take aim with it. Trackless forest made for difficult transportation as well as nearly impossible targeting, the trees providing thick screening of major objectives.

The natural obstacles to an advance through the Argonne dissuaded the French from providing for its defense and therefore spurred Falkenhayn's order to march through the forest. On September 21, the Sixteenth Army Corps, commanded by General Karl Bruno Julius von Mudra, attacked elements of the French Third Army west of the Meuse near Montfaucon and Varennes-en-Argonne. An aging commander—he was in his sixties—Von Mudra was nevertheless an innovative one who had revised the role of the *Pioniere*—military engineers—into combat engineers, a specialty well adapted to fighting in a forested environment. Von Mudra's Pioniere were armed with small mortars, including highly transportable Minenwerfers. This enabled him to position very transportable high-trajectory artillery close to the enemy, so that his men could lob explosives directly onto French positions. So portable were the Minenwerfers that Von Mudra deployed them not in separate artillery batteries but alongside his infantry riflemen. In addition, the Pioniere units were supplied with "inflammable projectors," immediate precursors of the flamethrowers that would play a significant part in the main Battle of Verdun in 1916.

General Maurice Sarrail, commanding the French Third Army, rushed forces to the densely forested Bois de la Gruerie in the Argonne, with the intention of arresting what he assumed was a German effort to make a major breakthrough toward the west. In fact, Von Mudra, a methodical engineer, was aiming at nothing so grand. Instead, his objective was to seize the heights of a butte called the Vauqois, from which he could direct artillery fire against the principal rail line supplying Verdun. Yet again, French commanders had failed to appreciate that the prevailing German doctrine was one of envelopment—strangulation—rather than head-on attack. Once he seized the heights, Von Mudra halted and began to rain down artillery fire on French infantry positions. Slowly, methodically, his guns annihilated one infantry position after another. When a position was wiped out, Von Mudra advanced his infantry—equipped with mortars and proto-flamethrowers—into that position. The German advance was slow and painstaking. Thanks to an envelopment by artillery firing from the high ground, the German commander was able to modestly advance his infantry every day or day and a half, so that, by September 26, his Sixteenth Corps had pushed back the French lines a full five miles across a front nearly twelve and a half miles wide. In the process, he took the town of Varennes-en-Argonne as well as the commanding heights of the Vauqois. Among other things, this rendered French rail transportation into the Verdun region all but impossible—except for the occasional train that managed to sneak in under cover of darkness. Von Mudra now had one hand on Verdun's throat.

The Sixteenth Army Corps of the German Fifth Army had made considerable inroads into the Argonne, while bypassing Verdun and most of the associated fortifications. In less than a week, however, the French were able to muster significant resistance in the Argonne, and on October 2 mounted counterattacks that pushed a bulging salient into the advancing German lines near the villages of Bagatelle and Saint-Hubert east of the Meuse. Von Mudra responded on October 4 with a new attack that, in keeping with his professional inclination, was also significantly innovative. For the first time in the war, he used Minenwerfers as well as hand grenades to supplement fire from the more conventional mortars he had employed earlier.

In essence, Von Mudra hurled at the French every weapon system he had at his disposal. Yet French resistance and counterattacking remained

French wounded at Verdun. AUTHOR'S COLLECTION

fierce. Believing that success depended on full coordination of forces throughout the Verdun sector, Von Mudra appealed to Falkenhayn to be given sole command of the entire sector. This was granted, and thus the general found himself with three divisions of infantry, two Jäger divisions (elite infantry, akin to the modern U.S. Army Rangers), three *Landwehr* (reserve) regiments, three battalions of Pioniere, and eight full artillery regiments. Von Mudra used these in a ruthlessly systematic fashion, always targeting a narrow section of the front for massive artillery bombardment to breach the enemy line. Once an opening had been made, a mixed wave of infantry and Pioniere would penetrate the breach, preparing the way for successive waves of infantrymen and machine-gun teams. Two-men light mortar teams also followed.

In contrast to the "first" Verdun battle, which was brief, the second presaged the 1916 battle by its length. Von Mudra mounted a series of small-scale assaults against various points in the French lines. General

Joffre liked to boast that he "nibbled at the Germans." Von Mudra likewise nibbled, but did not boast about it and, in contrast to Joffre's nibbling—which was strictly a process of attrition, hard on both defender and attacker alike—Von Mudra's made measurable, albeit agonizingly slow, progress. During November–December 1914, he mounted nine attacks, each using only a few companies of men. In January 1915, the attacks became larger but were still modest. Inexorably, the French casualties mounted in the Argonne. By March 1915, the French Third Army had lost some thirty thousand men to the methodical harassment of Von Mudra. Moreover, the Germans voraciously "nibbled" through the forest the French had assumed was essentially impenetrable by a modern army. On February 16, 1915, the German advance reached Le Four de Paris. This miniscule hamlet was inconsiderable in and of itself, but it marked the point at which the Argonne began to open out onto clear land to the west. Possession of Le Four de Paris signaled the imminence of a German breakthrough.

While Von Mudra chewed through the Argonne, General Hermann von Strantz was tasked with advancing through the Woëvre with the objective of seizing the so-called heights of the Meuse. This would give the Germans control over much of the territory between the Meuse and the Moselle rivers. To accomplish this mission, Von Strantz was promoted from command of the Fifth Army Corps to a combination of that corps plus the Third Bavarian and Fourteenth Army corps, a division of Bavarian cavalry, and the Austrian artillery batteries. This grouping of forces was christened the *Armeeabteilung von Strantz*, the "Von Strantz Army Detachment."

Von Strantz had learned an important lesson from the unsuccessful German assault on Fort Troyon: artillery bombardment was insufficient to neutralize fortified positions. Like Von Mudra, he believed the solution was what today is called a "combined arms" approach. Instead of using artillery to "prepare" the objective for a follow-on infantry assault, he created operational units consisting of infantry, artillery, and Pioniere. With these, he would move as quickly as possible southwest and take Fort du Camp des Romains, which would allow him to cross the Meuse to its west bank via the bridge at Saint-Mihiel. Once here, he would destroy the railroad into and out of Verdun. While Von Strantz faced a French line on his right flank, east of Verdun, he was confident that he could attack this force frontally and hold it in the attack while his main force advanced around it and targeted Fort du Camp des Romains. In World War II, U.S. general George S. Patton Jr., would describe this sort of tactic—one of his favorites—as "holding the enemy by the nose while kicking him in the ass." For Von Strantz it proved to be uncannily effective. He commenced his offensive on September 20. By September 24, the French Seventy-Fifth Division—the only French force defending the much-neglected, little-understood Woëvre—virtually ceased to exist. The Germans mowed it down as they marched into Saint-Mihiel, crossed the bridge over the Meuse, and destroyed the south–north rail route into Verdun.

Camp des Romains, on a butte south of Saint-Mihiel, was the next objective. If the Germans failed to neutralize this, the valuable Meuse bridgehead just established would be indefensible. To any civilian, Camp des Romains looked formidable because of its commanding position on a height overlooking both Saint-Mihiel and the Meuse. To Von Strantz and his engineers, the fort's position appeared not as its strength but as its vulnerability. The fort was isolated and, because the German general had used his howitzers and Minenwerfers to suppress fire from nearby forts, Camp des Romains received no crossfire support from the rest of the Verdun system. Rather than assault it directly, Von Strantz fell back on accepted German doctrine and, by September 24, completely surrounded Camp des Romains. Thanks to the sheer firepower available to his Armeeabteilung—firepower now focused on Camp des Romains from all directions—the garrison suffered far more than that of Captain Heym. By September 25, the shattered survivors of the bombardment huddled in the fort's remains, which were effectively no more than a cave. Units of Pioniere and infantrymen stormed the rubble from all sides and, after a three-hour exchange of fire, what remained of the French garrison surrendered.

Camp des Romains was the only fort of the Séré de Rivières era to be captured by a direct infantry assault. That was bad enough. Worse, the regular-gauge rail lines to Verdun were now completely cut. Supplying and reinforcing this major complex of forts would be supremely difficult.

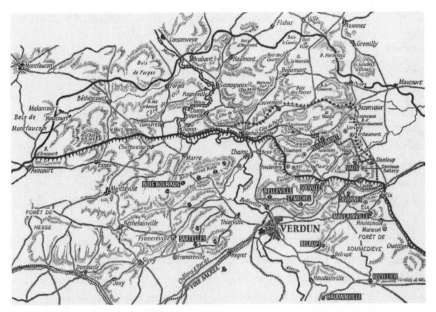

This map shows the major villages and towns, including the city of Verdun, and their relation to the system of forts (pentagon symbols) as laid out (chiefly) by Séré de Rivières. The heavy black line shows the German position at the start of the battle. The heavy black line with "barbs" shows the extent of the German advance by August 1916. WIKIMEDIA

Perhaps worst of all for the French was the fact that the German army, so soon after suffering defeat at the First Battle of the Marne, inflicted humiliation of French arms with a vigorous comeback counteroffensive.

OCTOBER 1914–DECEMBER 1915

A third battle in the Verdun sector began in October 1914 and ended in March of the following year. It was a succession of direct attacks on the German position that had been established atop the butte of Vauquois. The objective of these attacks was to restore access to the rail line running to Verdun from the west.

Simultaneously with the French action against Vauquois came another series of French attacks on German-held high points at a ridge known as Les Éparges and elsewhere in the Woëvre. These actions, intended to relieve the envelopment of Saint-Mihiel, may be considered the fourth of the pre-1916 battles of Verdun.

Histories of World War I devote little attention to the fighting in the Verdun vicinity prior to February 1916—an amazing fact, since the French government secretly reported that some 200,000 French soldiers were killed or wounded in this sector from the outbreak of the war in August 1914 through the end of 1915.[5] The high level of losses may be attributed in large measure to a French shortage of heavy artillery and, even more critically, to an acute shortage of high-explosive shells. At Verdun—not only in 1914–1915 but through the main battle in 1916 and elsewhere on the Western Front to the very end of the war in November 1918—the French often lacked artillery capable of sufficient range to conduct an effective counterbattery campaign against German artillery positions. Most German heavy artillery had substantially greater range than the biggest French guns and could therefore be positioned within range of French targets but out of range of French artillery.

During 1914 through most of 1916, the artillery the French did have was inadequately supplied with ammunition. Budget cutbacks before the outbreak of the war—cutbacks high command not only accepted but, in its contempt for heavy artillery, actually endorsed—meant that gunners' specifications of shell requirements were never met. The official French prewar estimate of ammunition was 700 to 1,200 shells per gun, depending on caliber. To his credit, Joffre, though by no means an advocate of artillery, upped this to between 1,200 and 1,500 shells. In reality, however, the need was a continuous 3,000 shells per gun.[6]

Chronically and critically outgunned, the French had no high-trajectory artillery—no heavy mortars with appropriate high-explosive ammunition—capable of aiding in the multiple attempts to recapture the high ground at Vauquois. In consequence, the only option for attacking this strongly held butte—1,300 feet long and nearly a thousand feet above sea level—was to attack it uphill and head-on. Any uphill attack is extremely difficult and bound to be costly. The Germans occupying the Vauquois made it a downright suicidal proposition by combining artillery fire with extensive runs of barbed wire. Stymied by the wire and an abundance of shell holes, the French infantry advance up the slope was extremely slow, the attackers making easy targets for the defenders. At first, few French troops even made it across the level no-man's-land separating the occupied butte from the nearest French positions. As more French artillery arrived, attackers were sometimes able to overrun the first line of German trenches, which had been largely abandoned. Once the attackers began their climb, however, they were blown up by artillery shells or mowed down by machine-gun fire. Wave after wave of head-on, uphill assaults suffered the same bloody fate without even coming close to retaking the butte. As the French writer and military volunteer George Boucheron described one assault, that of October 28, 1914, "We advance . . . always progressing . . . but suddenly, a muted detonation, followed by a hiss, makes itself heard: an explosion, then others, and on the slopes, big black clouds," which were the earth and dust raised by shells. These, Boucheron wrote, invariably fell "exactly on the positions we occupied." He recalled how men are "harvested by the shells," so that, in just "a few minutes after the first shell has hit, you can't see the dark blue tunics or the red trousers . . . only the dark green grass. All is quiet."[7]

Although Boucheron described only the assault of October 28, 1914, those that had preceded it were similarly futile, as were those that followed it, over and over, through December 1914. The next month, on January 5, 1915, Joffre replaced General Auguste Yvon Edmund Dubail as First Army commander with General Pierre Roques. Like Joffre, Roques was a military engineer, and the chief of staff therefore had a degree of faith in him. At the same time, Third Army commander Maurice Sarrail, apparently undeterred by the unproductive slaughter his forces had endured since September, continued to believe that the current offensive would—somehow—ultimately prevail against the Vauquois. Sarrail tasked General Joseph Alfred Micheler to make a new assault with Third Army's Fifth Corps. That unit had heavy mortars—220-mm and 270-mm weapons—which was impressive; however, having been cast in 1878, they were also obsolescent. Although they could achieve the steep trajectory required when attacking high-ground fortifications from below, they needed to be very close to their targets. And there was the rub. The German positions looked directly down on the French. The German howitzers installed on the heights were much smaller than the French weapons, but they had far greater range. German counterbattery fire would either quickly destroy the French mortars or, more likely, prevent their in-range positioning altogether. Big though the 220s and 270s were, they were essentially useless. Moreover, Sarrail moved without any sense of urgency as he formulated the attack with Micheler. The most recent French offensives had failed in December 1914. It was February 17, 1915, before the new offensive even got under way.

As before, the first French assault waves withered under German artillery fire. Yet early reports—remarkably enough—indicated success. The village of Boureuilles on the Vauquois butte had apparently been retaken from the Germans, and the men of the French reserves waiting to join the assault were awakened at 1 a.m. on the 18th by the regimental band playing "La Marseillaise." Dawn of that day revealed a very different reality. Although French troops had managed to scale the butte, the German defenses were quite intact. The French "occupiers" of Boureuilles were nothing more than a handful of tattered troops, survivors of an assault that had cost the lives of more than half of the men in the two participating regiments. Before the end of the day on the 18th, the few Frenchmen in the tiny village climbed back down the slope of the butte, feeling fortunate to have escaped with their lives.

The failure duly reported to Joffre, Joffre instantly ordered Sarrail to mount a new assault. For this, Joffre sent a railroad train hauling a pair of 100-mm naval guns into position. Although this heavy artillery was welcome, the guns were actually incapable of high elevation and so were of very limited value against high-ground fortifications. One witness, a platoon leader named André Pézard, contemptuously described the French barrage of February 28 as "a very feeble cannonade" and posed the rhetorical question, "Is that the 'magnificent artillery preparation' of which the colonel spoke?"[8]

Nevertheless, French infantry once again entered the rubble that had been Boureuilles and began digging in atop the butte, which had been won through two days of combat and at the cost of three thousand men. Throughout much of March 1915, fighting atop this rise was fierce. It unfolded as part of a larger French offensive raging below. All the struggle resulted in nothing more than stalemate—or, more accurately, a qualified

German victory, since the Germans remained in possession of the Vauquois high ground. In consequence, the railroads below were unavailable to the French. The main point at which men and materiel were fed into the Verdun sector was at Bar-le-Duc, a town almost due south of Verdun. Now the rail line connecting Bar-le-Duc with Verdun was entirely under German control and would remain that way at the outbreak of the 1916 battle.

Below Ground and Above

Between January and March 1915—with the main Battle of Verdun still a year in the future—General Sarrail had already managed to lose nearly 27,000 men, of whom 4,534 had been killed and 5,770 were missing and unaccounted for. While German losses were much lighter and the fighting had left the Germans in control of some of the Verdun sector forts as well as favorable positions menacing Verdun itself, there was frustration on both sides. Having failed to achieve definitive results above ground, both armies tried tunneling into the butte. On May 14, 1916—with the main Verdun battle by then under way—the Germans detonated a mine beneath the west end of the butte, which was still occupied by the French. The blast excavated a crater nearly a hundred feet deep, instantly killing eight hundred members of the French Forty-Sixth Regiment.

Yet the blast was, in its way, counterproductive even for Germany. The great crater made a German advance against the French position, tenuous though it was, impossible. The positions of German and French troops on this portion of the Verdun-sector high ground would remain relatively unchanged until the Americans moved in on September 26, 1918.

While the struggle for possession of the Vauquois was under way on the left bank of the Meuse, a larger butte, Les Éparges, on the right bank, loomed as an objective both sides coveted. The Germans seized it in September 1914, not only entrenching its rugged top but also excavating shelters within it. Possession of Les Éparges gave the Germans a position from which they could deliver flanking fire against French columns as well as protect the flow of their own supplies and reinforcements. General Roques, commanding the French First Army, was assigned to take Les Éparges. He used a combination of regular infantry and *Chasseurs*,

French soldiers watch the detonation of a mine dug under a German position at Verdun. Both sides "undermined" one another's trenches, detonating explosive charges intended to bury their adversaries alive. WIKIMEDIA

elite heavy infantry units equipped with machine guns. The initial assault was synchronized with General Sarrail's February 17, 1915, assault on the Vauquois. After climbing the slope to the top of Les Éparges, Roques's troops were relieved to find the first line of German trenches all but deserted. No sooner, however, had the assault troops occupied these trenches than the German defenders unleashed an artillery barrage from their rearward positions. The barrage was followed by fierce infantry counterattacks that quickly wiped out the French first wave—six hundred killed or missing, a thousand wounded. This represented more than half the paper strength of a French infantry regiment, but it was really almost all of the regiment's actual deployed, effective strength. By February 20, the French withdrew from Les Éparges only to return to make a second assault on March 18, which managed to regain what had been lost in February—but nothing more. Nine days later, a third assault was mounted.

This effort was quickly swallowed up in the failure of the general French offensive throughout the Woëvre. That action had begun on April 5 and collapsed utterly before the end of the month. At Les Éparges alone, the three assaults cost thirty-five thousand men killed, wounded, or missing. Today, a historical marker placed at the entrance to what remains of Les Éparges (the original butte or hillock was much reduced by artillery and mine explosions) bears a quotation from a survivor of one of the pre-1916 battles: "You cannot know what man is capable of doing to his fellow man: after five days my shoes are greasy with human brains, I crush thoraxes, I encounter entrails."[9] Such horrific combat in this region was virtually continuous during the nineteen months between the start of World War I and the commencement, on February 21, 1916, of what history calls the Battle of Verdun.

CHAPTER 5

Blood Judgment

My friends, we have to take Verdun. It must be over by the end of February, and then the Kaiser will hold a grand review on the Place d'Armes of Cerdun and peace will be signed.
—WILHELM, PRINCE OF GERMANY, MESSAGE TO THE TROOPS OF THE FIFTH ARMY DELIVERED PRIOR TO THE ASSAULT ON VERDUN[1]

BY THE CLOSE OF 1915, THE VERDUN SECTOR HAD BEEN THE SITE OF AT least four battles—some count more—none of them decisive, most of them partial, incomplete, temporizing efforts, yet all of them costly. The French were largely victims of their own ill-conceived strategic and tactical policies, especially the failure to adequately maintain and man their system of fortresses and the even more egregious failure to acquire modern heavy artillery. The Germans were far better furnished with advanced heavy artillery but could not seem to recover from the collapse of the Schlieffen Plan. Falkenhayn and his field commanders favored envelopment over head-on assault and a defensive posture over attack. This combination led to an excess of caution—greater concern over avoiding defeat than achieving victory. It also resulted in missed opportunity. By the fall of 1914, the Germans were building a substantial salient that threatened Verdun and the forts and strongpoints in its vicinity. Yet the doctrinal imperative under which Falkenhayn operated, a strong inclination to assume a defensive position, discouraged him from exploiting French deficiencies by mounting a concerted attack from this salient. This meant that, by the end of 1915, the Verdun sector loomed for Germany as a field of frustration, cautiously squandered resources, and so much unfinished business.

Until recently, most historians paid little detailed attention to the pre-1916 fighting in the vicinity of Verdun. Ignoring these battles gives the false impression that Falkenhayn's decision to launch a major assault against Verdun was something like a strategic epiphany, a bolt-from-the-blue realization that the French would do anything to defend Verdun, which (somehow) had suddenly emerged as a place sacred to the honor of France. We now know, of course, that Joffre and the others who dominated French high command had shown remarkably little interest in defending Verdun from the outbreak of the war in the summer of 1914 right up to the end of 1915. We also know that the pre-1916 fighting in this sector, bloody as it was, failed to be decisive because Falkenhayn and his top field commanders saw no particular reason to seize this particular territory or even devote lives and other resources to breaking through at this point.

In short, there was nothing special about Verdun—not to the French, and not to the Germans.

But then came the infamous Christmas Memorandum to Kaiser Wilhelm II, in which Falkenhayn explained that Verdun was so sacred to the French that Joffre would feel "compelled to throw in every man" he had. "If they do so *the forces of France will bleed to death*—as there can be no question of voluntary withdrawal."[2] As Falkenhayn explained it, a German breakthrough at Verdun would be a desirable bonus but not necessary to achieve victory. Although a breakthrough to the French interior via Verdun would be a massively demoralizing blow to France, Falkenhayn argued, possibly even prompting surrender, it was hardly the only way for Germany to win the war and perhaps not even the best way. The longer the German army took in its assault on Verdun, the more slowly it advanced, the more it employed the tactics of defense in this offense, Falkenhayn proposed, the more French soldiers would bleed. As Falkenhayn portrayed it in the Christmas Memorandum, Verdun was less a point vulnerable to German penetration than it was a wall against which the French army would be lured into beating itself into a bloody pulp.

The historians who more or less ignore the pre-1916 fighting in the Verdun sector are the same historians who take and have always taken the Christmas Memorandum at face value—that is, as a genuine communication between Falkenhayn and the kaiser written by the general to explain his strategy and objective in making a major attack on Verdun. But as we have already noted, some recent historians have questioned the authenticity of the memorandum, arguing that it was fabricated by Falkenhayn after the war to justify his apparent failure to bring about the fall of Verdun. Other than the fact that the manuscript of the memorandum has never been found—it is known only by the text Falkenhayn "reproduced" in his own postwar memoir—there is no definitive evidence that the memorandum was fabricated ex post facto. There is, however, significant circumstantial evidence, including the vagueness surrounding Falkenhayn's December meeting with the kaiser at which the memorandum was supposedly presented and discussed. This "Christmas" document may have been handed over anytime between December 15 and 22. Or it may not have been written, let alone handed over, at all. Indeed, in his memoirs, Kaiser Wilhelm II makes no mention of meeting with Falkenhayn at this time and, for that matter, no mention of Verdun.

But by far the most compelling item of circumstantial evidence challenging the authenticity of the memorandum is the complete absence of any reason for Falkenhayn to believe, let alone tell the kaiser, that the French would invariably sacrifice everything in defense of Verdun. On the contrary, Joffre had already stripped the sector and its forts of garrison troops and most of the artillery that was not permanently fixed in place. Would he have thus desecrated a "sacred" place? (Add to this the fact that neither Falkenhayn nor his predecessor, Helmuth von Moltke, had made Verdun a priority before 1916.)

Even if we willingly suspend our disbelief and accept the authenticity of the memorandum, a close reading of it reveals a key ambivalence built on an oxymoron. Falkenhayn posits two theses: First, Verdun is sacred to the French, who will therefore bleed themselves white to save it. Second, this very fact—that the French will do anything rather than lose Verdun—makes Verdun a relatively cheap objective. Why? Because it is a battle Germany cannot lose. If the German army breaks through at

Verdun, the moral effect on France will be fatal. If Germany *fails* to break through at Verdun, the French army will bleed itself white in the course of the fight. Either outcome would be a German victory.

If Falkenhayn actually presented the kaiser with the Christmas Memorandum or if he even verbally discussed terms that appeared later in a fabricated memorandum, he would have found a ready audience. The collapse of the Schlieffen offensive and Germany's reversal at the First Battle of the Marne devastated Wilhelm II. Reportedly, throughout the bleak autumn and winter of 1914 and into 1915, he was heard to mumble, "I never wanted this," referring, presumably, to the war—the contest from which, he had promised, the troops would return before the leaves had fallen from the trees. Now, Erich von Falkenhayn, a general for whom few of his colleagues had any affection but who was a longtime favorite in the kaiser's court, presented his discouraged sovereign with a handful of magic beans in the form of a proposed battle that, win or lose, could result only in a victory both cheap and decisive. How could the kaiser resist?

GERICHT

Whether the Christmas Memorandum actually existed in December 1915 or not, by Christmas Eve, when Falkenhayn returned after his interview with the kaiser to his Western Front headquarters at Charleville-Mézières, the word *Gericht* began appearing in an avalanche of dispatches, orders, and telegrams. Most commonly, the word means "court," "court of justice," or "tribunal," but it may also mean "judgment" or "justice." Occasionally, its meaning is stretched to include the "place of execution." In any and all of these senses, it was the code word Falkenhayn (or the two officers he charged with planning the operation's details, Schmidt von Knobelsdorf and Crown Prince Wilhelm) chose as a label for everything relating to the campaign against Verdun.

In all its forms, Gericht had the ring of finality about it. And yet the German crown prince, whose Fifth Army was assigned the major role in the assault on Verdun, wrote in his own memoirs of a mixture of eagerness and disquiet over Falkenhayn's plan. He was thrilled by the prospect of leading his "tried and trusted troops once more to battle against the enemy," yet he confessed himself "disquieted" by Falkenhayn's "constantly repeated expression . . . that the French Army must be 'bled white' at Verdun." He had "a doubt"—or so he reports in his memoirs, originally published in 1919—"as to whether the fortress could . . . be taken by such means."[3] Of all the meanings of Gericht, "place of execution" would appear to be the most final. The crown prince seemed to imply, however, that mere bloodletting was not necessarily compatible with the finality of breaking through Verdun. If the objective was to get the war moving again, wouldn't it have been far better simply to concentrate on breaking through the system of fortifications? Falkenhayn, if we take him at his word, did not think so. He seems to have lost all faith in attaining a "final judgment" by strategic means. With the collapse of the Schlieffen Plan and its great checkmating blow, Falkenhayn *said* he believed (but may have said it only after the war) that nothing less than the utter destruction of the enemy's army could possibly be decisive. He did not *need* a breakthrough. He did not *need* a few forts. He needed a mountain of exsanguinated corpses.

Yet what of the crown prince? If he doubted the plan's priorities, should he not have voiced his doubts? Given the fact that his military experience was far from adequate to merit command of an entire army—he held his command only because he was the kaiser's son and heir—and given his nearly slavish reliance on his second-in-command, Schmidt von Knobelsdorf (whose enthusiasm for the attrition-through-slaughter approach was truly boundless), it is difficult to believe that the crown prince fretted much about his doubts. On the other hand, if, by expressing them, he was merely trying to make himself look good in his postwar memoirs, wouldn't he have gone a step further? At a time when much of the world was condemning Falkenhayn as a fiend, less interested in military victory than in mass slaughter, wouldn't the crown prince have attached to the expression of doubt a personal addendum denouncing killing for its own sake?

Or perhaps his doubts and disquiet were strategic rather than moral in origin. We know that the German crown prince pushed back when Falkenhayn insisted that the Fifth Army attack only the right bank of the Meuse, the eastern bank, rather than both the right and the left. Falkenhayn was determined to hold back at least a third of his reserves in anticipation of Allied counterattacks launched in an effort to relieve the beleaguered front lines. Instead of mounting a maximally ambitious infantry offensive, Falkenhayn proposed to attack with just nine divisions. Both the crown prince and Knobelsdorf objected, arguing that it was essential to attack on both sides of the river, but Falkenhayn remained adamant. What is more, he sought to disseminate his caution to other commanders. In January, he summoned Sixth Army chief of staff Herrmann von Kuhl, whose forces were fighting Douglas Haig's British forces in the north of France. Falkenhayn warned him that the offensive in Verdun would likely trigger a British offensive in the Sixth Army sector. Kuhl thanked Falkenhayn for the warning but noted that the Sixth was facing soldiers of what was called "Kitchener's army." In contrast to the majority of British political and military leaders, many of whom believed the war would end by Christmas 1914, Secretary of State for War Lord Horatio Kitchener predicted it would last years and would require forces far greater than the nation's all-volunteer professional army. He recommended creating a "new army"—the people called it "Kitchener's army"—through an intensive recruitment campaign. He approved a policy promoting mass recruitment in local areas, with the promise that the men who joined together would serve together. The result was the creation of numerous "Pals battalions." While they greatly enhanced morale, the Pals battalions also often resulted in particular communities suffering massive losses of their sons, fathers, uncles, nephews, and cousins. For Britain, the emotional impact of loss in World War I was often amplified in this way. The devastating impact of heavy losses in Pals battalions—some were virtually wiped out in single battles—drastically reduced the rate of voluntary enlistment by the start of 1916. This prompted Britain to resort to conscription. During the period of exclusively voluntary enlistment, Kitchener's army had an ample supply of enthusiastic recruits but an acute shortage of proper equipment, from uniforms (some men wore scarlet jackets salvaged from First Boer War supplies) to weapons. Worse, the newly created regiments lacked experienced officers to train as well as lead the men. Add to these deficiencies the reduced zeal of conscripts—who were first sent to the front in massive numbers by the start of 1916—and the poor reputation of Kitchener's army was well deserved.

Despite General Kuhl's generally merited confidence, Falkenhayn repeated his warning about the counteroffensive the Sixth Army should expect as a result of what he, Falkenhayn, was doing with the Fifth Army against Verdun. Kuhl believed this warning betrayed Falkenhayn's congenital excess of caution. What disturbed Kuhl even more, however, was Falkenhayn's prediction that the Sixth Army's successful repulse of any British counteroffensives would benefit Germany's position by bringing "movement into the war again."[4] Kuhl dutifully reported this exchange to his boss, the commanding officer of the Sixth Army, Crown Prince Rupprecht of Bavaria, who despaired. As he later lamented, Falkenhayn "himself was not clear as to what he really wanted." He was doing nothing more or less than "waiting for a stroke of luck that would lead to a favourable solution."[5]

Operation Gericht—the name of which implied the finality of an absolute judgment—bore conflict and confusion at its very core. Whereas Falkenhayn called for nothing more specific than "an offensive in the Meuse area in the direction of Verdun," Crown Prince Wilhelm issued orders to his Fifth Army to conduct an offensive against Verdun with the objective of capturing "the fortress of Verdun by precipitate methods."[6] In comparison with the orders from the top commander in the German military, the crown prince's order appears very specific—until one realizes that there was in fact no single "fortress of Verdun." Rather, Verdun was more or less ringed by numerous forts, some widely dispersed. Thus the crown prince's phrase is itself actually quite vague. Somewhat more specific, however, is the specification of "precipitate methods." Yet even this falls well short of stipulating a maximum effort battle. In fact, "precipitate methods" may be interpreted as implying storming of the fortress of Verdun—whatever this actually meant—rather than laying siege to it. Thus the crown prince may have envisioned a short, sharp battle—a kind of blitzkrieg attack—whereas Falkenhayn intended to force the French to stand and fight for a sufficiently long time to suffer a bleed-out.

Only after the war did all of the German commanders who commented on Verdun appear to get on the same page, insisting that actually capturing Verdun was *never* the real aim of the offensive; the destruction of the French army was. If, in the process of this destruction, Verdun happened to fall into German hands, well, so much the better. But this postwar expression of consensus could not erase the confusion that reigned on the verge of battle. What seems indisputable is that Falkenhayn, chief of the German General Staff and, until January 21, 1915, Prussian minister of war, ordered a vague offensive in the direction of Verdun, whereas the commander of the principal army tasked with conducting the offensive, Crown Prince Wilhelm, ordered something like a blitzkrieg—hard, fast, and intended to overwhelm and capture.

And the confusion actually deepens. In the armies of the democracies, and in none more than the army of the United States, so-called soldiers' battles are common. Notable American examples of soldiers' battles include, in World War I, Belleau Wood (June 1–26, 1918), in which a comparative handful of U.S. Marines held a small patch of the Western Front against the most desperate of Erich Ludendorff's all-out offensives, and, in World War II, the breakthrough inland from Omaha Beach during the Normandy landings (June 6, 1944). Both engagements were won not by executing plans issued by higher headquarters but by the improvisation and enterprise of on-the-scene field and company commanders as well as enlisted troops. In the armies of autocracies, soldiers' battles are rare. In the Imperial German Army of 1916, independent initiative was, if anything, sternly discouraged. In truth, the order Crown Prince Wilhelm issued to *capture* Verdun did not somehow inadvertently slip past the scrutiny of Erich von Falkenhayn. Wilhelm adhered to the chain of command. He both sought and secured Falkenhayn's approval before he published his orders to the Fifth Army. In effect, therefore, Falkenhayn acted in a way that implied his wholehearted endorsement of Verdun's capture by "precipitate methods"—something very like what would be termed "blitzkrieg" in World War II.

So did the chief of staff somehow profoundly misunderstand Wilhelm's intentions? Almost certainly not. They were clear, except for the precise specification of "fortress of Verdun"—an objective that, in the strictest sense, did not even exist. Did, then, Falkenhayn fail to see that Wilhelm's orders effectively contradicted his own? This, too, is difficult to imagine. For whatever else Erich von Falkenhayn was and was not, he *was* an officer in the Prussian mode, as thoroughly committed to hierarchy of authority, to the sanctity of the German military's command structure, as any military leader could possibly have been. He would never have let a contradictory order stand—unless he had a precise motive for doing so. This leaves only one possible interpretation. Erich von Falkenhayn was deliberately deceiving the commander of the principal force he had tasked with the Verdun offensive. Falkenhayn *wanted* the German crown prince to believe that his mission was not merely to bleed the French army white but also to heroically seize the complex of fortresses that was Verdun.

But why the *need* for deception? As chief of staff, Falkenhayn's authority was beyond challenge. His prerogative was to order whatever action he wanted. Issuing an order, however, is one thing. Achieving enthusiastic "buy-in" from subordinate commanders and the troops themselves is another. More disquieting than the confusion and contradiction that enveloped Operation Gericht—the template that would launch one of the deadliest and least productive battles in history—is the almost certain purpose behind it. Falkenhayn knew that ordering an operation with the objective of attrition, while perfectly within his authority, was nevertheless hard to sell. Attrition, after all, was an objective that had already produced and was continuing to produce slaughter without victory all across the Western Front. Like a slick salesman practicing bait-and-switch, Falkenhayn allowed the German crown prince to believe that he was leading his army in a bold operation to take a "sacred" bastion of France. All the while, however, Falkenhayn's real intention was the attrition of French forces in and around Verdun. His approval of Wilhelm's orders implied a very different mission than the one he actually contemplated—which was a mission that even he, Erich von Falkenhayn, knew would likely demoralize his subordinate commanders as well as the soldiers they led.

Erich von Falkenhayn was liked and admired by virtually no one except for Kaiser Wilhelm II. He was thought of as cold and calculating. In the Prussian-led German army of the time, these qualities were hardly disqualification for high leadership. On the contrary, they were expected, even demanded. The deception of the German crown prince was far more than rhetorical sleight-of-hand practiced by an unethical salesman. Falkenhayn made specific promises—*tactical* promises—to the commander of the Fifth Army. Chief among these was his guarantee that adequate reserves would be available for Wilhelm to draw upon in time of need. What Falkenhayn did *not* do, however, was surrender to Wilhelm direct control of these units. The reserves "promised" to the Fifth Army were, in fact, under the *direct* command and control of Erich von Falkenhayn. It is, of course, possible to designate any body of troops as "reserves." Those Falkenhayn designated, however, four divisions in all, were held too far from the Verdun sector to be in good faith deemed reserves intended for this sector. Two divisions were located two full days away. (Falkenhayn pleaded a shortage of adequate accommodations closer to the anticipated battlefield.) Two others were domiciled not even in France but in Belgium. Falkenhayn knew that the German crown prince would call on reserves only in case of extreme and urgent need. Yet he kept them far away, presumably to discourage the Fifth Army commander from being too "precipitate" in the actions he ordered. The remoteness of these reserves ensured that the crown prince would conform to Falkenhayn's cautious wishes.

It is precisely the content of Falkenhayn's wishes that remains, to this day, uncertain. But let us assume that everything Falkenhayn did to deceive the German crown prince was the product of deliberate thought rather than error in judgment or deficiency of clarity. The conclusion we must reach is that, at bottom, Falkenhayn thought of the German Fifth Army less as an offensive force than as bait, raw bait to lure the French army into spending itself in one futile counteroffensive after another.

"Humanity must be mad," Second Lieutenant Alfred Joubaire wrote under fire at Verdun. If we accept as valid the well-worn definition of insanity attributed to Albert Einstein—"doing the same thing over and over again and expecting different results"—the goal of mutual attrition at the heart of Falkenhayn's Verdun strategy, a strategy already discredited over and over again, may well have been madness.

METHOD IN MADNESS

Some lunatics rave. The demeanor of others, however, is coldly rational. Those who knew him, worked with him, invariably described Erich von Falkenhayn as both cold and rational—in other words, the ideal Prussian officer.

Despite an objective that was ill-defined, ambivalently defined, or deceptively defined—an objective to capture Verdun, but not really—preparations for Operation Gericht were both massive and massively methodical, incredibly efficient, and scrupulously thorough. As mentioned, both the French army and the French government showed remarkably little interest in the Woëvre plain, the boggy, wooded, rugged expanse separating the Metz ridges from the heights that run along the Meuse. Roads in this region were scarce, and those few were neglected and overgrown. If French military planners wanted to claim an excuse for their negligence, they might have pointed out that the difficulty of traversing the Woëvre would work a greater hardship on invaders than on defenders. It was, in fact, a valid point, and no one understood this more clearly than *German* military planners. In preparation for operations in this remote and largely neglected sector, German military engineers built ten new rail lines and no fewer than twenty-four stations to serve them. Under orders from Falkenhayn, Crown Prince Wilhelm organized many of his Fifth Army troops in work battalions to rapidly lay seven spur lines running from the main rail lines into Spincourt Forest, a rugged woods near the village of Gincrey. Here, the big artillery would be planted, and the railway spurs would ensure that they would be fed their lethal ration of ammunition without interruption throughout the battle.

Spincourt was not the only platform from which the battle was to be launched. Military authorities evacuated dozens of small villages in the sector, either appropriating or razing buildings to prepare cantonments and other facilities for more than 140,000 troops assembling to attack. The first order of business for the early arrivals was to process the supplies that arrived on the new rail lines, distributing ample caches to each key position. Those prepared positions—the springboards from which the attack and the follow-ups would be launched—ranged from rapidly dug trenches and even more hasty field fortifications, such as firing pits, to *Stollen*. These were major construction projects, capacious underground galleries reinforced with poured concrete, each large enough to hide as well as shelter a half battalion or more from French infantry *and* artillery. By 1916, the Western Front was scarred by a complex of trenches. World War I had become unmistakably a *trench war*. To the German planners, however, the inadequacy of trenches—especially the forward trenches, closest to the enemy, the trenches from which men would "go over the top" to make their attacks—was abundantly apparent. Instead of lamenting this and simply muddling through, as the French and British did, Falkenhayn intended to use the Stollen as a means of preventing the futile and premature loss of attacking troops to enemy counter-bombardment. He knew that attacking troops would be killed, but he wanted them killed *after* they had gained a thousand or more yards of no-man's-land, not while they huddled in trenches or struggled to survive for ten or twenty-five yards beyond those trenches. The longer a soldier lived, the more of the enemy he could bleed.

Stollen were intended to increase the effectiveness of infantry. The higher priority in Falkenhayn's mind, however, was artillery. Most of the laborious preparations—the rail spurs, the evacuation of villages, the accumulation of ammunition—was devoted to serving the big guns. As major an endeavor as the assault on Verdun would be, Falkenhayn hoped to achieve his purpose, the destruction of a large fraction of the French army, as cheaply as possible. Much as many politicians and military leaders use air power today, as a hopeful alternative to boots on the ground, a means to a relatively cheap victory that will raise the fewest objections on the home front, Falkenhayn proposed to substitute the devastating effects of relentless artillery barrages for infantry assaults. In this, his thinking was very much in line with German doctrine of the era, which was precisely the opposite of the thinking that prevailed among French high command. Whereas the top French generals disdained heavy artillery and paid homage to the celebrated "French 75," the light and highly portable field gun capable of keeping pace with swiftly advancing infantry, the Germans relied first and foremost on heavy firepower. The great cannon of Krupp, the venerable munitions firm in Essen, had won the victory in the Franco-Prussian War. They would, it was believed, do the same now.

The butcher's bill of World War I validated the German reliance on artillery. High-explosive shells, not rifle bullets, created the great majority of casualties. In the specific case of Verdun, artillery would be essential not only to killing men but also to destroying forts and breaching fortifications. Although Falkenhayn would deny that his priority was to break through the Verdun sector, he did intend to use his guns to blast gaps into the French lines, filling those gaps with his infantry, which would thereby be positioned to flank and enfilade the broken lines. Would his soldiers break through to the French interior? Perhaps. But that mattered less than what they could do to roll up tens of thousands of *poilus*—"hairy ones," the French nickname for its soldiers—from the flanks and from the rear as opposed to engaging in a head-on shootout. As Falkenhayn saw it, artillery, used effectively, did not achieve a definitive *breakthrough* but an opportunity for *envelopment*, for attacking masses of the enemy from the most advantageous positions. And *that* killed them, lots and lots of them.

The key to achieving maximum slaughter was massive and relentless bombardment. This, of course, required a great many guns—guns of all calibers but with a generous complement of the very heaviest weapons—and it required ungodly quantities of ammunition. Falkenhayn's methodical logistics supplied both.

No fewer than 542 heavy cannon were arrayed along a concentrated eight-mile front. Infantry was supplied with an additional 306 field pieces and 152 Minenwerfers. Along the heights along the margins of the main attack front were another 220 cannon, positioned to augment the principal fire.

The artillery arrayed against the French was drawn from the full range of the bulging German arsenal. There were thirteen of the celebrated "Big Berthas"—a 420-mm Krupp behemoth some believe was nicknamed in dubious honor of Gustav Krupp's wife, Bertha, although the original German, *Dicke Bertha*, means Fat Bertha, and Frau Krupp, though tall, was hardly fat. A giant howitzer—a high-trajectory weapon intended to be used against massive fortifications—Big Bertha was officially called the Gamma Gun. It weighed 47 tons, and it fired a shell weighing more than 1,800 pounds. Some Berthas were mounted on steel wheels to be transported intact via railroad and fired from specially built sidings. Those used at Verdun, however, were broken down into 172 pieces, which were distributed into a dozen huge horse-drawn wagons and then reassembled on site—that job took about twenty hours.

Big Bertha was a high-trajectory siege gun. In addition to it, the army also modified a number of 380-mm naval guns for land use. In contrast to the stubby-barreled Big Berthas, the naval cannon had long barrels designed for accuracy over great range at a relatively shallow trajectory.

They could be fired from far behind the lines with impunity and, big as they were, they were capable of rapid fire. Their purpose was to pound a target relentlessly.

The Berthas and the naval guns were supplemented by Beta guns, which were 305-mm mortars, and by more portable 210-mm guns. Both of these guns were often aimed directly at trenches and, of the two, the 210-mm weapon, capable of very rapid fire, created the greater terror among French poilus. When a 210-mm shell detonated nearby, anyone who survived knew that the entire line was doomed in short order to be swept by many more high-explosive projectiles. Heavy and yet maneuverable, the 210-mm cannon could be fired, rapidly relaid (re-aimed), then fired again in order to probe a target area both tenaciously and mercilessly. Much the same was true for the even more numerous 150-mm cannon, which were heavy fieldpieces.

It was, however, the 130-mm "whizz-bang" that poilus most deeply feared and hated. This cannon was first and last an antipersonnel weapon. It fired very rapidly at a low, raking trajectory that made the fire virtually impossible to evade. No sooner would soldiers hear the characteristic *whizz* of the incoming shell than the *bang* would follow, without any interval in which to seek cover.

The artillery pieces that fired shells of 130 mm or greater were offensive weapons. Whereas the French, early in the war, neglected heavy artillery in favor of producing more and more light 75s, the Germans, who relished their heavy guns, by no means neglected fieldpieces. German infantry was equipped with light but deadly 77-mm artillery used to unleash defensive barrages against attacking troops. In addition, the German infantry was well supplied with heavy machine guns, including Maxim guns and so-called revolver cannon. The Maxims fired at full automatic and enabled a two-man gun crew to defend against hundreds of incoming attackers. The revolver-cannon were semiautomatic, but they fired a larger-caliber projectile than the Maxim. Together, all of these defensive field weapons were force multipliers that enabled a relatively few soldiers to kill many attackers.

But Falkenhayn's hope and intention was that his big guns would preempt both costly attacks by his own infantry and counterattacks by the French. Before the battle commenced, he issued stern orders that no French "line [was] to remain unbombed" and that the barrages should be of such intensity and scope as to produce in the enemy the conviction that nowhere on the eight-mile-wide field of attack was safe.[7] To ensure this scope and intensity, Falkenhayn furnished 2.5 million heavy rounds, a quantity calculated to be sufficient for six continuous days of intensive bombardment.

SECRECY IN MADNESS

We have already seen that French high command was remarkably obtuse. Joffre and his immediate circle clung fiercely to their contempt for fortifications and artillery and their enthusiasm for a heedless policy of headlong infantry attack. Nevertheless, it would seem that no degree of blindness should have been able to shield from French military intelligence and reconnaissance any preparations as massive and elaborate as those under way near Verdun. Yet the efficiency and thoroughness of German preparation was more than matched by German stealth.

The secrecy began internally. None but those directly involved in Operation Gericht knew of its existence. Everyone outside of the Fifth Army was kept in the dark. In a move that invites comparison with Operation Mincemeat, the elaborate Allied campaign of deception that preceded the Normandy invasion of June 6, 1944, in World War II, Crown Prince Wilhelm, commander of the Fifth Army, was sent on a tour of the Western Front during the ramp-up of the Verdun attack. The objective of this quite public exercise was for him to be seen anywhere and everywhere *except* in the Verdun sector. In addition, German agents fabricated rumors of a great impending offensive, set to fall—well, anywhere and everywhere except Verdun. They circulated the rumors both within Germany and Austria as well as throughout the neutral countries. On a more tactical level, the Fifth Army enlisted the aid of a legion of German artists to create highly sophisticated camouflage paint schemes and elaborate netting and canvas coverings to conceal even the biggest guns. Most prominent among these masters of camouflage was the great German expressionist Franz Marc, by 1916 a painter of international renown. Far from resenting being pressed into this service, Marc delighted in inventing novel forms of camouflage, using as his models the illusionistic techniques of painters as diverse as Edouard Manet and Wassily Kandinsky. Even as he worked at the Verdun front, the German government identified Marc as one of a small group of artists and literary figures so important to the cultural life of the nation that they were to be withdrawn from the haz-ards of frontline combat. Tragically for the artist, the orders calling for his withdrawal arrived after a shell splinter had fatally penetrated his skull on March 4, 1916.

The work of Marc and others was intended to exploit the features of the rugged woodland landscape to hide the German army and its weap-ons until the very moment that both went into action. Although it was relatively easy to hide people and things from ground-level observers, aer-ial reconnaissance was just beginning to play a major role in warfare dur-ing the run-up to the main Verdun battle. As the French high command was slow to adopt modern heavy artillery, so they were initially resistant to military aviation. By late 1915, however, Germany was already making extensive use of both Zeppelins and heavier-than-air craft—airplanes—for purposes of reconnaissance and mapping. To forestall the possibility that some French aviator might glimpse the preparations, Falkenhayn assembled most of Germany's military air power at Verdun: 168 airplanes, four Zeppelins, and fourteen tethered observation balloons—called "sau-sages" after their elongated shape.

The French regarded this sudden increase in aerial activity as an effort to reconnoiter *their* positions in and around Verdun. Falkenhayn, how-ever, used the aircraft less for intelligence than to lay down a continual "aerial barrage." During the battle, this would supplement the ground-based artillery barrage. In the days before the battle, however, its purpose was to keep French reconnaissance aircraft, comparatively few in num-ber, from even getting airborne. At Verdun, the world was about to see the most savagely atavistic spectacle of slaughter on an unprecedented scale. Erich von Falkenhayn intended to ensure the success of this primal bloodletting by employing the civilization's most advanced technology, military aircraft, to deprive the enemy of intelligence—indeed, of sight itself. Fought in the mud, the Battle of Verdun began in the sky with the world's first campaign for total air supremacy.

CHAPTER 6

The Matter Is Serious

"... something terrible is going to happen."
—GERMAN DESERTER CAPTURED BY THE
FRENCH AT VERDUN IN JANUARY 1916[1]

VERDUN, A FORTRESS TOWN SINCE THE ERA OF THE ROMAN EMPIRE, had a reputation as an unassailable citadel, a landlocked Gibraltar. Although combat had swirled around it since the beginning of the war— coming close enough so that we can call each of at least four pre-1916 World War I engagements nearby a "Battle of Verdun"—the town itself was repeatedly bypassed. And while Verdun was a kind of byword for *fortress*, no one with significant standing in the French government or the French high command showed any concern for it before the end of 1915. In the thick of the First Battle of the Marne (September 5–12, 1914), Joseph Joffre effectively cut the sector loose, first ordering his Third Army commander, Maurice Sarrail, to pull back and then stripping Verdun's fortresses of their nonfixed artillery and the bulk of their garrisons.

And so Verdun was left naked for the taking. When the Germans did not bother to take it, Joffre withdrew even more troops and threw them into an attack in Champagne during September 1915. There, Erich von Falkenhayn observed as French generals hurled their poilus against his defensive positions. The French bled. If it was not literally mass suicide, it was something very close to it. All the while, Joffre and his lieutenants continued to ignore Verdun the way a man, looking into his shaving mirror, might ignore a dark, strangely shaped mole in the hope that it would simply go away as imperceptibly as it had appeared.

Alarms

Joffre's subordinates did not protest in September 1915 when the chief of staff transferred men from what was now called the "Fortified Region of Verdun" to participate in the Champagne offensive. But in October, when relatively few of those men returned to the Verdun sector after the collapse of the Champagne operation, General Frédéric Herr, in command of the fortified region, raised the first alarm. Herr was an Alsatian who had immigrated to France after Germany annexed his native region following the Franco-Prussian War. He remained partial to the portion of France bordering the enemy. After graduating from the prestigious École Polytechnique in 1874, Herr entered the army. Nine years later, he married into great wealth. His bride was Anne Peugeot, heiress to what was at the time a maker of everything from umbrella frames to bicycles. Instead of contenting himself with a life of genteel privilege, however, Herr led troops in the colonization of Madagascar, earning a reputation for enthusiastic and competent leadership that set him on a steadily upward path. By the outbreak of World War I, in 1914, he was a general of division—but, nearing sixty, the zeal of his colonial days was a distant memory. He had quietly complied when Marshal Joffre took so many of his men to use as fodder for cannon and machine guns in the Champagne. But now that so few had returned, his competence overcame his senior passivity. He informed Joffre of the obvious. Left with just eighty thousand men and precious little in the way of artillery, he could hardly be expected to resist any serious German attempt along the seventy-five miles of the operational perimeter for which he was responsible.

A calm and competent observation, it proved insufficiently alarming to disturb Joseph Joffre. Fecklessly, Herr next pleaded with an aide to General Philippe Pétain—Pétain having just returned from the costly Champagne offensive. "Every day I tremble," Herr told the man. "If I were attacked I could not hold; I've told the G.Q.G [Grand Quartier Général, French high command, led by Joseph Joffre], and they refuse to listen to me."[2] When this failed to penetrate, Herr went directly to Joseph Galliéni. Retired by the time of the outbreak of World War I, Galliéni returned to service as the military governor of Paris and, in this role, was instrumental in the French victory at the First Battle of the Marne. He

115

became a genuine popular hero by commandeering the celebrated taxi-cabs of Paris to rush garrison troops from the city to attack the German west flank, thereby helping to prevent an enemy breakthrough into the capital. Shortly after this, he was appointed minister of war. Ordinarily, Herr would not have broken the chain of command by talking directly to Galliéni, but Herr had served under him in Madagascar, over which Gal-liéni had been colonial governor. The two had formed a bond of mutual respect. Herr explained that the "Young Turks of G.Q.G" replied to every request for reinforcement of artillery by *withdrawing* more of what little artillery he had. They attempted to placate him, Herr said, with assur-ances that Verdun would not be attacked because it is "not the point of the [German] attack." To cap this circular argument, high command added the dubious assurance that the "Germans don't know that Verdun has been disarmed"![3]

It was at this point that Galliéni confided to his notebook, "The mat-ter is serious."[4] He brought it up with the rest of the cabinet and President Raymond Poincaré.

Their inquiries provoked a curt reply from Joffre: "Nothing justifies the fears you express in the name of your government." Rather than leave it at that, Joffre continued by threatening to resign rather than endeavor to "answer vague insinuations" made by sources unknown to himself.[5]

Despite the record he had compiled thus far—except for the First Battle of the Marne, made up chiefly of disappointment or outright defeat—"Papa" Joffre was tremendously popular not only with the French people but also among the entire Allied public. The *Evening Post* (Wel-lington, New Zealand) noted on March 24, 1915, that "a baby boy was born to a British officer at the front, and he requested that the child should be named 'Roberts Joffre French,' after the famous generals of those names." (One of the great imperial generals of nineteenth-century Britain, Frederick Roberts, 1st Earl Roberts, died on November 14, 1914, of pneumonia, at the Western Front—still in harness at age eighty-two. Field Marshal Sir John French became a national hero during the Great [Second] Boer War and was commander-in-chief of the British Expedi-tionary Forces for the first eighteen months of World War I.) The *Eve-ning Post* singled out "Joffre," pointing out that the name "has already

Raymond Poincaré, who struggled to maintain his presidency even as the French army struggled to survive Verdun. WIKIMEDIA

been many times exploited as a patronymic for male infants, but 'Joffrette' as the feminine appellation is something quite new. Yet it has made its appearance, and doubtless will be borne by a good many baby girls who make their first appearance in this year of international disaster."[6] Fearful of provoking the general into resignation, President Poincaré and his cabinet backed off.

One man, an ostensibly lowly colonel, persisted pushing, however. And he pushed hard and sharp.

Ordinarily, an officer of Émile Driant's rank would not presume to question, let alone criticize, the policies of the senior-most soldier in the French army. But Driant was not just any field-grade officer. He was a member of the Chamber of Deputies (a representative of Nancy) and the son-in-law as well as former aide-de-camp of the late Georges Ernest Boulanger, an enormously popular Revanchist general—a right-wing nationalist who had led a movement to avenge France's ignominious defeat in the Franco-Prussian War. Driant, who was sixty at the time of the Battle of Verdun, was also a prolific author, among whose works were novels and nonfiction studies devoted to the nature and conduct of war. The best-known of his fictional works was *La Guerre en fortresse* (*Fortress Warfare*), which begins, presciently enough, with a German assault on France via its great fortresses.

As a Catholic, Driant was repeatedly passed over for promotion and finally resigned his commission in 1906. He never let up on his criticism of the weakness and vulnerability of the French army, however, and, elected to the Chamber of Deputies in 1910, he sounded the alarm that much more stridently. When the war broke out in 1914, he rejoined his old unit of *Chasseurs-à-pied*, an elite army organization roughly equivalent to the Rangers of the modern U.S. Army. A reserve captain in 1914, Driant was assigned to the staff of the Verdun garrison. Eager for a combat assignment, he requested—and secured—active command of two Chasseur battalions, the Fifty-Sixth and Fifty-Ninth, which were positioned in a woods, the Bois des Caures, on a rise some two miles long and a half-mile wide northeast of the town of Verdun. This would prove a critical position, located on the right bank of the Meuse, at the very center of the first French line facing the Germans.

Lieutenant Colonel Émile Driant (with cane, third from right) stands with his doomed *Chasseurs* at Le Bois des Caures, prepared to make his stand against the attacking Germans. WIKIMEDIA

A soldier with strong military instincts, Driant possessed the faculty of *coup d'oeil*—the ability to take in, at a glance, all the tactical advantages and disadvantages of the terrain. One look at the landscape from the perspective of Bois des Caures was sufficient for Driant to understand the enormous significance and vulnerability of the Verdun sector. It had nothing to do with the mythology of Verdun as a place "sacred" to France and French honor and everything to do with Driant's strategic sense of Verdun as a wide-open back door to the nation's interior. Toward the end of August 1914, he wrote to the president of the Chamber of Deputies, Paul Deschanel, that the German "sledge-hammer blow will be delivered on the line Verdun-Nancy." He believed that the capture of *either* Verdun or Nancy—or both!—would have a devastating "moral effect" on France. "We are"—by which Driant really meant *I am*—"doing everything day and night to make our front inviolable," he wrote to Deschanel. But, he warned, there was "one thing about which one can do nothing; *the shortage of hands*." He asked that Minister of Defense Galliéni be told that if the first line should fall—*Driant's* line, the line closest to the Germans—the second line, short of soldiers and short of barbed wire, would rapidly collapse.[7]

When word of Driant's missive to Deschanel reached him, Joffre protested that he would not be a party to soldiers violating the chain of command by appealing directly to the government—especially when the matter concerned "the execution of my orders." Verdun in danger? The *only* cause for alarm Joffre chose to recognize was the threat to "the spirit of discipline in the Army" posed by Driant's insolence.[8]

THE AWAKENING

Throughout the late fall and during December 1915, Driant and Herr did what they could with what little they had to strengthen the front line running through Verdun. The rest of the army, including high command along with the political class, spent December either thinking about other sectors or simply fretting about Verdun without doing anything about it. In January, Crown Prince Wilhelm's message to his troops—"My friends, we have to take Verdun. It must be over by the end of February"—was discovered by French intelligence, and some evidence of German preparatory movements was beginning to accumulate. Although Joffre continued to dismiss reports of Verdun's dire straits, he nevertheless issued orders in January to prepare defensive positions in the Fortified Region of Verdun. More important, he backed these up by countermanding orders to transfer yet more troops out of the Verdun sector, organizing an entire corps to reinforce the sector, and deploying engineers to assist with defensive preparations.

The French picked up one unexpected ally in January. Verdun and vicinity have the dubious reputation of suffering through the worst weather in France, especially during the winter months. Throughout January, snow, freezing rain, clouds, and fog hampered German reconnaissance efforts. The weather also put a crimp in French intelligence, but the Germans needed reconnaissance more urgently, especially now that the French were at long last making preparations. Falkenhayn had brought in large numbers of aircraft, intending to rely heavily on aerial reconnaissance. These were now all grounded. Nor could he move his men into advance positions for an attack. Up to January 17, when the weather finally broke, the French enjoyed more than two weeks of valuable preparation time. Given the prevailing state of neglect in and around Verdun, this was hardly sufficient, but it was far better than nothing.

When the weather cleared—for a short time, as it turned out—on the 17th, both sides sent up aerial reconnaissance sorties. The Germans learned much in a short time, the French comparatively little. French pilots did, however, bring back the reassuring news that they had detected no new advance trenches, the hastily dug jumping-off points for an attack. The absence of these works suggested that no attack was imminent. Now the genius of having excavated those concrete-reinforced Stollen was apparent. Instead of visible trenches, the Germans had created subterranean galleries, invisible springboards from which the first wave of the attack would be launched. French intelligence was thoroughly deceived and accordingly conveyed to Herr a false sense of security.

But the Germans could not hide all signs of impending battle. French artillery spotters began to report that, in towns behind the German lines, church steeples were being torn down. A landmark steeple would be visible one morning—and gone the next. The French artillerymen understood instantly that the Germans were methodically removing anything that could be used for spotting—the aiming and ranging of artillery. Steeples and other towers made ideal reference points. One by one, these were vanishing.

January passed into February. On the 12th of that month, a few artillery rounds issued from various places in the German lines. Their meaning was unmistakable. German gunners were "ranging," determining the appropriate elevation of their guns for the initial barrages of what would doubtless be a long and terrible artillery preparation. Over the next three days, reports of the erection of field hospitals arrived, and the rumble of troop transport by train and truck could be heard—and even seen. German deserters—there were a few—captured by French pickets reported that their commanders had summarily cancelled all leaves. There was, they said, a feeling of something big, something truly terrible, about to take place.

At last, on January 24, Joseph Joffre sent his top lieutenant, Noël Édouard, Vicomte de Curières de Castelnau, to ride herd on Herr. He ordered that Herr concentrate all of his entrenchment work on the right bank—the eastern bank—of the Meuse. Joffre directed Castelnau to order not only the first and second lines reinforced but another line of trench works to be interposed between them. Under no circumstances were the Germans to be permitted to cross the Meuse. Later that day, President Poincaré toured the defensive front, riding about on a narrow-gauge railcar drawn by a pair of mules. Then came none other than Joseph Joffre himself—and, to his credit, he did not arrive empty handed, but brought news of the arrival of reinforcements: two entire divisions.

WHITE OUT

Joffre's promised divisions arrived on February 12, whereupon General Herr began the laborious process of deploying them along the newly entrenched lines. He was in a dreadful hurry. Intelligence had made clear that the tipping point was very close. The German attack would come—well, certainly any day and quite possibly any minute.

Herr did not know just how right his instinct was. February 12, 1916, was the very day scheduled for the crown prince's assault to begin. On that day, some twelve hundred guns—about 850 arrayed behind the core of the attack, the remainder arranged on the heights flanking the planned front—were ready, placed, ranged, manned, and amply supplied with ammunition. In the vanguard of the attack, no fewer than seventy-two battalions—about seventy-five thousand soldiers, all drawn from the best troops the Fifth Army had to offer—were prepared to advance. At this point, with reinforcements just getting into position, the French had no more than 270 artillery pieces in position. Many of these were the light 75s. The few heavy guns in the French artillery park were serviceable but distinctly obsolescent. Ammunition was in short supply. In the front two lines of defense were no more than thirty-four French battalions—thirty-five thousand men. The forts behind them were thinly garrisoned. Most of the troops occupied newly dug trenches, many of which were far from complete.

If the crown prince had been able to order his men over the top that day, the French defenders in and around Verdun would not have stood a chance. The battle would have been over quite quickly. Two full divisions would have been caught on the move, in the very act of deployment. Slaughter between entrenched forces was horrible enough. Attacking a fully exposed pair of divisions in the laborious act of getting into position would have been far more destructive and, what is more, one-sided.

But the German gunners were blind on February 12. In his 1851 "Dover Beach," the British poet Matthew Arnold wrote of a "darkling plain" on which "ignorant armies clash by night." On the morning of February 12, 1916, as the pale sun, poor ghost of itself, struggled in vain to shine, its feeble light illuminated two armies enveloped not in darkness but all in white. The weather was a mix of thick mist and driving blizzard. Neither side could see the other. Artillery preparation was impossible. A creeping barrage to precede the troops even less possible.

There would be no attack. The "god of weather," Crown Prince Wilhelm wrote in his memoirs, deranged "all our plans."[9]

On the French side, the miserable weather worked its customary hardship on each lowly poilu. The new arrivals moved into position through the icy mist and pelting snow. They neither understood nor appreciated that this chill, wet presence was a life-saving cloak.

On February 13, Herr issued a general alert, followed almost immediately by an order to stand down as the blizzard increased in intensity and the mercury plummeted. Over the eight days that followed, the temperature fluctuated, but if it was not the blowing snow that forestalled the German attack, it was the dense fog created by thawing ice and melting snow, accompanied by cold and heavy rain, punctuated by renewed bouts of heavy, windblown snowfall.

The weather provided a reprieve, but no one really understood, let alone appreciated, this. To the poilus, huddled in open trenches or miserable wooden shelters, it was a wretched tedium. "You couldn't even think about lying down," Corporal Louis Barthas wrote in the remarkable journal he kept throughout the war, "or sleeping sitting up. The terrible cold which reigned throughout the night obliged us to head frequently to a place where the duckboards [wooden boards that formed the crude floor of a trench] weren't covered with water, to stamp our feet furiously in order to struggle with frostbite, keeping our feet from swelling up, turning blue, and cracking painfully."[10]

To do battle with the cold, instead of giving us more fortifying meals or an extra ration of pinard [cheap wine furnished to French soldiers as part of their rations], our captain could himself find nothing better to do than to send us on work details, nonstop. This hard work consisted of ridding the trenches of water, mud, and snow. But rain or snow fell every day, almost without stopping; the sides of the trenches caved in, and the water bubbled up in thousands of little springs, between the edges of the duckboards.[11]

The icy, foggy storms that saved French lives were nevertheless an agony to the French soldiers. The effect of this weather was, however, much harder on the Germans. Arguably, those in the Stollen had the advantage of shelter. But while these subterranean galleries kept out the snow and wind, they were icy damp, dark refrigerated tombs. Worse, nothing, save defeat itself, is more demoralizing to a warrior than waiting to attack. The longer the wait, the greater the impact on morale; the more elite the troops, the greater the degradation of performance. Going over the top to attack an entrenched enemy required working oneself up to a frankly suicidal degree of energy and passion. Waiting in the cold, the gloom, and the icy mist, day after day, sapped precious strength, will, and concentration.

As the snow alternately froze and thawed, water seeped into the Stollen from below, from the sides, and from the ceiling. Pumps had been supplied, but their number was insufficient and fuel too precious to squander on their operation. The only alternative was to wade knee deep in the freezing, foul liquid and bale it out with mess kit pans, buckets (when available), or helmets.

Much has been written about World War I as a killing machine. Unlike the wars of centuries past, it was not—the argument goes—a contest of warrior against warrior, sentient man against sentient man, but, rather, of indifferent machine against helpless human flesh and blood. A bullet fired by one soldier aiming at another more often than not missed its mark. No, the great killer in World War I was shellfire: high explosives— the products of modern chemistry and physics—propelled at high velocity over great range by cannon that were the products of cutting-edge metallurgy and manufacturing techniques. Heavy shells were meant to penetrate fortifications and explode within or simply bring the structure down. Thousands of troops were blown to bits, buried alive, or both. Shells from lighter field weapons were intended specifically as antipersonnel munitions. They were designed to explode into many thousands of razor-like fragments. As a modern historian has written, "The large-caliber guns of artillery warfare with their power to atomize bodies into unrecoverable fragments and the mangling, deadly fallout of shrapnel had made clear, at the war's outset, that mankind's military technology wildly outpaced its medical: 'Every fracture in this war is a huge open wound,' one American doctor reported, 'with a not merely broken but shattered bone at the bottom of it.'"[12]

The barrelmaker-turned poilu Louis Barthas described how a school-teacher named Izard struggled to return to the French trenches after "an explosive bullet [had] torn his guts to shreds" and then how another, crawling toward the trench, "suddenly leapt up and fell right in the middle of us. . . . This man had almost no face left. An explosive bullet had blown up in his mouth, blasting out his cheeks, ripping out his tongue (a piece of which hung down), and shattering his jaws, and blood poured out copiously from these horrible wounds." The man's comrades wrapped bandages "around what was left of his face" and finally got him to a first-aid station hours later, toward evening.[13]

It is not difficult to find horrific descriptions such as these. Less well documented is the misery between the intervals of action. Even without the shelling, the poison gas, and the explosive bullets, a trench would not have been fit for human habitation. It was always wet and frequently flooded. It was infested with lice and rats—particularly aggressive lice and especially big rats. German and English noncommissioned officers were typically insistent in their efforts to keep the trenches as clean as possible. French trenches, however, became notorious for their lack of even the most elementary hygiene. They were invariably squalid. A ration of *pinard* was invaluable in coping with the elements, the vermin, and the despair. Under the best of conditions, French rations—in contrast with German—were abundant and tasty; however, the system of supply frequently broke down. Moreover, while each French army company was supposed to be equipped with its own complete mobile kitchen, approximately half the kitchens ordered from manufacturers either failed to be delivered or proved too defective to be usable. More often than not, troops were forced to make do with field rations. In these, the staple item was tinned beef that the French troops called *singe* and the British Tommies (as well as, later, American doughboys) called "monkey meat." This was supplemented at times by heavily salted cod.

When they weren't focused on merely surviving the cold or bailing out their flooded trenches, soldiers indulged a passion for tobacco. The older troops tended to smoke pipes, the younger chain-smoked cigarettes, which soon became a standard part of soldiers' rations. Reading also passed the time but even more important were the reading and writing of letters from and to home. The commanders of every nation's army considered correspondence so valuable to morale and motivation that significant resources were devoted to maintaining large and efficient military postal services. The British Army Postal Service alone handled two billion letters and 114 million parcels over the war's four years.[14]

Card games were a universal pastime among soldiers. Although gambling was officially forbidden in all the combatant armies, the ban—in all of those armies—was blithely ignored. Behind the lines, outside of the trenches, football (soccer) was popular. No young soldier was ever too tired to play and, whenever possible, matches were more or less formally organized, often by senior noncommissioned officers. Company commanders also highly approved of such competitive sports as boxing—which encouraged physical competitiveness—and various team sports, which promoted esprit de corps as well as discipline.

The anxiety of war encourages friendships, but the continual company of others—often in cramped quarters—also creates an urgent need to be alone. A surprising number of soldiers spent time in solitary search of battlefield debris such as shell fragments and the nose caps of shells, as well as large-caliber rifle and machine-gun ammunition casings, which they turned into "trench art." Shell cases could be fashioned into remarkable flower vases or tobacco jars. Driving bands, made of copper and used to create a tight fit between an artillery shell and the cannon barrel, might be fashioned into letter openers or other implements. Poilus were especially skilled creators of trench art, the most inventive of which were the improvised instruments of "trench orchestras." Horns and percussion instruments were hammered out from debris, and musically inclined comrades were recruited to serenade themselves and others.

Although, between battles, soldiers were often left to their own devices, commanders did their best to keep the men busy. In part, they were concerned to keep fighting skills honed. More important, however, they believed that boredom and idleness were destructive to discipline. Work details were abundantly assigned. By 1916, however, the French army was suffering from an acute shortage of junior—company-level—officers, among whom the combat death toll was especially high. As a result, unit efficiency as well as discipline suffered, and punishment—especially punishment by example—was liberally applied. Although the French army was a military force ostensibly in service to a democracy founded on *liberté, égalité, et fraternité*, a strict class system was imposed to segregate privates from noncommissioned officers and both from commissioned officers. In addition, military "justice" was meted out in the French army with a severity that reportedly scandalized even the "autocratic" army of the kaiser. French disciplinary courts were, in effect, drumhead courts martial, convened ad hoc and hurling verdicts like thunderbolts. All verdicts were final and subject to no appeal. Sentences were carried out immediately. These ranged from assignment to labor details to exile to a "penal company," whose members were assigned the most disagreeable and dangerous of tasks. For the most serious offenses, such as demonstrated cowardice (perceived or actual) under fire, summary execution by firing squad was prescribed. Conviction for desertion, disobedience, or abandoning one's post in the presence of the enemy usually also carried a death sentence, and a report commissioned by the French war centenary commission in 2013 determined that, during 1914–1918, between 600 and 650 French soldiers were executed by firing squad for various issues of military disobedience.[15] Such executions were public and formal, explicitly intended to inculcate discipline by example.

The truly remarkable thing about the horror and misery of life and death in World War I, especially at hellish places like the Verdun sector, is not the gruesomeness of wounds or the degree of suffering with bad food, brutal discipline, general squalor, and boredom punctuated by terror. The *truly* remarkable thing is the degree to which soldiers, most of them pressed involuntarily into military life, endured and adjusted. Yes, punishment and other coercions were available, present, and practiced. By and large, however, French—and German, British, and American—soldiers sacrificed willingly, not only under the crush of industrial warfare's indifferent machinery but also in the face of unfeeling and, it seemed, heedless and irrational superior officers, top commanders, and national leaders.

SUNBURST

February 19, 1916, was distinguished by something that had not been seen in the Verdun region for well over a week: the sun. Joseph Joffre took advantage of the gentler weather to take another tour of the sector. He was pleased with the progress General Herr had made in erecting new defenses. He said nothing about those Herr had scrambled to restore, artillery emplacements and barbed wire obstacles that had been dismantled pursuant to Joffre's own orders in 1914 and early 1915.

The next day, February 20, was downright brilliant. The trenches dried out. The mud of no-man's-land hardened. There was a bright yellow sun in a bright blue sky. Ordinarily, these would be reasons to rejoice and celebrate. Men like Lieutenant Colonel Émile Driant, however, were well aware of the grim significance of the fair weather. In command of the position he knew would take the initial brunt of the attack the radiant sun would now enable and unleash, Driant wrote to his wife: "The hour is near." He assured her that he felt "very calm," but he also assured her that his front trenches would "be taken in the first minutes." And so he sighed for his "poor battalions, spared until now."[16]

To all of his field commanders, Driant included, and to the troops, General Frédéric Herr published his stern orders concerning the battle to come. His chief command was to "resist whatever the cost; let yourselves be cut to pieces on the spot rather than fall back."[17] Verdun—it seems—had become land sacred to France.

CHAPTER 7

The Guns of February

The method of the Germans is simple: to eliminate our ability to respond through their heavy artillery fire.

—GENERAL ÉMILE FAYOLLE, DIARY
ENTRY, SEPTEMBER 8, 1914[1]

AT 7:15 ON THE MORNING OF FEBRUARY 21, 1916, AN EXPLOSION IN THE courtyard of the Bishop's Palace in Verdun sent skyward a great geyser of earth and debris, higher, much higher, than the tower of the cathedral. Erupting rocks, shell fragments, or perhaps the shockwave of the blast itself tore the corner off the building.

Construction of the cathedral began in the year 990. Its corner was blown off by the explosion of a 380-mm shell fired from one of the great modified naval guns manufactured by the Krupp armaments works, which had been founded in Essen exactly 599 years after the cathedral began to rise. Many years separated the cathedral from Krupp, and a full twenty miles separated the Krupp-made weapon from its target in 1916. The artillerymen feeding the biggest guns aimed at Verdun were always far away and never saw what they hit. The unseen targets might be forts, cathedrals, homes, or human beings.

By no means, in fact, were the gunners actually aiming to hit a house of God. Their assigned targets were the bridges crossing the Meuse. The shot that hit the cathedral was only the first of about a million shells the Germans would fire during the next ten hours along a front that was some nineteen miles long and a little over three miles wide. (The Germans had budgeted two million shells for the first six days.) With the naval gun

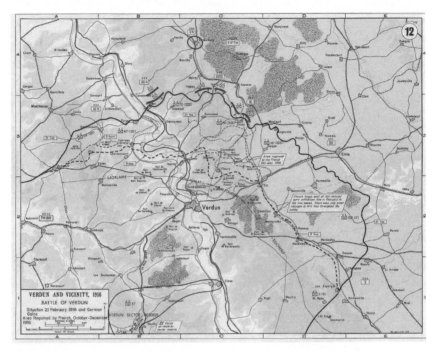

The Battle of Verdun at its start, February 21, 1916. Moving from right to left, the solid black line is the line of battle on which the German and French forces fought on Day 1; the gray dashed line is the area regained by the French during October–December 1916; the thin dashed line is the area regained by the French early in October; and the heavy dashed line is the front to which the French withdrew in the opening phase of the battle, late in February 1916. UNITED STATES MILITARY ACADEMY

planted approximately twenty miles away, it was understandably difficult to be very accurate. To be honest, the Germans were perfectly willing to reduce the town of Verdun to rubble, but it was of far greater tactical importance to destroy bridges, roads, railroads, and rail yards in order to cut off the Verdun sector from supply, reinforcement, and rapid communication while also preventing the French soldiers there from making a strategic retreat intact. And while the naval guns were aimed mainly at the bridges, the biggest weapons of all, twenty-six of them firing 420-mm shells, were trained principally on the forts throughout the Verdun

131

Pounded by artillery, many of the trenches at Verdun were transformed into deadly ruins. The uniforms of the soldiers identify this as a German trench. AUTHOR'S COLLECTION

fortified region. All of the other artillery the Germans arrayed against Verdun and environs, a total of 808 pieces, pounded trenches, supply depots, vehicles, and the earth itself. The idea was to transform the field of battle into a killing field, a veritable storm of universal disintegration.

"A STORM, A HURRICANE, A TEMPEST"

Lieutenant Colonel Émile Driant had predicted that his section of the front, the Bois des Caures, would be the first to feel the German onslaught. His time would come—and arrive both gallantly and terribly—but he had failed to factor into his calculations the scope of the enemy's preparatory artillery barrage. The Bois de Caures took its first hits at the same time as the rest of the front took theirs and not before. It was, however, terrible enough.

Early risers at the Bois had caught sight of a solitary German aircraft flying overhead. But what of it? A Corporal Stephane—those who served with him called him *Gran'pere* because he was all of forty-six years old—saw it, but now he was more interested in eyeing two of his comrades as they began to grind coffee to prepare a morning's cup. That is when the shells began to fall on the Bois de Caures. The two men in the midst of making coffee seemed disturbed only by the interruption in that vital rite of the morning routine. One of them cursed as they both quickly withdrew into a dugout. Stephane could not force himself to be so blasé. He later recalled that he felt swept up in "a storm, a hurricane, a tempest growing ever stronger, where it was raining nothing but paving stones."[2]

Stones, whirlwinds, and dust were added to tree limbs and branches splintered by the incoming shells. The big boughs fell to earth, only to be kicked up again—wildly—by the next detonation.

Destruction? Absolutely. Chaos? Not quite.

Driant had not dug contiguous trenches to defend the Bois de Caures, but instead excavated a ring of independent dugouts around another ring of larger redoubts, also dug into the earth. Behind these two lines was a line of concrete fortifications. Stephane was in a redoubt that contained his company's headquarters. Set apart from the ranks of the other redoubts, it was, at the moment, probably the safest place to be while under attack. And so, without panic but with intense interest, he studied the process of destruction. No, it was not chaotic. On the contrary, it was relentless in its orderly progress. The shells fell and detonated. As they detonated, another series of shells began falling in a rank behind the first, followed by another, and another. The shells marched, advancing like an army deeper and deeper into the encampment of the Chasseurs. Actually, Corporal Stephane saw it less as an advancing army than as a garden hose wielded by a patiently diligent gardener. First the nearest rank was thoroughly "soaked," then the rank behind that one, and then behind that, and so on. Stephane noted that, at first, most of the big shells were not directed at his dugout or the other outposts, but at the "Grande Gardes," the circle of redoubts between the outer dugouts and the concrete fortifications. Then, at last, he saw the barrage creep farther back, to the concrete positions. Once the barrage had completely "soaked" the outmost redoubts, rank by rank, and then hit the concrete fortifications, it started all over again—from the outer redoubts, back, rank by rank, toward the fortifications. Each iteration of the cycle took about fifteen minutes. The progress was relentless: a garden hose wielded by a maniacally patient gardener.

But, suddenly, that gardener lost his patience. The methodical pattern of rank after rank abruptly shifted, and four large shells impacted very close to Stephane's redoubt. A stretcher-bearer's shelter—a small covered excavation intended to afford a modicum of protection to the wounded—absorbed all four hits and collapsed. This was followed by a fifth incoming shell, which landed directly in Stephane's redoubt. Much of the blast was swallowed up by the earth and, remarkably, the close hit failed to harm him.

Corporal Stephane was lucky. The fact that he lived to describe the barrage tells us this much. Most of his comrades were silent on the subject for the simple reason that they had not been as lucky as he.

Armies kill people and break things. An enemy killed is an enemy who won't kill you. But a sustained artillery barrage did even more than kill. It left the survivors profoundly shaken, often transforming them from upright soldiers into cowering beings. Some became obvious victims of "shell shock," a kind of emotional paralysis or walking catatonia. Historian Denis Winter described the effect of a barrage as destructive of "the body and mind of the front line." In a contest between combatants on an open battlefield, the individual soldier could—at least sometimes—feel he was making an impact on the enemy. In a trench or a dugout under artillery bombardment—perhaps from guns as much as twenty miles away—each soldier "saw himself as the rodent occupier of a pockmarked, grassless zone, whose forward limit was determined by the very limit of human endurance." Rodent? Maybe even that was too grand a self-image. Under barrage, the very "order of life . . . seemed beyond . . . comprehension . . . the future greyer and more unthinkable, even if a man could gather himself to contemplate anything beyond survival."[3] Under barrage, those who survived often felt they had been reduced to mere ciphers.

The 420-mm gun was intended to destroy fortifications. In the concentrated arena of the Verdun sector, however, the shells from that gun often exploded in or among the trenches. Each massive projectile fired from this behemoth traveled upward at 1,700 miles per hour to an altitude of more than fifteen thousand feet before descending to earth. The combination of impact and explosion blasted a crater large enough to swallow a large house—or the equivalent in whatever men were hunkered down in the trenches it hit.

The smaller, more mobile guns were not intended to crater the earth but to maim or kill anyone who dared to walk upon it. The shells they fired were designed to detonate above the enemy target, disgorging thousands of shrapnel fragments in a puff of dirty white smoke. A properly detonated air burst would produce a conical cloud of high-velocity metal fragments six hundred feet deep and nearly a hundred feet wide. Whatever came within this cloud was penetrated, torn, often ripped limb from limb.

Again, the destruction, certainly horrific, was far less chaotic than one might expect—and therefore that much more diabolical. Experienced soldiers quickly learned to separate the sound of a distant artillery piece being fired from the shell's explosive impact seconds later. Frightened men on the receiving end of a barrage became, in spite of themselves, connoisseurs of the instruments of their own demise. They learned that the "small field gun went off with a crack like a fat man hitting a golf ball. The shell . . . arrived with a screaming shriek." In contrast, the firing of a larger medium artillery piece "sounded like a giant newspaper being torn, its shell a farm cart coming down a steep hill with its brakes on." And the shell from a truly big gun? Its firing "rapped a man's head with a heavy cane." Then the sound "rolled in a leisurely arc across the sky, a man on a bicycle whistling slowly and pensively." There was a teasing sense that the shell was moving slowly enough to be outrun. But just as one began thinking this way, the sound "speeded up like an express train rushing down a tunnel." If a shell passed overhead, it echoed. If it fell in an enclosed place—like a building—there was a double bang. A projectile that just missed you "would whistle or roar, with debris raining down long after the burst." Nobody *wanted* this knowledge and these sensations, but they came nonetheless, and the "strain of listening for all these sounds did something to the brain. A man could never be rid of them."[4]

At Verdun, in the French lines that bleak February day, men who had lived through barrages in earlier battles comforted themselves by recounting how shells often exploded next to a comrade or next to oneself without doing any real harm. The mud, they said, swallowed the blast. Those who had never been through a barrage before listened eagerly to such men—men who might or might not share the sights they had also seen: how soldiers hit by shrapnel or debris lost eyes or entire faces, lost limbs, lost guts. The blast wave alone could rupture kidney and spleen, even if neither shrapnel nor debris actually hit you. Some men died from explosive decompression. The blast literally took their breath away, asphyxiating them. In contrast to bodies shredded by shrapnel, the corpses of these men appeared uninjured, spotless, without a blemish. Just dead.

You could die. You could be blinded or deafened or both. Disfigured, perhaps. Maybe crippled for life. Or you could be unhurt but forever haunted. Shell shock might come after a prolonged barrage, like that at Verdun. "No one was immune. Some stared at their hands clasped on their knees in a state of catatonic fear. Some hid their heads in their greatcoats in a state of torpor. Others would sit in certain positions, touch particular objects, whistle so many bars of a particular tune to ward evil off with ritual. Some wept; others joked hysterically, but all shook and crawled, white-faced in dull endurance, 'How long? How long?'"[5] Shell shock might come with a single experience. One British soldier recalled an "eighteen-year-old trembling for twenty-four hours after a dud dropped ten yards from him."[6] Or it might come, at last, after having lived through just one too many barrages.

Torture

Cursory histories of World War I treat the "artillery preparation" that customarily preceded an attack as an all-out pounding with little method to it. As Corporal Stephane saw for himself, German gunners were in fact highly disciplined, working over their targets with relentless method.

German intelligence had been sufficient to reveal that the French were terribly outgunned—by at least four to one in number of artillery pieces, but far more lopsidedly in terms of explosive power. Falkenhayn's commanders were not content to rely on the numbers, however. German counterbattery fire—artillery attacks intended to knock out the enemy's artillery—made liberal use of poison gas shells to disable the French gunners.

Not that the French had much artillery of sufficient range to reach the biggest German guns. As long as the barrage continued, the battle was terrifyingly one-sided. It was torture, really. Torture is more than the infliction of pain. It is the infliction of pain on a victim who is effectively helpless. The torturer controls everything. The object of the torture can do nothing but endure—or break. At Verdun that opening day of combat, the Germans surely inflicted both pain and torture. They dominated the battle. They controlled its terms. The barrage had begun at 7:30 in the morning. At about midday, the torturers seemed to relent. The barrage ended.

To deprive men of hope is a terrible thing: *This barrage will never end.* To give them hope—and then crush it—is even worse. As soon as the barrage stopped, survivors emerged from their dugouts and forts to survey the damage. The German commanders had expected as much. They launched reconnaissance flights, which were able to estimate the numbers of troops, exposed as they now were. The pilots were also able to note what forts and other structures were intact and still capable of action and which positions had been damaged beyond repair or wiped out entirely.

As for the psychological effect of emerging to see what had happened, those at Bois de Caures, who had been told they would take the brunt of the opening attack, could now look around and see that *no* portion of the Verdun sector had been spared.

THE LIMITS OF DESTRUCTION

The German barrage resumed sometime after 2 p.m. and reached a high intensity within an hour. By 3:40, it was at its most intense. The Fifth Army infantry was on the verge of advancing to attack.

From their forward-positioned Stollen, the concrete galleries built in place of exposed advance trenches, the infantrymen of Crown Prince Wilhelm must all have been greatly heartened by what they beheld. It appeared that the frontline French defensive positions had been entirely swallowed up in the great barrage. From the rising columns of smoke marking the French trenches closest to them, not a single living figure in horizon blue was to be seen. The French returned no fire. A German aviator landed after completing a reconnaissance flight during the lull in the barrage. "It's done," he reported to his CO. "We can pass. There's nothing living there anymore."[7]

And so it must have appeared—both to the men waiting in the Stollen and to the aviator. A cratered moonscape is by definition devoid of life, and that was the appearance of much of the Verdun sector by afternoon of the first day.

Eyewitnesses as well as four generations of historians have written about the destruction wrought by artillery in World War I. The impression both leave is of complete devastation. "A chicken could not live on that field when we open on it," Porter Alexander, commanding Confederate general James Longstreet's artillery battalion at Fredericksburg, remarked just before that battle began. Even more than half a century before Verdun, during the American Civil War—a conflict often deemed the first war to be thoroughly fought with the weapons of the Industrial Revolution—commanders habitually overestimated the effectiveness of artillery. Yes, Confederate artillery fire helped turn Fredericksburg into a Union catastrophe. And yes, German fire was devastating to the French defenders of Verdun. But neither of these facts is surprising. What is astonishing, however, were the limits of destruction, both in 1862 and 1916.

German artillerymen were confident that their big Krupp guns would destroy all the forts and strongpoints of Verdun. They did not. More important, they did not destroy the earthwork defenses. Those shells that exploded in or near trenches could be terribly destructive—yet, with much of the explosive force absorbed into the earth itself, these impacts left many men alive and structures standing. More important, most shells missed entirely. In missing, they cratered the battlefield, creating the impression of total devastation that the men in their Stollen and the aviator in his aircraft saw and reported. But it was, finally, more an impression than a reality.

The cratering of no-man's-land—the territory separating the combatants—not only misled observers, it also created extraordinarily difficult obstacles for the attacking infantry. Going over the top—climbing out of the trenches, or emerging from the Stollen—to attack the enemy trenches exposed the attackers to defensive fire. Craters in no-man's-land were formidable obstacles that slowed the advance, often with fatal results.

A hundred years after World War I, we have an overly simplistic view of the nature of combat in that war. We tend to think of the Western Front as two opposing lines of trench separated by no-man's-land. In fact, each "line" of trenches was far more complex. Typically, each side set up *three* lines of trenches: a front line closest to the enemy, an intermediate line behind it, and a third line behind that. Short trenches perpendicular to these allowed covered passage from one line to another. The front trench was often used as a stepping-off place for launching attacks. When soldiers spoke of "going over the top," it was the top of this front trench they were speaking of. The intermediate trench was the principal defensive trench, and the rearmost trench was the "last ditch" defensive position.

Attackers were usually able to overrun the first trench. In the process, however, they were slowed down as they came up against the stronger middle trench, which was steadily reinforced by men sent forward from the third trench. As Corporal Stephane observed in the methodical shelling of French positions at Bois de Caures, a standard preparatory artillery barrage swept the front, middle, and back line of trenches. Many shells, of course, failed to hit any of these lines of trench and instead impacted between them. Thus the ground between the first and second and second and third trench lines was almost always badly cratered by the time infantry made its attack. Having to negotiate this inter-trench cratering slowed the attack and made the attackers highly vulnerable targets.

Going into the Battle of Verdun, the French were tragically crippled by their high command's groundless belief that fortifications and heavy artillery were somehow passé and that nothing was superior to a fierce infantry attack or counterattack. Although the Franco-Prussian War had taught the Germans many lessons about industrialized warfare, the most valuable of which was the critical importance of heavy artillery, they, too, nevertheless went into the battle burdened by critical errors. The Germans had faith in heavy artillery as the ultimate weapon. They believed that the heavy guns would win the war. In fact, the German military's unconditional reliance on their big guns had two critical limitations:

1. As discussed, heavy artillery preparation cratered the battlefield, making an infantry attack very difficult and potentially very costly. In

this sense, the use of heavy artillery, while devastating to the enemy, was also—in some degree—inevitably self-defeating.

2. As destructive as relentless shelling was, it was rarely decisive. Even more than eight hundred guns firing for ten hours could not and did not kill everyone and destroy everything. While badly damaged, most forts remained sufficiently intact to continue functioning. While many soldiers were blown to bits, most were not.

This second point was especially important at Verdun. The impression that both French and German troops had—that the massed artillery barrage of February 21, 1916 was, in extent and destructive effect, unprecedented in the history of warfare up to that time—was indeed accurate. Nothing like it had ever been unleashed before. Nothing like it had ever been suffered before. This was true not only with regard to intensity but also extent. The German barrage stretched from Avocourt on the left (west) bank of the Meuse to the most easterly French forts on the right (east) bank. It covered a large slice of the Woëvre, hitting about 60 percent of the seventy-five-mile-wide Verdun front. Yet the destruction was far from total.

By the time the German infantry was ordered over the top at 4 p.m. on the afternoon of February 21, the French certainly looked beaten. And yet they were not. "Home before the leaves have fallen from the trees," the kaiser promised his troops and their families back in August 1914. He could not keep his promise. Yet now it looked as if Verdun would actually fall very quickly. But this, too, would prove untrue—and within its untruth was a very difficult, counterintuitive lesson. It turned out that attacking with the purpose of achieving annihilation by bombarding the enemy relentlessly, by attempting not merely to kill but to overkill, was not the way to win the battle. The effort to destroy the enemy with explosives ended up hobbling one's own ability to attack. The secret was to calibrate the use of artillery so that it paralyzed rather than destroyed the enemy. Instead of cratering no-man's-land and the intervals between trenches, it would have been better to bombard most heavily the positions *behind* the front lines, thereby isolating the troops who were in direct contact with the attacking force. Cut off from sources of supply, reinforcement, command, and control as well as routes of orderly retreat, the frontline defenders would become targets far more feasible and far less costly.

At 4 p.m., the men of the German Fifth Army were poised to do what both sides had repeatedly attempted to do ever since the collapse of the Schlieffen Plan at the First Battle of the Marne in September 1914. They were poised to break through a front.

There was, of course, nothing remarkable about such an objective. Since the very first battle of which there is any record—at Megiddo, between Egypt and the Mitanni kingdom about 1469 BC, the battle that gave birth to the concept of ultimate battle: Armageddon—combat has been about two armies clashing along a front. The army that breaks through that front wins. The army whose front is broken through loses. Little wonder that the armies of World War I, some 3,500 years after Armageddon, persisted in seeking a breakthrough—even though industrialized war was teaching them another, very different lesson.

Long-range heavy artillery was less effective at helping an infantry break through a front line than it was at disrupting everything behind that front line. Paralyzing the enemy was better than killing him, it turned out.

If heavy artillery was imparting the first lessons of this new warfare, the emergence of military aviation—in many ways, an extension of conventional artillery—was, in 1916, on the cusp of imparting lessons significantly more advanced. The German artillery barrage on day one of the Battle of Verdun was unprecedented in extent and destructiveness. Also unprecedented, though less noticed by the battered French, was Germany's use of tactical airpower. Erich von Falkenhayn assembled for use at Verdun most of the German air force, 168 fixed-wing aircraft. He used these, along with captive balloons and untethered dirigibles, for aerial reconnaissance and for what would be called in the *next* world war close air support, or tactical bombing. The aircraft augmented conventional artillery by bombing trenches and other enemy positions. During the first week of the battle, German aircraft dropped about five hundred bombs, representing some eleven thousand pounds of high explosives. Given the extremely limited payload capacity of aircraft of the period, this is highly impressive.

But there was more. At Verdun, German aircraft hit targets too far behind the front lines for even the longest-range artillery to reach. Before

Verdun as well as simultaneously with it, the biggest German bombers were also dispatched to drop bombs far behind the front lines—on Paris and London. In this way, tactical bombing was developed into strategic bombing: bombing aimed at civilians and the civilian-run industries that supplied the war.

Of course, the number of aircraft and the bomb-carrying capacity of each plane were too limited for either tactical bombing or strategic bombing to be decisive. But, at Verdun, a battle destined to stand as an icon of futile trench warfare on the Western Front, the seeds of a revolution in warfare were being planted. The ongoing evolution of an industrial civilization that had given nations the ability to pound each other across a static no-man's-land was beginning to produce the means to fight wars without any fronts at all. World War I would not become what President Woodrow Wilson promised it could become when he took America into the war in April 1917. It by no means proved to be "the war to end all wars." But, at Verdun, it did begin to become the war that transformed all wars by ending the possibility of winning the war by breaking through any particular front. At Verdun, World War I was becoming the war to end all fronts.

CHAPTER 8

Los!

There's going to be a battle here, the likes of which the world has not yet seen.
——MEMBER OF THE HESSIAN EIGHTH FUSILIER REGIMENT,
LETTER TO HIS MOTHER ON THE EVE OF BATTLE[1]

AT THE HEIGHT OF ITS INTENSITY, THE ARTILLERY BARRAGE OF FEBRU-
ary 21, 1916, dropped shells across the entire Verdun front at the average
rate of forty per minute. There was great devastation, obviously. Far less
obviously, that devastation was not nearly as complete as the Germans
confidently believed it would be. The toll in injury and death was terrible but not decisive. The damage to military hardware and fortifications
was extensive but far from complete. Nevertheless, one French military
asset suffered more than the rest. It was information. The barrage virtually stopped its flow from and to the Verdun front. The defenders on the
front line were, virtually from the beginning of the battle, in every sense,
on their own.

Early in the barrage—by eight that morning—all telephone communication between the frontline outposts and higher command in the rear
were cut off, blasted. Individual unit commanders, some of them, improvised by hastily organizing relays of runners. They did not undertake this
lightly. For to be assigned as a runner through a front under heavy artillery bombardment was tantamount to a death sentence. Yet, throughout
that first day of battle, the runners were very nearly the only link between
Verdun and everything to the west.

If runners had a slim chance of survival, reinforcements had, for all practical purposes, none—certainly not as long as the sustained bombardment continued. The men of Verdun were captives under fire. They were held in a kind of collective solitary confinement. They knew nothing of the world outside of their sector. In fact, for them the only certainty was the barrage itself. Nothing reached them from the rear. For eight or more hours, it was as if the command structure of the French army ceased to exist, at least above the level of the smallest units. Squadrons and platoons retained some semblance of command hierarchy. In some areas, companies remained recognizable organizations. Beyond the dozen, fifty, or two hundred men closest to one another, the army no longer existed. For these men of Verdun, under bombardment, France itself did not exist. The world? The whole world was contained within the next exploding shell.

INFANTRY ATTACKS

At four in the afternoon, the barrage ended. Within the Stollen, all along the eight-mile front the crown prince and General Schmidt von Knobelsdorf had staked out, platoon commanders cried out, "*Los!*"

Go!

It was the simplest possible command. And, one hundred years later, most of us imagine its having produced the simplest possible result. At the sound of this word, hundreds, thousands of men emerged from their trenches (in the case of the Germans at Verdun, we may envision them sallying forth from their concrete galleries) and swarmed toward the enemy trenches in a single, great, massed attack.

Or so we imagine.

In fact, had it been the French or the British who were attacking the Germans at Verdun and not the other way around, this simple picture would be quite accurate. The pattern of Allied assaults rarely varied, even though they produced the same tragic result time and time again. Officers blew their whistles, and thousands of men, often loaded down with full field packs, tumbled "over the top" to begin a suicidal advance across no-man's-land. Many met a bullet or a blast the second they poked their head above the lip of their trench. Shot, they slid back down its steep wall. Others became mere molecules in a wave sweeping over no-man's-land, each able to do no more than hope for survival amid the lethal stream issuing from machine guns that were inevitably arrayed to deliver inescapable crossfire all across no-man's-land. As the machine-gun fire swept no-man's-land, field artillery let loose with air bursts of shrapnel shells that cut down men as if by the action of numberless scythes. It was, we imagine, a greatly reduced swarm that finally reached the enemy trenches, there to engage the defenders bayonet to bayonet and hand to hand.

Yes, in the case of an Allied assault, this crude picture would be reasonably accurate. The Germans, however, did things differently. Although the Fifth Army staked out a wide front and unleashed a barrage all across it, gunners also identified small sections of the enemy's front trench line to receive the most intensive bombardment. At these places, the goal of the German heavy artillery was total annihilation. Instead of attacking in one huge swarm, the Germans assembled relatively small units, each of which headed for the most intensely bombarded portion of the enemy's advance trench line. The units—think of them as "fighting patrols"—were not the customary combination of infantry riflemen backed up by a unit of machine gunners and yet another unit of field artillery, each under different command, at best cooperating but ultimately quite separate from one another. Much as the Germans at Verdun closely integrated air power with artillery and infantry (in close-air support), so they created what today would be called "combined-arms units." The fighting patrols consisted of infantry, machine gunners, and combat engineers working together under single command. This was in stark contrast to the Allied order of battle, in which these three groups operated independently from each other, segregated in infantry platoons, machine-gun battalions, and engineer units, each under its own commanders. As the war progressed, such German combined-arms fighting patrols were designated as *Sturmabteilungen*, Storm Troopers.

Despite their name, Storm Troopers did not customarily take an enemy position by storm. Instead, they tended to probe carefully, looking for ways to avoid costly head-on attacks by dividing themselves so as to attack isolated objectives from multiple positions. General Joffre liked to say that he "nibbled at" the enemy. More often than not, this was little more than an excuse for failing to make significant progress. In the case

of German assault tactics, however, "nibbling" produced highly significant results. The fighting patrols infiltrated enemy lines where they had
been broken by intensive artillery bombardment. They carefully targeted
isolated, dazed, and disorganized survivors of the barrage, flanked them,
and then killed them. In this way, they rendered the front line increasingly
porous, ultimately vulnerable to a larger breakthrough. Far from being
a rapid "storming" attack, it was a methodical approach that exploited
weakness.

Some contemporaries as well as later historians have criticized
the nibbling, probing approach as yet another symptom of Erich von
Falkenhayn's excessive caution as a commander. Indeed, there is a valid
argument to be made that he and his field commanders failed to precisely delineate the point at which the probing and nibbling should give
way to more massive exploitations of an opening. Be that as it may, it is
undeniable that the German approach was far less costly than the Allied
practice of pouring masses of men into no-man's-land, thereby creating a
human carpet to be pounded out by the defender's artillery and machine
guns.

Deploying small packets of men in fighting patrols had another
advantage. It was an inherently deceptive tactic, giving the French at Verdun (and elsewhere, for that matter) the false impression that they were
inflicting far more casualties on the Germans than they actually were.
Historians have long understood that Allied estimates of enemy casualties were routinely inflated during World War I. They assumed that the
inflation was part of a systematic and deliberate effort to deceive politicians and public—that it was propaganda, plain and simple. More likely,
however, the inflation was due at least in part to the Allied assumption
that the Germans attacked in mass, the same way as the Allies themselves did. If fewer troops were visible coming across no-man's-land, they
assumed that this paucity was the result of casualties inflicted on what
had somehow started out as a massed assault. Thus, the German fighting
patrol, the probing and nibbling approach was not only effective, it also
made very difficult the task of accurately estimating the attacker's effective strength.

THE AUDACITY OF HANS VON ZWEHL

On day one of the assault against Verdun, Erich von Falkenhayn had hugely ambitious goals for his artillery but distinctly limited aims for his infantry. It can be argued that he overestimated the effect of a massive—unprecedentedly massive—artillery barrage and underestimated the effect of a follow-on infantry assault. It can also be argued that, in contrast to French commanders, who were wedded to the dictum and doctrine of attaque à outrance—attack to excess—Falkenhayn had a genuine battle plan.

In either case, whether out of an excess of caution or true tactical ingenuity, Falkenhayn neither demanded nor expected—let alone, counted on—making a breakthrough on February 21, 1916. His orders to the Fifth Army made it clear that he was not interested in pressing the battle to a rapid conclusion. On the contrary, he saw the first-day role of his infantry not as conquest but as a combination of mopping up survivors of the ten-hour artillery barrage and probing for the weakest areas in the French lines. Any attempt at major breakthroughs would be directed to these identified areas—and that would commence on day two of the battle, February 22.

Those who study the European theater of World War II often remark on a major difference between the German army on the one hand and the British and American armies on the other. Whereas German commanders tended to defer to higher headquarters rather than risk exceeding their authority by exploiting ad hoc opportunities in the field, both British and American field commanders assumed greater initiative and acted more independently of rear echelon authority. Soldiers' battles, engagements clearly won as a result of frontline initiative rather than rear-echelon strategic planning, are relatively common among Allied units in World War II but rarely found in German operations. In World War I, however, it was the Allies—at least the British and, even more, the French—who habitually deferred to higher headquarters. The German army of that time, while very hierarchical, nevertheless accorded field commanders great latitude. Three Fifth Army corps participated in the infantry attacks that immediately followed the artillery barrage of February 21, 1916. Two of the three rigorously toed the mark inscribed by Falkenhayn's order: On day one, mop up and identify weak points. On day two, break through these weak points.

A third corps, the VII Reserve Corps commanded by General Johann "Hans" von Zwehl, diverged from Falkenhayn's timetable. Driven by his bias for action, Zwehl, on day one, threw against the French line a large infantry force immediately following the action of his fighting patrols.

General Zwehl was a Prussian officer, but his face bore an expression that looked downright exuberant compared to the typically stern, drum-tight, severely close-cropped image most of his brother Prussian officers self-consciously cultivated. He was sixty-five in 1916, having been called out of retirement at the outbreak of the war two years earlier. Yet he had already proven himself a commander of youthful zeal. In the first month of the war, he was assigned to lead the VII Reserves and was tasked with laying siege to the formidable French fortress of Maubeuge, located on the Sambre River about five and a half miles from the Belgian border.

Zwehl commenced the siege on August 24, 1914. Two weeks later, on the evening of September 6, he forced the surrender of the entire Fortified Region of Maubeuge. For this achievement, he was decorated with the coveted Pour le Mérite—one of the very first German officers so recognized in World War I. (He had already earned an Iron Cross for action in the Franco-Prussian War.)

From Maubeuge, Zwehl led his VII Reserves to the Aisne trenches, from which, in October 1915, he and his command were transferred to the Verdun front. On February 21, 1916, the bulk of the VII Reserve Corps faced the Bois d'Haumont, a patch of dense woods just to the northeast of the Bois des Caures. Lieutenant Colonel Émile Driant deployed a portion of his Chasseurs here to protect the flank of his main position in the Bois des Caures. The detachment at the Bois d'Haumont had absorbed terrific punishment during the barrage. Those who survived it were physically and mentally exhausted. Some slept at their posts. Others were stuporous with shell shock. When a lookout suddenly sighted a line of German troops—the leading edge of a larger VII Reserve Corps attack—advancing no more than three hundred feet from the Haumont, the alarm he sounded was more than sufficient to rouse the mentally and physically battered troops.

The Germans anticipated something of a cakewalk. They did not know that they weren't facing ordinary poilus but elite Chasseurs. French defensive fire proved highly effective, especially at close range. The men of the approaching line stopped and flattened themselves.

In the meantime, in the Bois des Caures itself, the situation was turning more critical for the French. Here the bombardment had totally obliterated many of the trenches and dugouts. There was a paucity of cover. Worse, the troops here had taken heavy losses, not only among men but also equipment. Impacted by high-explosive shells, the very earth had swallowed up rifles and ammunition alike. Weapons that had to be dug out of the ground were often fouled and useless. Not only were the troops traumatized and shell shocked, they were physically spent by the frantic labor of digging themselves and their comrades out of a living burial under great geysers of dirt and debris.

The advance units of the VII Reserve infantry seized and occupied two outposts in the Bois des Caures without much of a fight. In the meantime, at the Bois d'Haumont, German reinforcements arrived and now rolled over the first line of trenches. With a foothold firmly established, machine gunners took over weapons captured from the French, and combat engineers busied themselves cutting through barbed wire to clear the way for more attacking units.

In fact, barbed wire was about all that the bombardment had left reasonably intact in the Bois des Caures. Concrete emplacements were smashed, entire platoons buried within them. Driant's command bunker was badly damaged, burying ten men. One was dead. Nine were rescued. Of this number, one broke free from the hands of his rescuers and ran off, alternately screaming wildly and laughing demonically. Relentless shelling and living burial had driven him mad. Driant's Chasseurs, 1,300 men, had suffered more than 50 percent casualties, either killed or wounded.

Driant, unhurt, responded to the approach of the German infantry by taking up a rifle, mounting his badly damaged command post, and summoning those closest to him.

"We are here!" he called out to his surviving Chasseurs. "This is *our* place. They shall not move us out of it!"[2]

Lieutenant Colonel Émile Driant's Chasseurs, as gallant as they were hopelessly outnumbered, defend Le Bois des Caures during the opening days of the Battle of Verdun. WIKIMEDIA

At this point, Corporal Marc Stéphane delivered to Driant a note his company commander, a Lieutenant Robin, had given him. Explaining that the advance positions had all been overrun, it asked urgently for artillery support.

Driant read it and then turned back to Stéphane. He told him that he himself had been begging for the 75s to open up on the advancing Germans. But, so far, there had been no French fire at all.

"Frankly, Corporal, I think we shall have to count largely on ourselves."[3]

As for Lieutenant Robin, a stealthy German infiltrator was on the verge of shooting him at pointblank range with his revolver when a sergeant shot the infiltrator dead, saving Robin's life. Without pause, that same sergeant shot down another half-dozen members of a 150-man German patrol making its way into the French position. Robin pulled his company—what remained of it—back to a concrete blockhouse known as S6. Here they took a stand, fighting hand to hand and with bayonets. They managed to fend off the attackers in front of them, but a portion of the patrol had crept around the flanks of S6, forcing Robin and the eighty or so men left to him to retreat to a cluster of concrete pillboxes.

While Lieutenant Robin struggled to hold on, the company to his right, commanded by a Captain Séguin, was approached by some two hundred of the enemy. Discovering that their damaged machine-gun emplacement had been flooded, some of the Chasseurs began frantically to bail it out, but the situation was hopeless, and Séguin ordered his men to fall back on blockhouse S9. It was already occupied by a platoon under a Sergeant Major Dandauw, and no sooner did Séguin's men arrive than another group of men approached. All that Dandauw could make out through the smoke and dust of the recently ended bombardment was that the newcomers had white brassards on their sleeves. These, in fact, were insignia distributed to members of the fighting patrols of the VII Reserve and were intended to aid in identifying themselves to one another. In the fog of war, it was the brassards that stood out, and the Germans therefore looked to Dandauw like French stretcher bearers. He ordered everyone to hold their fire—until he suddenly realized that the blockhouse was about to be overrun not by French medics but by German soldiers.

In a sudden panic, Dandauw ordered a retreat out of S9. When he and his platoon reached R2, the damaged command post, Lieutenant Colonel Driant personally blocked the communication trench through which Dandauw and his platoon were retreating.

In dramatic contrast to the typical French field-grade officer of the era, Driant neither scolded, threatened, blustered, nor shamed. Instead, he spoke calmly to Dandauw.

"Get your men under shelter," Driant told him. "Rest them. Before dawn you will retake your post."[4]

But the blockhouse, it turned out, had not yet been lost. A Sergeant Léger, belonging to Séguin's company, had the presence of mind to bring with him a machine gun. While Dandauw withdrew in panic, Léger set up the weapon and opened fire against the infiltrating German patrols. He took a heavy toll on them—until he ran out of ammunition. Additional German soldiers poured in, once again employing the tactic of flanking and encirclement. Determined to keep his machine gun out of German hands, Léger smashed it, then fought the infiltrators hand to

A rare photograph of the Chasseurs fighting in forward positions in Le Bois des Caures. WIKIMEDIA

hand. With the dozen men of his platoon, Léger fought on. One by one, however, the members of the platoon fell in battle. Léger, seriously and repeatedly wounded, collapsed. After having been slowed, the German infiltration resumed on this outpost of the Bois des Caures.

NIGHT

Lieutenant Robin, badly wounded, nevertheless continued to hold out in and around the pillboxes. As the terrible day finally turned to night, he rallied his men to make a bayonet attack against the infiltrating patrol. Stunned at the ferocity they encountered, the Germans retreated, and Robin succeeded in retaking two positions. Encouraged, he and his soldiers next attacked a group of Germans who, satisfied that all the French had fled or were dead, bedded down for the night in a French frontline

trench. Their sleep was violently interrupted at the point of French bayonets. Amid the shouts and cries of their comrades, the surviving Germans
hastily withdrew.

A wounded German, now a prisoner of war, told Lieutenant Robin
that he was nothing more than a member of a patrol, a mere probe. The
main infantry attack was yet to come, he warned. Robin found this hard
to believe, probably because Zwehl, audaciously exceeding his orders, had
sent in additional troops. What Robin witnessed certainly looked like
more than a "patrol"—although also less than a full-on attack. In any case,
he made his way through the dark back to Driant's command post. Relay-
ing what his prisoner had told him, Lieutenant Robin looked plaintively
at his colonel.

"What am I to do against this"—meaning the anticipated main
attack—"with my eighty men?"

"My poor Robin," Driant answered, "the order is to stay where we
are."[5]

CHAPTER 9

Driant's Last Stand

"You know very well they've never hit me yet!"
—Lieutenant Colonel Émile Driant, at Verdun[1]

THE GERMAN PROBES, AS WELL AS THE MORE AMBITIOUS ATTACKS ZWEHL ordered, abruptly ceased after dark. The cratered no-man's-land and the even more devastated French lines were impossible to navigate in the dark, much less do battle on. But as the attackers withdrew, the German artillery resumed its hellish barrage. Lieutenant Colonel Émile Driant sent, by runner, a hastily scrawled situation report to his divisional commander, General Étienne André Bapst (Seventy-Second Division). He promised to "hold against the Boche although their bombardment is infernal."[2]

But what, really, did it mean to "hold out" against a bombardment—especially when you lacked the artillery to mount a meaningful counter-battery barrage? (It meant enduring the shells. There was nothing more it could mean.)

For the French, it was a night of utter misery—not just because of the bombardment but also because of the mounting uncertainty. All over the front, troops labored under fire to rebuild battered trenches and other means of cover and concealment. As their men worked the shattered ground, field commanders planned counterattacks for the next day. Their plans proceeded on the mere assumption that the reinforcements necessary to carry out the plans would arrive with daylight. Since the Germans had directed much of their heaviest shelling against bridges, roads, and rail lines, however, it was doubtful that many reinforcements would arrive. Still, the commanders plotted.

Strange to say, the misery that night was not confined to the battered French. Falkenhayn and his field subordinates were themselves painfully disappointed. All had expected much more from an artillery bombardment of unprecedented intensity and duration. There were many French corpses, to be sure, but why were so many poilus still upright, still walking? Why had so many survived?

As for the German fighting patrols that had been sent out following the barrage, losses among them were heavy—some six hundred casualties among the small probing forces. Yet many of the leaders of these probes, satisfied with what progress they made, urged Fifth Army high command to do what General von Zwehl had already done—defy Falkenhayn and commit more troops to the assault immediately. Indeed, Zwehl's VII Reserves had managed to seize and hold the Bois d'Haumont, a highly significant objective. Encouraged by Zwehl's progress, General Schmidt von Knobelsdorf was receptive to the pleas of others to send in more troops, but he could not issue his order quickly enough. Night fell before more troops could be deployed.

Whether hunkering down in the benighted ruins of their defensive positions or laboring to repair them, the French were unaware of their enemy's disappointment. Thanks to the policies of high command, the doctrine espoused by Joseph Joffre, they had been left disastrously unprepared for the attack they all knew was coming. But thanks to individual company and even platoon commanders—indeed, thanks to the individual soldier—the French units farthest in front had nevertheless achieved remarkable things with remarkably few men. They performed like the Spartans against Xerxes's Persians at Thermopylae 2,500 years earlier. Handfuls of desperate soldiers held far larger, far better armed invaders at bay—although all bets were off at the few places where the German combined-arms units included a weapon new to the war: the flamethrower. To men who had just endured hours of bombardment with high explosives and, in some parts of the front, poison gas as well, the prospect of being incinerated where they stood was just too much to take. The flamethrowers of World War I were difficult weapons to use. Heavy and cumbersome, they typically required a crew of three to operate. As soldiers on both sides became accustomed to the presence of the weapon, they learned to target the flamethrower crews as soon as they made their appearance on the battlefield. On day one at Verdun, however, the first sight of the flamethrower in action was sufficient to induce panic. Men and their officers surrendered at the first blast of flame.

But that was the exception. At daybreak on February 22, the situation in Verdun was this. The Germans were stunned by how few men (comparatively) their artillery had killed. The French, horribly battered and in many places on the verge of collapse, were still in the fight.

FURIA FRANCESE

The depth of disappointment among the German field commanders—we don't know how Erich von Falkenhayn felt—was immediately evident on the morning of February 22. Crown Prince Wilhelm's second-in-command, Schmidt von Knobelsdorf, issued an order removing the previous limits on Fifth Army objectives. He spoke directly to the chief of staff of XVIII Corps, pinned down at the Bois des Caures as of nightfall the day before, to spare nothing in taking the woods that day. In the meantime, the Germans renewed the artillery bombardment, intent on using the morning to visit destruction upon French lines that, against all odds, continued stubbornly to hold out. The infantry assault would resume in the afternoon.

Viewed from the perspective of a century's passing, it seems like massive overkill—something that might happen at a mismatched prizefight in the absence of a referee. The poor man was down, yet the champion continued to beat him without mercy. From the German point of view at the time, however, what had happened on February 21 appeared to be confirmation of the very mythology that had moved French high command so foolishly, that had prompted them to scorn heavy artillery and fortifications in favor of attaque à outrance, élan vital, and furia francese. By sheer force of will, it seemed, the bleeding French held the whip hand at sunup on the 22nd. In obedience to doctrine inculcated by high command, French field commanders were determined to reclaim yielded ground instantly, eager to trade lives for real estate. Thus the French did not merely hold out. At numerous points along the line, they counterattacked. True, the blows were delivered by small units—often individual companies—but those on the receiving end of these blows were likewise small units, the fighting patrols that had probed and in many places pricked or even pierced the front line.

The gains the French managed to make before dark on February 21 proved impossible to sustain. The morning's bombardment drove many French units back. Those who held their ground were, for the most part, swept by machine-gun fire. During the bombardment, the Germans brought fresh machine gun and machine-gun crews to the very verge of the French lines.

BATTLES OF THE BOIS

At dawn on February 22, Sergeant Major Dandauw, who felt he had disgraced himself by panicking as Germans overran blockhouse S9, was sufficiently bucked up by Lieutenant Colonel Driant to lead a counterattack against German positions. It was as spirited as it was hopeless. Dandauw was outnumbered, which was bad enough. Far more damaging to the counterattack, however, was the friendly fire incoming from *French* artillery batteries. In contrast to the German attacks, which were well coordinated with the artillery barrages, the French artillery was deployed almost catch-as-catch-can. There was very little communication, let alone coordination, between artillery commanders and infantry commanders. Almost certainly, the French gunners were entirely unaware of the counterattack Dandauw led. As a result, the shelling of the German lines fell equally on the Germans *and* Dandauw's men. His Chasseurs—those who survived—were soon compelled to withdraw—not from the Germans, but from the rain of their own countrymen's ordnance.

While Dandauw made his valiant effort, a Major Bodot rounded up as many of his men as he could, troops who had been dispersed in panic the day before by German flamethrower attacks at Herbebois. As they prepared to retake a blockhouse there, however, they were turned back—again, not by German troops, but by French artillery fire.

Just north of the Bois des Caures, Lieutenant Colonel Bonviolle frantically worked to cobble together a battalion-strength unit from the tattered remains of his 165th Infantry Regiment. He and his men had been forced out of the Bois d'Haumont the day before, and he was determined to reclaim it. Try as he might, however, he could not gather more than half a battalion. With this group, at 5 a.m., Bonviolle prepared to mount an assault on the southwest corner of the Bois, hoping to gain a foothold in the forest, build up more strength, and force the invaders out.

Just as he was about to commence his attack, a runner arrived from General Bapst. The general had more troops for him, and he wanted Bonviolle to use them to mount an attack on the *entire* Bois d'Haumont. In position to seize the moment now, Bonviolle did not want to wait. Nor did he want to attempt an attack along the *entire* woods, even with more men. Better to move now, he believed, against a manageable objective, than to wait, risk losing the element of surprise, and attempt a less focused attack.

It was not that General Bapst had issued a last-minute order, but that the bombardment through the night had been so intense that it had taken the runner five hours to traverse the four miles from Bapst's 72nd Division headquarters to Bois d'Haumont. The general had cut the order at 11 p.m. on the 21st. In any case, discovering that telephone communications had been restored with divisional HQ, Bonviolle pleaded his case with Bapst over the static-choked phone line. Against Bonviolle's protests that he was ready to attack immediately, the general was adamant about making a more ambitious attack with more men. He did acknowledge, however, that, given the runner's delay in delivering the order, the attack would be postponed until 8:30.

A general trumps a lieutenant colonel any day of the week. Bonviolle capitulated, salving his wound with the consolation that at least he now had more time to deploy his additional troops for the attack. Of course, that attack would now take place not in the predawn gloom but in broad daylight, when the heightened visibility would be to the advantage of the Germans.

In the meantime, seventy minutes before the 8:30 H-hour, Major Bertrand, commander of a battalion of the 165th Infantry, was handed his orders to join the counterattack. This was news to him. His battalion was a full two miles behind the Bois d'Haumont, yet all he could see in front of him were the multiple earth geysers created by the renewed German barrage. In his judgment, he was already completely pinned down—two miles from where he was supposed to join a counterattack. Flummoxed and lacking telephone communication, he dispatched a runner to General Bapst's headquarters with a note asking for additional orders. While waiting, Bertrand assembled his battalion so that it could move out en masse—if and when higher headquarters told him how to advance into the teeth of a barrage without committing mass suicide.

The sun rose higher with every minute that ticked by. German aircraft flew over Hill 344, where Bertrand had arrayed his battalion. He and his men were still awaiting orders when the planes suddenly swooped down, dropping bombs and strafing the area with machine-gun fire. Men neatly assembled for the advance fell where they stood. The air raid meant that Bonviolle's counterattack, now scheduled for the broadest of daylight and with the last vestige of surprise quite lost, would be short a battalion.

Even as German artillery continued the barrage, Hans von Zwehl, who had so boldly exceeded his orders the day before, fudged them again. Without waiting for the barrage to be lifted, he unleashed his infantry against a woods just west of the Bois d'Haumont, the Bois de Consenvoye. Being relatively in the rear of the French lines, it was occupied by a regiment of French Territorials—soldiers long in the tooth (they were age forty and older) and/or less than physically fit for service in a frontline unit. They were placeholders only, and upon them Zwehl's attack would fall.

The German commander did not deploy against the Territorials his own third-string team. He sent his Jägers. *Chasseur* is French for "hunter." *Jäger* is German for the same. Applied to military units, both terms were labels for the deadliest elite. Unsurprisingly, the Jägers rolled over the Territorials, who, grossly overmatched, simply crumbled before them. After the Jägers deployed flamethrowers, one entire company of Territorials hightailed it nonstop from the Bois de Consenvoye to the village of Samogneux, on the Meuse River—a run of nearly four miles. When an entire battalion of the 351st Regiment—regular frontline poilus—rushed in to engage the Jägers, they, too, were rolled over. The result was a large gap in the French line. Since Bapst had sent most of the reserves to join Bonviolle's counteroffensive, no one was available to plug the hole made by the Jäger onslaught.

Worst of all, the build-up Bapst had ordered proved futile. As Lieutenant Colonel Bonviolle had feared, the delay the general had imposed proved fatal. Just as he was about to order the counterattack to commence, Bonviolle saw large numbers of German infantry emerging from the Bois d'Haumont, with a heavy German barrage immediately preceding them. There was no way to retake the woods. Bonviolle and his men would have all they could do to try to hold onto the adjacent village of Haumont. Accordingly, minutes before the 8:30 H-hour, Bonviolle issued orders calling off the attack. One company of the 165th Regiment, under a Lieutenant Derome, failed to get the word. Accordingly, at the appointed hour, the dutiful Frenchman led his men directly into a German barrage. Those who somehow survived the shells were then confronted by an entire German infantry division, against which Lieutenant Derome, in the lead, could do nothing more than brandish his saber. He was soon shot and, severely wounded, was taken prisoner along with the fifty men left to him.

Having reassembled most of his battalion, which had scattered during the German bombardment of Hill 344, Major Bertrand watched the lone lieutenant and his company get swallowed up by a far superior German force. As for Bertrand, he continued to wait for further orders from his general.

As it turned out, Lieutenant Derome's charge was not the total failure it should have been. Zwehl's Jägers were astonished, stunned to the point of paralysis, by the fierce heroism of his company's action. Assuming that Derome must be part of something much larger, they significantly slowed their advance. This gave Lieutenant Colonel Bonviolle time to plug some holes along the four miles separating the Bois de Consenyoye, now held by the Germans, and the village of Samogneux. Bonviolle believed he could arrest the German progress toward Haumont village—*if* enough men could be found.

But they could not be. Ahead of the Jägers—still advancing, albeit more gingerly—a heavy artillery barrage crept closer to the village. By three in the afternoon, Bonviolle's force of about two thousand men had been reduced to five hundred, with virtually all officers dead. By four o'clock, the Jägers had enveloped the village on three sides. Bonviolle's machine gunners, holed up in the cellars of the villages, opened fire on the advancing Jägers, taking a heavy toll on them. That is when the Germans ordered their flamethrowers forward. This time, the poilus did not flee. In consequence, they were swallowed up by fire. Bonviolle withdrew along with the sixty men that now constituted the sum total of his remaining force. Now the woods as well as the village of Haumont were in German hands. It was the first substantial prize the defenders had yielded. From here, Zwehl's troops could advance south to nearby Samogneux and north to hit the left flank of the Bois des Caures.

Driant's Men

Gratified by the progress made, Schmidt von Knobelsdorf nevertheless remained all business—which, for a Prussian military man, meant directing all resources toward killing the enemy army first and, only afterward, seizing territory. He therefore ordered Zwehl's men to advance against the Bois des Caures and all other units nearby to join in that assault. On a front in a war that relied chiefly on manmade entrenchments, the dense and rugged woods of the Woëvre was a highly effective *natural* fortification. Knobelsdorf was not about to yield any of it to the French.

As planned, the assault would be deliberate overkill. The XVIII Corps, augmented by units from two other corps, would hit Driant's two battalions of Chasseurs, which had already been very badly mauled. By the time the German infantry would be set into motion, the Bois was to have been pounded by massed artillery. The barrage began at 7 a.m. and was intended not only to kill French soldiers but also to blast holes in the maze of barbed wire barricades Driant had erected.

By early afternoon, the outer entrenchments and fortifications had been reduced to rubble. The barrage was lifted, and the XVIII Corps—on paper, about forty thousand men, although its fielded strength was surely much smaller—advanced against perhaps two thousand French troops. The Germans were deployed in waves separated by 1,500 feet. Moreover, possession of the Bois d'Haumont gave the attackers access to Driant's flank, so that while the main body hit him head-on, some five thousand Hessians approached on his right. Driant used signal rockets to call for a barrage from the 75s that should have been available nearby—but were not. Still, Driant was able to claim many lives on the flanking attackers with his machine guns, which were deployed to provide heavy crossfire.

Despite their overwhelming superiority, the German XVIII Corps assault was not the juggernaut Knobelsdorf had counted on. Once again, the German attackers were victims of the cratered and chaotic landscape created by their own relentless bombardment. The neat waves of attackers broke upon the craters and debris like waves upon a rocky shore. Sent in an overabundance of strength, the German units fragmented. Fighting was accordingly shattered into many small fights. It was serial murder more than organized warfare.

But, even disorganized as the attack became, the numbers were unquestionably with the Germans, and the numbers were all that mattered. When a fight broke out, it soon attracted more attackers, so that, little by little, Driant's Chasseurs were defeated in detail. It was a kind of whittling down, inexorable. Captain Séguin's reduced company of eighty men was soon halved. By the time the German penetration of Séguin's corner of the Bois des Caures reached its fullest extent, the French captain had just ten effectives, who were forced to share six rifles. It was at this point that the nearby detonation of an artillery shell blew off Séguin's right arm. The company sergeant-major attended to the hideous wound, hurriedly applying a tourniquet. While he was thus engaged, the remaining fragment of Séguin's command was overrun, and they all became prisoners.

Hunkering down in the rubble of a bunker, Lieutenant Robin found himself surrounded by Germans. He ordered the few Chasseurs who were with him to open fire.

"Shoot, for God's sake shoot!" Corporal Marc Stéphane later recalled the lieutenant demanding.

"It's impossible! They're there, hundreds of them, six meters away," a Chasseur replied.

"Never mind, fire!"

"It's mad, Lieutenant, they're here, I tell you, more than a hundred have encircled the post!"

With that, Robin sobbed: "What are we going to do then?"

As if by way of answer came a question posed in German-accented French: "Is anybody inside there?"[3] And so the battered Chasseurs emerged from the rubble, hands up, now prisoners of war.

LA GLOIRE

With the fall of the outposts held by Séguin's Seventh Company and Robin's Ninth, both on the western face of the Bois des Caures, Driant's command post—the battered blockhouse known as R2, located within the inner defensive perimeter, at the heart of the Bois—was exposed. The Germans bore down on it, preceded by Pioniere wielding flamethrowers, which they used like hoses to flush out—albeit with flame rather than water—those who hid in the bunker rubble.

The "R line" was the last-ditch defense for the Bois des Caures. Emerging from cover, Driant saw that Blockhouse R1, 2,400 feet to the right of his command post (R2), had already fallen to the infiltrators. Driant therefore seized a rifle, took a stance in front of R2, in full view of the enemy, and directed the fire of the small knot of Chasseurs around him. When his men begged him to take cover, he replied, "You know very well they've never hit me yet!"[4] Remarkably, the initial attack on R2 melted away, the Germans driven off.

Or so it seemed. Falling back on their previous small-unit tactics, the infiltrators made a tactical withdrawal from R2, which offered the most resistance, and repositioned themselves between R2 and R3, which was to the left of Driant's stand. This allowed them to attack from the rear. The combined forces of R2 and R3 drove this attack back—but no sooner had the Germans once again pulled back then an entire German regiment emerged from the Bois d'Haumont and launched a vigorous frontal attack against R3, driving out its defenders by 4:30 in the afternoon.

R2, defended by Lieutenant Colonel Émile Driant and no more than eighty Chasseurs, was entirely alone in the heart of the ruined woods. Unbelievably, they managed to beat off a battalion-strength assault. The respite this provided was a matter of minutes. A pair of German 77s suddenly opened up on R2. Driant sent a lieutenant with a machine gun and crew to fire on the battery. The position was quickly set up, and the machine gun opened fire—just as a 77-mm shell scored a direct hit on it, killing the French lieutenant and his gun crew and destroying the machine gun. Nearby, those manning a second French machine-gun post fled. The commander of the Eighty-Seventh Hessians took this action as a signal to charge R2.

Driant was a patriot and a warrior, not a madman. He calmly ordered his two battalion commanders to effect a withdrawal. He explained that he believed doing so was now "prudent."[5] This matter settled, Driant withdrew into the blockhouse to burn his papers, lest they fall into enemy hands. He then divided the Chasseurs who had stood by him into three groups, instructing them to fan out toward the rear of the Bois des Caures and make for the village of Beaumont.

Driant assumed the lead of the second retreating group. He must have seen that the fleeing Chasseurs were being cut down as they ran across open ground. German soldiers, on both sides of the avenue through which the French soldiers sought survival, double-enfiladed them, firing from the two sides directly through their longest axis. As Lieutenant Colonel Driant paused in this deadly double stream to aid a wounded Chasseur, he met his end.

A German sergeant of Pioniere saw him raise his hands to the sky and cry out, "Oh! Là, mon Dieu!" The sergeant rushed to the Frenchman's aid. The French colonel was dead when the German sergeant reached him, shot through the temple.

It was, as Driant's commanders saw it, a glorious death, an enviable death for a soldier and a leader of soldiers. For most of the French public, Émile Driant instantly became a hero. For a significant minority of that public, he was, more precisely, a martyr—crucified on the cross of military arrogance, stupidity, and madness. He who had pointed out—in the Chamber of Deputies, no less—the fatal inadequacies of the Fortified Region of Verdun, stripped of men and stripped of artillery, was now the heroic victim of a willful policy of magical thinking, a doctrine that sought to substitute the mythology of war for the machinery of war, that elevated the theory of élan vital over the kinetic reality of high explosives.

On balance, it is surprisingly difficult to say who saw Driant more accurately. To be sure, it was he, having warned against the willful unpreparedness of others, who was forced to pay the price for that unpreparedness.

Yet his achievement at the Bois des Caures was not merely spiritual, patriotic, and gallant, a grand gesture, the ultimate *beau geste*. It was also of significant tactical value. With 2,400 men against perhaps 20,000 actually deployed, Driant and those under his command inflicted sufficiently heavy casualties on the Germans to shake their confidence in achieving what Erich von Falkenhayn claimed to want: a relatively cheap victory at Verdun. The cloud of doubt Driant's stand created was not exclusively emotional. The end of combat on February 22 was supposed to see Germany in possession of the entire French front line across some eight miles of front. This objective had not yet been attained, and the battle revealed a hint—the slightest hint—of ultimately settling into stalemate.

Verdun was becoming ugly and bitter, like every other front in this war. What little glimmer of chivalry and humanity that remained after day two of the battle was concentrated entirely in the earthly remains of Émile Driant. The Germans accorded him a solemn burial. (He would later be reburied, where he fell, by the French.) The wife of the officer who found his body, a baroness, accepted Driant's personal effects from her husband and then conveyed them, through a neutral Swiss intermediary, to Madame Driant. The German lady enclosed in the parcel her personal letter of heartfelt condolence.

CHAPTER 10

The Third Day

The C.O. and all company commanders have been killed. My battalion is reduced to approximately 180 men. I have neither ammunition nor food. What am I to do?
—FRENCH LIEUTENANT (HAVING ASSUMED COMMAND OF THIRD BATTALION, SIXTIETH REGIMENT), MESSAGE TO HEADQUARTERS OF 143RD BRIGADE, FEBRUARY 23, 1916[1]

IT MUST HAVE BEEN HARD FOR LIEUTENANT COLONEL ÉMILE DRIANT to order the sixty or so men remaining under his command to make a "prudent" withdrawal from the Bois des Caures, which he had held at such great cost. Hard? Actually, in a sense, it was impossible.

When General Joseph Joffre raided the garrisons of the Fortified Region of Verdun to mount a counteroffensive against the Germans in the Champagne during December 1914–March 1915, he did so in the belief that the enemy would either attempt to hold their positions at great cost to themselves or break and yield territory to the French. In fact, they did neither. German strategy had no place for the equivalent of attaque à outrance. To be sure, it was the Germans who invaded France, so that the war on the Western Front was fought on French soil. Instead of demanding that field commanders only advance, only move forward, and only to claim more French soil, German high command allowed for a strong component of defensive tactics in their strategic thinking, which included the option of falling back. Forward German positions were always backed with a second and third line, which were meant to be used as necessary. In contrast to the French, for whom any

166

retreat meant yielding French soil, which was regarded as a sin both against strategy and patriotism, the Germans freely moved between their first and second lines. So when Joffre's field commanders threw the men from Verdun against the German front lines in the Champagne, the Germans withdrew to their second line, from which they took a ruinous toll on the depleted French forces that occupied the positions they had just yielded.

Being a Frenchman in the French army, Driant was bound by French rules. He ordered a withdrawal from Bois des Caures but, in truth, he had no place to go. Behind Bois des Caures were no prepared defensive positions. Between the Bois and Vacherauville was an entirely unprepared distance of six miles, through which the survivors of the defense of Bois des Caures had to pass. As a result, a considerable French expanse was left undefended once the front line was lost. At the Champagne, the existence of a well-prepared second line gave the Germans a place from which to continue the battle and exact a heavy toll. At Verdun, the nonexistence of such a second line left the French with only two options: either simply yield substantial territory or try—somehow—to reclaim the positions that had been lost on February 22, 1916.

CHAOS

The commanding officer of the French Seventy-Second Division, Étienne André Bapst, was sixty years old during the Battle of Verdun. This was not an unusually advanced age for a French *general de division*, but it was very old for a human being in a war of steel and high explosives against mere flesh and blood. During the First Battle of the Marne in September 1914, General Ferdinand Foch had endeared himself to France with his famous message, "My center is yielding. My right is retreating. Situation excellent. I am attacking."[2] Alas, Bapst was no Foch. He had spent far more of his pre-1916 career administering artillery depots than commanding battlefield forces. His headquarters, in a little schoolhouse at Bras, was distant from the action on February 21. Ordered to transfer it forward to Vacherauville, he did just that. It was closer to the action, which meant that it was closer to the falling shells, and that made exercising meaningful, well-informed command next to impossible. By ten o'clock on the morning of February 22, he was given leave to withdraw back to his original headquarters at Bras.

Moving from one HQ to another, setting the new one up, hunkering down in it against the incessant barrage, and then moving back to the headquarters from which he had just come took time. Given his oscillation between headquarters, how could Bapst have exercised much in the way of meaningful command during the first day and a half of battle? He had no time, and he had no firsthand knowledge of what was going on. Thus Bras, on February 22, was chaotic. The commander of the Seventy-Second Division did his best to settle in, but the news that arrived after noon was hardly conducive to settling. His entire left flank, he learned, was near collapse with the loss of the Bois de Consenvoye and the capture of both the Bois d'Haumont and the village adjacent. That left another village, Brabant, which was on the Meuse and anchored the principal line of the Seventy-Second, fully exposed to German encirclement. Brabant lay between Consenvoye to the northwest and Samogneux to the southeast. Consenvoye was lost.

If it was unthinkable to next yield Brabant, the prospect of giving up Samogneux was even worse, as it was closer to Verdun. As far as he could tell from the perspective of Bras, Brabant was almost certainly doomed. Yet he was under orders to make no retreat. A French commander, after all, must yield no territory. Since, however, much territory had already been yielded, this imperative began to ring hollow. To save Samogneux, Bapst reasoned, he needed to withdraw from Brabant to its defense. And so he sent a runner to the commander of XXX Corps (of which the Seventy-Second Division was a part), General Adrien Paul Alexandre Chrétien.

In contrast to Bapst, Chrétien was combat-seasoned, a veteran of grim French colonial warfare in Indochina, with a dramatic facial scar to prove it. To Bapst's runner, he snapped *No. No, he would not give the Seventy-Second Division permission to retreat.* But then he ordered the runner to wait before conveying the response to Bapst. After cooling his heels for two hours, the runner received General Chrétien's revised response. He told the man to tell the general that, since he was closest to the situation, the decision was his. Chrétien had yielded not to Bapst but to the prevailing chaos.

168

By the time Chrétien's message reached Bapst, it was 12:45 on the morning of February 23. While awaiting orders from corps HQ, Bapst had been the recipient of increasingly grim news, including the surrender of at least one company at Brabant. Taking Chrétien's response as the permission he sought, Bapst sent an order to Brabant for its complete evacuation. A copy of this order arrived at General Chrétien's headquarters at about 3 a.m., by which time the corps commander had received assurances of the imminent arrival of reinforcements. Chrétien spent the next three and a half hours weighing this promise against the evacuation of Brabant and concluded that Bapst should *not* have evacuated without his explicit permission; therefore, at 6:30 on the morning of February 23, he issued a peremptory order that Bapst's Seventy-Second Division must retake Brabant. Astounding as this was, he followed the 6:30 order with a modification at 7 a.m. that directed General Bapst to avoid deploying a large number of men for that operation.

That Chrétien was battle-hardened did not, apparently, make him decisive. Bapst had already frittered away time and attention moving back and forth between headquarters. Told to do as he judged best, he had just executed a withdrawal from a forward position—only to be commanded to retake it. General Bapst had been grateful that a dense mist enshrouding Brabant had made for a nearly bloodless withdrawal. We do not know how he felt about being ordered to retake the village, but we do know that he did obediently order a counterattack—only to receive word that no one, not a single poilu, could be found in the vicinity of Brabant to mount that counterattack. Confronted with the impossible, Bapst countermanded his own order.

With Brabant now vacant, General Hans Zwehl ordered its immediate occupation. This became an instant scandal in the French press and within the inner circles of high command. In due course, Bapst would be skewered and even threatened with court-martial—though, in the end, he was simply relieved of active command and, unofficially, given a new assignment: scapegoat for the failure of the early phase of the Battle of Verdun. He would become known as the man who sacrificed Brabant, thereby allowing the Germans to take a giant goose step closer to Verdun itself. Subsequent historians concluded that either Bapst could have done nothing or that nothing he could have done would have saved Brabant and would only have needlessly spilled more French blood. But these vindications came long after the general's death.

THE JUGGERNAUT SLOWS

February 23 was marked by orders given, orders countermanded, orders denied, new orders given, and those orders countermanded. Against this background of a breakdown in command at the level of corps and division, miscellaneous units of the Seventy-Second Division were hurled against the new German positions in an effort to buy back lost French land with fresh French lives.

An entire battalion under Major Bertrand was ordered to attack the German-occupied Bois des Caures and reclaim it. The soldiers of the German XVIII Corps who held it were stunned by the sheer audacity of an understrength battalion going up against them—more than half a corps in number. Suicidal gestures can be highly impressive, especially on a mass scale. Temporarily paralyzed by the spectacle confronting them, the German occupiers reeled under French blows they should have been capable of brushing aside. Bertrand might have succeeded in capitalizing on this effect had he been joined in a timely manner by another battalion under a Colonel Vaulet. Through no fault of his own, however, Vaulet did not receive orders to join Bertrand's early morning attack until after noon. Well aware that it was probably too late to save the attack, Vaulet nevertheless obeyed his orders—and ended up advancing directly into a newly arrived German regiment. Spectacularly outnumbered, Vaulet's men were all but wiped out—without ever having made contact with Bertrand's forces.

There were numerous other, much smaller French counterattacks and ripostes. Tactically, all failed. In fact, anyone who contemplates the events of February 23 from the distance of a century must conclude that the French were well on their way to validating the strategy that Erich von Falkenhayn claimed to be pursuing. For, truly, the French army in this sector was bleeding itself white. That is a fact. Yet in this case what proved stronger than fact was irony. The very process of committing mass suicide, of fiercely throwing smaller numbers of soldiers against larger numbers of soldiers, was so unexpected that German commanders found it impossible to feel any confidence in victory. Instead, intimidated by the prodigious willingness of the French to die, they became increasingly cautious. Instead of rolling over the inferior numbers that confronted them, the German XVIII Corps slowed, hesitated, and then held back.

As Falkenhayn had planned it, day one, February 21, was nothing more than a preparation for a breakthrough. At that, it had gone very well. The progress on day two, however, while impressive, resulted in no breakthroughs and heavier-than-expected losses. And now, incredibly, at day three, the German juggernaut was once again slowing. Astoundingly, the more the German forces experienced victory, the more cautious they became.

It was not just the ferocity of the doomed French ripostes that so discouraged the attackers. On the French right, to the southeast of the Seventy-Second Division, the French Fifty-First Division continued to hold Herbebois. By the afternoon of February 23, this was the only stretch of the first French line that the French still held. After three days of fighting, the poilus, who had become accustomed to incessant shelling, were now also becoming inured to the horror of the flamethrower. Intent on breaking the Fifty-First Division line and seizing Herbebois at last, the Germans unleashed Pioniere with multiple flamethrowers. Instead of panicking, however, the French responded with snipers, who found easy targets in soldiers loaded down with the heavy tanks of compressed air and highly flammable fuel oil. It was not even necessary for a sniper to hit the man. In fact, it was far more effective to send a round into the tank strapped to his back. Its detonation killed him and anyone near him. The weapon of terror, it turned out, was readily transformed from battlefield asset to liability.

What flamethrowers could not accomplish, however, 305-mm mortars did. Under heavy mortar bombardment, orders were issued from Fifty-First Division headquarters at 4:30 p.m. to withdraw from Herbebois. By six, this woods, like other densely forested outposts, was delivered into German hands—but at a cost so unexpected that it chastened rather than cheered the attackers.

And there was worse to come.

THE BATTLE OF VERDUN

Beaumont, a village midway between the Seventy-Second Division line to the north and the Fifty-First to the south and well to the east of the German gains at Consenvoye and Haumont, occupied high ground that the Germans desperately wanted to possess. Given the extent of German penetration along the northern portion of the front, Beaumont threatened to become a French salient—a dangerous bulge—into the German line. Repeated assaults against the position had failed, as German infantry fell to well-entrenched French machine guns firing down at them from the heights. Whereas, in the face of mounting casualties, German commanders had been cautious elsewhere, at Beaumont they responded by unleashing wave after wave of infantry. Looking down upon them, the French gunners had the sense that one wave actually forced the wave ahead *into* the machine-gun fire. It was as if an unseen hand pushed the *Feldgrau*-clad troops into a great killing machine. This process continued throughout the 23rd. But, by the 24th, superior numbers prevailed. Both sides were worn down, but the French, fewer in number, were worn down more. Reportedly, only the quick action of a German lieutenant saved the captured French commander from the vengeance of the German soldiers who had lost so many comrades to his machine gunners.

Throughout February 23, the combination of machine-gun fire and artillery bombardment emanating from the Bois de Wavrille, alongside Beaumont, also took a terrible toll on the attackers and, combined with the long resistance at Beaumont, enabled the battered Seventy-Second Division to hang on along the line between Beaumont and Samogneux throughout most of February 23.

THE BREAKING OF THE SEVENTY-SECOND

The cost of this defense was the attrition of the French Seventy-Second Division. Officers were rapidly being killed. In the 143rd Brigade, for instance, the Third Battalion of the Sixtieth Regiment, normally under the command of a lieutenant colonel, was now being led by a mere lieutenant, who sent a desperate message to brigade headquarters reporting the commanding officer and all company commanders killed in action, his effective strength reduced to 180 men, and his supplies of both food and ammunition entirely gone. His question to HQ was simple: "What am I to do?"[3]

This is the way even large French units dissolved at Verdun, not just man by man, but company by company, battalion by battalion, even regiment by regiment. There was heroism, to be sure. But as the leaders were killed and the smaller units vanished, men had a tendency to stop being soldiers and start becoming human beings, discouraged, terrified, and bent on nothing more than survival. There was increasing fear of mutiny. The commander at Samogneux—a village still firmly in French hands, the place at which what was left of the Seventy-Second was to try to reorganize itself—was ordered to hold ready one machine-gun unit "to enforce obedience upon those who might forget their duty."[4]

Before the breaking of the Seventy-Second reached the point of mutiny, however, General Chrétien ordered General Bapst to withdraw from Samogneux and take to the high ground along a pair of ridges, Talou and Côte du Poivre (Pepper Hill). The division's place in Samogneux would be filled by colonial troops of the Thirty-Seventh Division.

The relief came as a godsend, but getting out of Samogneux would not be easy at this point. The Germans were concentrating an artillery bombardment on the village, much of which was now in flames. Zwehl's infantry was on the periphery along two sides of the village. The third side fronted the Meuse. The side still open was under a hail of shells. An orderly withdrawal became impossible, and those troops who managed to leave the village now did so on their own and without orders. They emerged with claims that Samogneux had fallen to the Germans and that they were the only survivors of the garrison. Hearing these claims, General Bapst sent a runner to the lieutenant colonel commanding the beleaguered garrison. He sent back word that the stragglers spreading rumors were "cowards and panic-mongers" and that he was still holding but expected very soon to be cut off, so that it would be impossible to continue to communicate.[5]

He was correct. Nothing further emerged from Samogneux. Now, despite having been advised that communication would soon be impossible, General Bapst concluded that the village had fallen. He therefore ordered its recapture. The first step in this was, of course, an "artillery preparation." Fifteen minutes after midnight on what was now February 24, French artillery shelled Samogneux, creating some casualties among the German attackers, but slaughtering many of the French defenders and effectively wiping out what little remained of the Seventy-Second Division on the very verge of its evacuation to higher ground. At Samogneux, it seemed, those poilus the Germans did not kill were killed by the French themselves.

CHAPTER 11

Imperfect Storm

In reality, they [the Germans] maneuvered by infiltration, under the protection of heavy fire from their artillery.
—FERNAND MARIE ALBERT CHALIGNE,
HISTOIRE MILITAIRE DE VERDUN, 1939[1]

AS THE OLD SAYING GOES, "TO MEN WHO HAVE ONLY HAMMERS, THE whole world looks like a nail." At the outbreak of World War I, the French army marched into combat carrying nothing but hammers. The stern doctrine of attaque à outrance permitted only head-on, headlong expressions of élan vital—all-out infantry assaults that knew only a single direction, forward, and that could refuse no bargain offering the exchange of lives for territory. Writing in 1939, on the very verge of blitzkrieg warfare—the mature development of the combined-arms approach the Germans tried first at Verdun—French military historian Colonel Fernand Marie Albert Chaligne noted that, at Verdun, the German infantry had not attacked in massive waves, as the French customarily did, but "In reality, . . . maneuvered by infiltration." When they encountered resistance, "they did not try to continue," but instead "waited until shellfire had resolved the problem . . . or until the advance of one of their neighbors had opened a way forward."[2]

Chaligne's introductory phrase, "In reality," speaks volumes. The French found it all but impossible to believe that the Germans did not conduct warfare the way they themselves did, namely with suicidal abandon. For years after the war, French historians as well as those from the other Allied countries wrote of assaults, including those mounted at

175

This still from *Verdun, visions d'histoire*, a 1928 film about the Battle of Verdun, is so realistic that it was long believed to be a rare action photograph from the actual battle. WIKIMEDIA

Verdun, as if they were all and always massive charges. For this reason, Chaligne felt obliged to begin with the qualifying phrase "In reality." Yet, where the subject of Verdun was concerned, myth persistently proved stronger than reality.

In his 1965 *The Great War, 1914–1918*, British military historian and screenwriter John Terraine could not bring himself to describe the German attacks as deliberate infiltrations but insisted that they were a kind of spiritual aberration. "The German bombardment of February 21st was more destructive than anything yet seen," Terraine correctly observed, "and yet, when the time came to follow it up, the Germans appeared to lose faith. Very slowly, preceded by large patrols and probing parties, the infantry came forward."[3]

In truth, it was not a loss of faith but an intelligent recognition that big artillery, destructive as its effect was, did not destroy everything. It was not a loss of faith but an approach to warfare that differed from the

French in refusing to see an absolute guarantee of victory in a heroic willingness to sacrifice everything. The German approach was more *conservative* than that of the French in the fundamental sense of that word. It was purposely aimed at conserving infantrymen by substituting the expenditure of German artillery shells for the expenditure of German lives. It was not a loss or a lack of anything but was, rather, a deliberate strategic and tactical choice. Nevertheless, General von Falkenhayn and most of his field commanders do seem to have taken caution to an extreme. When presented with clear-cut opportunities to make more extensive infantry breakthroughs, they did tend to hold back. Even more remarkable, German commanders at all levels were inordinately impressed with and intimidated by demonstrations of the French willingness to do precisely what Falkenhayn later claimed he wanted them to do, namely bleed themselves white. On February 23, the Germans repeatedly responded to frankly suicidal French attacks in which smaller numbers were heedlessly hurled against larger numbers, not by simply rolling over those smaller numbers but by slowing down or stopping entirely. It was rather like motorists on today's superhighways who slow to a crawl whenever there is some hideous wreck to be seen on the shoulder.

Even with this failing, however, the Germans, as of nightfall on February 23, had gained considerable territory, creating what historian John Mosier aptly describes as "two ominous bulges down into the French positions, reaching down on either side of Louvemont . . . and right up against Bezonvaux."[4] Louvemont was about four miles west of the German position on day one of the battle, and Bezonvaux about two. By the standards of stalemated Western Front warfare, this was highly impressive progress. Moreover, the "ominous bulges" constituted a salient, a heavily armed peninsula thrust into the imperiled sea that was eastern France in 1916.

DAY FOUR, FEBRUARY 24

Before nightfall on February 23, General Adrien Paul Alexandre Chrétien had desperately rushed the French colonial troops of the Thirty-Seventh Division to the line running from Beaumont to Samogneux. Precariously held by what remained of the tattered Seventy-Second and Fifty-First

Divisions, it represented the *second* line of French defense. Because, going into the war, French high command did not believe in defense in depth— if an army attacked as it should, with relentless élan, no such defense was necessary—the creation of a third line of defense at the Verdun sector had been at best an afterthought. The decision to establish one was made at the very end of 1915. Engineers dug trenches along a line beginning in the west, at the Meuse, from the Côte du Talou, which is between Samog-neux (to the north) and Vacherauville (to the south). From Côte du Talou, the line was extended east and slightly southward to the heights of the Côte du Poivre and thence almost due east through a rise designated as Hill 378. The line terminated, in the east, at Bezonvaux, which was about two miles due north of Fort Vaux and two and a half miles northeast of Fort Douaumont. It was hardly a fully developed third line and so, if you wanted to find the true "last ditch" of French defense at Verdun, it was probably more accurate to look toward Paris.

Despite the unpreparedness of the French positions at Verdun, the Germans, including the elite Jägers, were repeatedly impressed by the valor and sheer ferocity the ordinary poilu often demonstrated. What they felt about France's African colonial troops went beyond being impressed. The reputation of the colonials for killing rather than capturing their enemy intimidated, even terrorized, the ordinary German soldier.

Had French commanders devised a means of using the Thirty-Seventh Division replacements skillfully—as human weapons of terror rather than as so much cannon fodder fit only for plugging holes in a badly riddled line—they might have significantly delayed the break-through of February 24. Instead, they deployed the newcomers in a way that destroyed the powerful cohesiveness of their unit. They split them up into companies and put them under the command of regular French offi-cers. They were regarded as mere placeholders—except that there really were no "places" left for them to hold. Three days of bombardment had reduced many sections of trench and had obliterated most shelters. Not only were the Africans exposed to whatever the Germans threw at them, they were unshielded from the very elements. And the weather, which had been miserable in the run-up to the battle, had once again turned bitter cold and wet. Everyone suffered, but none more than men born and bred in Mediterranean Africa. Throughout the night of the 23rd, they shivered, even as they watched the retreat, ceaseless and formless, of a shattered army. Defeated men flowed right past them.

Early on the 24th, the customary artillery preparation began, the same relentlessly intense bombardment that had begun the three previous days. Whereas Driant and his men had had blockhouses and dugouts to give them some semblance of shelter from the onslaught, for the Thirty-Seventh Division there was nothing left but rubble. It must surely have dawned on them that they were no longer regarded as soldiers. They were now targets. And when the bombardment was lifted and the German infantry rolled in—this time in waves rather than probing units—they broke, and with their breaking, the French second line was breached.

On the French left (northwest), the village of Louvemont, perched on the key high ground of Côte de Poivre, was all but overrun—*behind* the second line. On the right (southeast), Chrétien had dispatched the Third Zouaves, a unit he had held as his final reserve. His instructions to them were to hold to the last man. They were the very same instructions that had been given to every other French unit at Verdun, most recently the Thirty-Seventh Division. The Zouaves, in fact, put up nothing but the most feeble resistance—so weak that at the Ravin de la Vauche, just east of Louvemont, the Germans captured a battery of French heavy artillery as well as *four* batteries of 75s without even having to contend with French infantry resistance. To this day, there is no official account of what became of the Third Zouaves. It is believed that the unit's commanding officer fell early in the onslaught and that the captain who was left to take his place simply could not rally the men to form a line. When this happened, *French* machine gunners behind the Zouaves opened up on them. Having failed to face German bullets, the Third Zouaves were cut down by French ones.

A TRAGEDY OF ERRORS

As evening closed in on February 24, the Germans were in position to begin an advance against Fort Douaumont, the largest and the highest of the nineteen forts ringing the city of Verdun. On the face of it, this menace presented a grave prospect to France—and yet Fort Douaumont,

An aerial reconnaissance photo of Fort Douaumont prior to the Battle of Verdun.
WIKIMEDIA

like the other Verdun forts, had been dismissed by French high command as obsolete and therefore stripped of all artillery that was not absolutely fixed in place and left virtually defenseless, save for a skeleton garrison.

It was now, at the worst possible moment in the Battle of Verdun, that Joseph Joffre and other top French generals suddenly reconsidered the wisdom of having failed to provide for the defense of Fort Douaumont. The French Twentieth Army Corps had been arriving at Bar-le-Duc, the main logistical transfer station from all points west to Verdun. Two brigades from this corps marched thirty-six miles—the railroad between Bar-le-Duc and Verdun having been bombarded to bits by the Germans—to Fort de Souville, between the city of Verdun and Fort Douaumont.

To this force fell the mission of blocking a German attack on Fort Douaumont. Astoundingly, however, the commanders of these brigades misinterpreted their orders and, instead of taking up a blocking position north of the fort, occupied the village of Douaumont, northwest of the fort itself. This left the fort entirely exposed to the east. Complicating the error was the inability of the newly arrived brigades to locate either the nearest French forces or the Germans, who were in position nearby throughout the forest of the Vauche.

To make a bad situation much worse, General Fernand de Langle de Cary, commanding the Armies of the Center—a total of fifty-two divisions—on the front facing Germany, decided to consolidate his forces by withdrawing from the Woëvre and forming a front from the Côte du Talou in the northeast, running through Louvemont, to Fort Douaumont, and to the nearby Fort Vaux. The magnitude of de Langle de Cary's consolidation was, in fact, breathtaking. He proposed to evacuate all French forces from the right (east) bank of the Meuse River, essentially ceding a huge swath of territory to the Germans—without a fight. After the war,

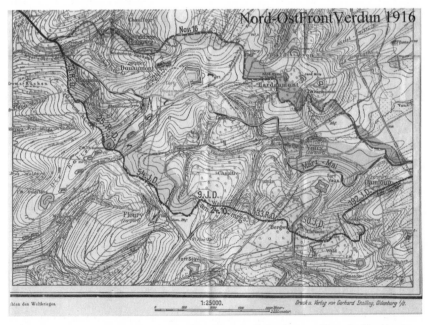

A German contour map of the right (east) bank of the Meuse River in the Verdun sector, focusing on Fort Douaumont (and the village of Douaumont), Fort Vaux (and the village of Vaux), and Fleury. WIKIMEDIA

he would be severely condemned for this order—condemned, that is, by those who conveniently forgot that French high command had deemed most of the Fortified Region of Verdun unworthy of being defended in the first place.

In the end, however, de Langle de Cary's order was not executed. Joffre was informed of this "General Order Number 18" at eight o'clock on the evening of the 24th, while he was enjoying his usual leisurely dinner. About an hour later, after he had finished his meal, Joffre telephoned de Langle de Cary and ordered him to hold the right bank, adding the customary injunction, "at all costs." Not only did this contradict Joffre's earlier assertion, which was that the right bank and its forts were not worth defending, it also contradicted the very same assertion made later, in his *postwar* memoir, in which he denied that the right bank of the Meuse was of any military value whatsoever. Yet even as he now ordered his general to hold the right bank, he did give him his blessing to carry out the other withdrawal he proposed, from the Woëvre. This had the effect of severing the river's right bank from the boggy plain beyond it, giving the defenders of the right bank so much less room in which to maneuver.

Joffre had a peculiarly passive-aggressive managerial habit of undercutting rather than firing commanders in whom he had lost faith. Such was now the fate of General de Langle de Cary. Joffre sent General de Castelnau to Verdun with extravagantly open-ended orders to take whatever actions he thought necessary. In this, Joffre consciously violated the chain of command. De Castelnau was a corps commander, whereas de Langle de Cary commanded the "armies of the center," which made him the equivalent of an Allied army group commander in World War II, an Omar Bradley or a Bernard Law Montgomery. Yet Joffre directed de Castelnau to bypass de Langle de Cary and report directly to him. Indeed, Joffre compounded this end run around the army group commander by dispatching yet another general, Henri Philippe Pétain, to follow de Castelnau to Verdun.

Although Joffre thus spectacularly mishandled their introduction into Verdun, de Castelnau and Pétain had undeniably shown themselves to be the kinds of commanders the desperate situation called for.

General de Castelnau had fought in the Franco-Prussian War, served as Joffre's chief of staff, and was instrumental in drawing up Plan XVII. The latter did not in itself bode success, since the plan produced disastrous results in the opening weeks of the war, but it is also true that de Castelnau averted total catastrophe by ably organizing the defense of the fortifications at Nancy. Not without at least a modicum of good reason, Joffre now hoped that de Castelnau could salvage another catastrophe-in-progress by organizing a credible defense at Verdun.

As for Henri Philippe Pétain, he had started the war by providing France with one of its very few victories during August 1914. As colonel commanding a brigade at the Battle of Guise on August 29, he played a major role in arresting a German advance and thereby delivering a significant, if strictly tactical, victory. Rapidly promoted to brigadier general, he commanded the Sixth Division at the First Battle of the Marne—another French success—and, promoted again the next month, he took command of XXXIII Corps, which fought in the Artois Offensive during the spring of 1915. Recognizing Pétain as one of his most successful commanders, Joffre assigned Second Army to him in July 1915, and it was this unit Pétain commanded at the start of the Battle of Verdun.

Trained as a military engineer, Joseph Joffre may well have seen the addition of Pétain to de Castelnau as the elegant solution to a simple mathematical problem. Verdun suffered from a deficiency of success. De Castelnau had brought a measure of success to an otherwise disastrous situation at Nancy, and Pétain had brought a significant measure of success to every command he had held. Add them together and the resulting sum would be even greater success delivered to a desperate situation that had so far yielded nothing but failure.

The trouble was that, given the poor condition of the battered French transportation system, de Castelnau could not arrive in Verdun until the 25th, and Pétain on the 26th. This meant that de Langle de Cary would be obliged to delay making any major decisions until both generals arrived—although it was by no means clear what the authority of each of the three men would be. As of the evening of February 24, no one—probably not even Joseph Joffre—knew who was in full and final command at Verdun.

The command situation, it would seem, could not possibly have gotten worse. But, come the morning of February 25, it did. Without question, the portion of General Order 18 calling for withdrawal from the right bank of the River Meuse was countermanded, and all commanding generals received the countermanding order. One, General Maurice Balfourier, whose territory encompassed the southeastern sector of the Fortified Region of Verdun, declined to transmit the countermand to those in his area. To this day, the reason for this refusal remains a mystery. Its result, however, is starkly clear. The French abandoned a large swath of the right bank after all, in the process leaving to the enemy a quantity—some 5 percent—of French heavy artillery. Combined with the authorized withdrawal from the Woëvre, this was yet another French disaster—and one entirely self-inflicted. Holding this portion of the front was not only strategically imperative for the French, it was tactically quite feasible. That is, in contrast to so many other French gestures of counterattack and riposte, which were ill-advised and sometimes even suicidal, holding ground to bar a breakthrough via Forts Douaumont and Vaux was eminently possible, since German coverage in this area was light. Even if there had been some good reason to evacuate the southeastern portion of the Verdun front, the dangers of evacuating only part of a front during an ongoing battle generally outweigh any possible advantages. Not only does the movement *away from* a battle create confusion and logistical bottlenecks, it spreads defeatism—which had been precisely the effect that the sight of retreating troops had on the Thirty-Seventh Division along the Beaumont–Samogneux line.

THE "PERFECT STORM"

By the night of February 24, as historian John Mosier puts it, the French had put in place all the conditions of a "perfect storm." They "couldn't stop the [German] advance; they had hopelessly intermingled their units. No one knew who was in charge, or what actual orders were to be carried out. Some units were told to advance, others to evacuate; others were abruptly halted."[5]

One can criticize French strategy and tactics, and these were indeed tragically flawed. The greater problem, however, was that, due to the delusions, errors, and incompetence of higher command, the French forces at Verdun had, at this point, effectively ceased to be an army. They were now a demoralized mass of men under grave and imminent peril. Having pulled back, most settled into entirely unprepared positions and did not even bother to dig in. This was a gesture of self-destruction—though it paled in comparison to what happened to the 240-mm naval guns, precious examples of scarce French heavy artillery. They were positioned at two extremes of the battlespace. One emplacement was at Fort Vaux, in the southeastern quadrant, not far from Fort Douaumont. The other was far to the west, on the *left* bank of the Meuse, near the village of Cumiéres. The gun crews abandoned the guns at both positions—after first blowing them up. Arguably, the Fort Vaux installation was vulnerable, but this was by no means true of the guns at Cumiéres. In any case, neither installation had even yet come under attack.

The demoralization was intensified by the spectacle of the French wounded. Of all the armies on the Western Front, the French earned an unenviable reputation for doing the very least for those wounded in battle. Many gravely wounded men were never even evacuated from the field but left to agonize where they fell. Others were retrieved from no-man's-land, laid out, and lined up like cordwood to await eventual transportation to a field hospital. In the bitter cold, their bloody, oozing wounds often froze solid. Any soldier who saw his comrades treated in this way had to feel two related but competing emotions: great pity for the wounded man and terrible dread for his own fate should he be wounded. The poilus were instructed to hate the enemy. What they saw, over and over again, was ample reason to hate their own commanders.

As of ten o'clock on the night of February 24, the situation of the French army in the Verdun sector was this: The entire corps commanded by General Chrétien had been, for all practical purposes, annihilated. There were no reserves, not even a single, solitary company. At this hour, Chrétien and what was left of his corps were officially relieved by General Balfourier, the same commander who had inexplicably refused to prevent the countermanded evacuation of the southeastern corner of the Verdun sector. His assigned corps, the so-called Iron Corps, had been led at the outbreak of the war by none other than Ferdinand Foch and, under him, had earned a reputation for boldness, valor, and efficiency. But, as of ten o'clock on the 24th, when he took over Chrétien's stretch of Verdun, the great bulk of the "Iron Corps" had yet to arrive on the front, despite a forced march to get there. Two advance regiments of the corps did arrive to take up positions sometime after ten but, because of the forced march, they had received no rations over the previous twelve hours, they had also left their heavy machine guns behind, and each man carried no more than 120 rounds of rifle ammunition.

Only one thing was more remarkable than the skeletal condition of the French forces holding Verdun, and that was the failure of the Germans to recognize it as dawn broke on Thursday, February 25. Verdun was wide open to them. They simply did not see it.

The French first line of defense was long gone. The second line was a cadaverous compound of demoralized flesh on bone. The third line, running, west to east, from the Meuse at Côte du Talon to Bezonvaux, above Fort Vaux and to northeast of Fort Douaumont, was thin but as yet fully intact. Moreover, up until the evening of February 23, it had been receiving something between a steady trickle and a sustained flow of reinforcements. When Joseph Joffre sent word that first one—de Castelnau—and then another—Pétain—were on their way to Verdun, General de Langle de Cary ordered the entire Thirtieth Army Corps to hold fast at Regret (the word has the same meaning in French as in English), a village along the road running from Bar-le-Duc, in the Verdun Sector Resérvé, to the city of Verdun. It was a road that would, in the course of the battle, be immortalized as La Voie Sacrée, "the Sacred Way." Regret, the village, was adjacent to Fort de Regret, and both were positioned some two miles southwest of the city of Verdun. With the corps held up here, the flow of reinforcements stopped. Why did de Langle de Cary keep this major unit back? Simple. Pending the arrival of de Castelnau and Pétain, he did not know what to do with it.

The bottling up of the main avenue of communication between Verdun and the rest of France had another adverse effect on the situation along the front. The troops in the second line as well as those in the third now believed they had no means of orderly withdrawal. Neither given a fighting chance by being fully reinforced nor provided with an exit route, they felt they had been abandoned to whatever fate the Germans had in store for them.

What that fate was, however, proved to be anticlimactic.

The Second Chasseurs, an elite organization positioned near Fort Douaumont, were now the easternmost body of French troops at Verdun. They were not overrun by the advancing soldiers of the Twenty-Fourth Brandenburg Regiment so much as they were infiltrated by them. The Germans, unaware of just how precarious French circumstances were, conducted their customary conservative probing advance, using small combined-arms packets rather than unleashing great rolling waves of infantry. It hardly mattered. Elite or not, the Second Chasseurs fell back toward Fort Douaumont, leaving the unit adjacent to them, the 208th Infantry Regiment, in the lurch. Surrounded by the Brandenburgers, some members of the 208th were able to slip away in retreat, but most surrendered with hardly a fight.

It was a victory for the Germans, to be sure. But it was not until late in the afternoon of February 25 that the Brandenburgers, now pursuing the retreating Chasseurs, realized they were approaching Fort Douaumont. It was not only the biggest and highest fort in the sector, it was also the very centerpiece of Verdun. In fact, when most people—civilians, that is—spoke of Verdun in a military context, they did not mean the ancient fortified city of that name. What they meant was Fort Douaumont. To the public, *this* was Verdun. And now a proud German regiment was perfectly positioned to take it.

CHAPTER 12

The Fall of Fort Douaumont

*The armored fort of Douaumont, the northeastern pillar of the chief
line of permanent fortifications of the Verdun strongpoint . . . is completely in the power of German troops.*
——GERMAN HIGH COMMAND NEWS RELEASE,
FEBRUARY 26, 1916[1]

IN 1916, FORT DOUAUMONT WAS THE BIGGEST CONCRETE STRUCTURE IN
the world. On February 25, it was also, doubtless, one of the world's most
severely battered concrete structures, having been bombarded by German shells for nearly five days and nights. Aside from any number of
ancient ruins, Fort Douaumont, going into the battle, might also have
been among the most neglected large structures in the world. Thanks to
the decrees of French high command, all but the two guns permanently
mounted in its massive turret had been removed for use in supporting
attacks elsewhere. With the removal of the guns, the fort's regular garrison of some six hundred men had been taken away, commandeered by
order of high command for other purposes. Most likely, many of these
men lay dead as of February 25, 1916, victims perhaps of the failed offensives in Artois and the Champagne or of the failed counteroffensives on
the Verdun front itself.

At the time of the German assault on the fort, the mammoth structure, intended to accommodate six-hundred-plus, was manned by about
forty Territorials, men aged forty or older, deemed unfit for service in
the front lines. The fort proper was in such an advanced—and ever-
advancing—state of semicollapse that it was no longer possible to see

188

Fort Douaumont early in the battle. Note the damage from artillery bombardment. WIKIMEDIA

the outside world from inside the principal building. The two 155s were functional, but they could no longer be sighted on a target from inside the fort. For this reason, the lieutenant who was put in charge of the forty-some caretakers took up a position in an outlying fortlet located in the nearby woods of Caillette. If anything, that small structure was even more battered than the main fort. Nevertheless, the lieutenant had a view to the east and was able to transmit orders to Fort Douaumont by field telephone. While he could see, all that he could see was the forest of the Vauche. He knew the Germans were out there—somewhere—in that dense tangle, even though he could not actually make them out. So, he ordered his old men to fire their guns in the direction of the forest on the off chance that they might hit something or someone. They obeyed, doggedly lobbing 155-mm shells eastward.

There is no evidence that any of that ordnance found human targets. Under fire in their general direction, the Twenty-Fourth Brandenburg Regiment slowly moved closer to the fort, pausing frequently to take prisoners among stragglers from the French 208th Regiment. The mission assigned to the Twenty-Fourth for the day made no reference to Fort Douaumont but did call for capturing nearby Hassoule Wood and then halting to form a line some 750 yards northeast of the *town* of Douaumont. The plan was for the German Twelfth Grenadiers and the Twentieth Regiment to join the Twenty-Fourth in its advance to this line but, thanks to delays in disseminating the order for the coordinated advance, the Twenty-Fourth moved forward on its own.

Had the French Second Chausseurs not fallen apart on the previous day, the Brandenburgers would have been in for a very nasty surprise. Instead, they found the way virtually undefended and therefore continued their solo advance, making prisoner of some two hundred French stragglers. Even after pausing to round these men up, detachments from the Second Battalion of the Twenty-Fourth Brandenburg reached their assigned line in less than a half hour.

A SKINNED KNEE

At the very forefront of the Second Battalion was a unit of Pioniere under the command of a thickly built soldier of peasant stock named Sergeant Kunze. As he rested after the rapid advance to the assigned line, Kunze gazed ahead at the great concrete dome of Fort Douaumont. The fort was laid out on a hexagonal floor plan. Behind the outer wall was a higher wall with a dry moat between the two. The walls and moat enclosed an open yard, more than 1,200 feet at the widest. The central structure was heavily reinforced with concrete and sheltered a barracks originally designed to accommodate a garrison of some six hundred. The largest guns, two 155-mm cannon, were permanently mounted in a single turret. Three tunnels connected the central structure with the outside world.

Although it had been pounded by German 420-mm howitzers since February 21, the fort remained a most impressive sight—and one Kunze simply could not resist. He summoned about ten combat engineers, all Pioniere, and pointed out to them that the fort was strangely silent, except for sporadic fire from the 155-mm guns in the turret. He told these men that he needed their help in carrying forward the unit's assigned mission, which, he said—quite accurately—was to eliminate obstacles impeding the advance of the infantry. By "obstacles," headquarters had clearly meant barbed wire and the like. Kunze did not dispute that; however, now pointing to the biggest concrete structure in the world, he identified it as a most significant obstacle indeed.

And that is how ten men and a sergeant commenced the assault on what was believed to be Europe's most formidable fortress.

Kunze and his party had the advantage of blowing frozen rain, a dense mist, and a sunless sky. The ground fog was thick. Apparently, the French machine gunners in the nearby village of Douaumont did see something moving toward the fort, but they assumed what they saw were *French* colonial troops returning from patrol. So they did not fire. For this reason, unmolested, the sergeant and his men soon reached the outer wall. Finding a portion of the wall from which artillery fire had bitten out a chunk, Sergeant Kunze directed some of his men to make a human pyramid and give him a boost. He topped the wall and lowered himself into the dry moat. The rest of his men soon followed. Making their way along the rubble-strewn moat, they discovered that the casemates at the corners of the outer wall—known as *coffres*—were unoccupied. Not only was the dry moat undefended, but each of the coffres had an access door opening into the dry moat. Kunze was able to force the door and climb inside one of the empty coffres. There he found another access door that, it was clear, opened onto a tunnel leading into the main fortress structure.

It was at this point, however, that the members of Kunze's party raised an objection. Surely, they were being lured into an ambush, they protested. Kunze did not deign to argue with them. Instead, rifle in hand, he went through the door by himself. The tunnel was pitch dark, but there was a handrail along the wall. He followed it until he heard the dull reverberation of the 155-mm guns being fired. He followed that sound until he also heard the periodic sharp metallic clang as each 155-mm casing was being ejected onto the turret floor. He walked toward a door from behind which the sound was coming. Pausing only briefly, Kunze laid his huge hand on the door handle, pushed it down, and flung the door open. Pointing his rifle at four overage gunners, he shouted *Händehoch!*—Hands up! Their eyes went wide in their powder-blackened faces.

Like the other members of the skeleton garrison, the four gunners had been holed up in the fort since the opening day of the battle. They had no idea of what was going on in the world beyond the concrete, the tunnels, the moat, and the wall. Who was winning? Who was losing? They did not know. Dazed from the incessant shelling—both incoming and outgoing—the only outside voice they had heard for the past five days was that of the lieutenant who phoned in orders from the fortlet outside. Now here was Sergeant Kunze, a German, from the outside, in the flesh, telling them exactly what to do. Unarmed, they put their hands up and waited.

In the meantime, a reserve lieutenant named Radtke had mustered another small group of Brandenburgers and, after speaking with Kunze's men who were still waiting by the access door, ventured through that portal. Discovering Kunze, Radtke summoned the sergeant's reluctant men and organized them into a patrol to sweep through the rest of the fort. Encountering a ragtag assemblage of aging mechanics, electricians, cooks, and other semiretired French Territorials, all unarmed, they took them prisoner.

A short time later, Captain Hans-Joachim Haupt and Oberleutnant (some sources call him a captain) Cordt von Brandis (or Brandeis) arrived with more men. Fort Douaumont was now a German possession. It was 4:30 p.m., about 45 minutes after Kunze walked through the access door. Not a shot had been fired at those who "stormed" the fort, and the only reported casualty was to one of Kunze's men who had scraped a knee while descending into the dry moat.

THE RIGHT BANK BECOMES GERMAN

Fort Douaumont, epicenter of the Verdun sector, the anchor of the system of forts General Séré de Rivières had designed to prevent a repetition of the humiliation of 1870–1871, fell without a fight, delivered into the hands of a peasant sergeant, a couple of lieutenants, and a captain. Only after its fall would a French divisional commander remark that its loss ultimately cost the lives of some 100,000 French soldiers.[2] This certainly seems a gross overestimate, but it was a significant setback. The fort was wholly commandeered by the Germans during the rest of the Verdun battle and used as a forward shelter and operational base just behind their front line. In a shambles, it must have been a most inhospitable environment, but it was preferable to an open trench. The German troops affectionately dubbed it "Old Uncle Douaumont."[3]

In the meantime, outside of the crumbling fort, the battle for possession of the right bank of the Meuse River rapidly unfolded. Since the territory had been substantially abandoned, it was by no means a momentous struggle. By twilight, every French position of military significance on the right bank was held by German soldiers.

The Battle of Verdun was now five days old. The German army had penetrated more than six miles across a front that had, in the course of combat, broadened to some 12 miles across. In addition, there was the Woëvre, about 125 square miles, which Generals de Langle de Cary and Joffre simply abandoned. The cost in French killed or missing was approximately seventeen thousand, nearly six times the number of wounded. Overall, the French casualty rate was 30 percent—although it would actually take quite some time to determine this. The fog of war was so thick among the French at Verdun that, initially, officials listed *95 percent* of the seventeen thousand in the killed or missing category as "missing." In other words, they were gone—but nobody knew where, whether on earth or in heaven.

THE FRENCH VERSION

French high command—the Grand Quartier Général (GQG)— scrambled to make up for the ignominious defeat of French arms in the field by issuing a bulletin intended to counter Germany's simple statement that the "armored fort of Douaumont, the northeastern pillar of the chief line of permanent fortifications of the Verdun strongpoint, was taken by assault by the Twenty-Fourth Brandenburg Regiment" and "is completely in the power of German troops."[4] The way GQG reported it—

> *A bloody struggle took place around the fort of Douaumont, which is an advanced element of the ancient organization of Verdun. The position was taken in the morning by the enemy after numerous fruitless assaults, that cost very high losses and was passed by our troops, who repulsed all the attempts of the enemy to throw them back.*[5]

Pretty much every word of the GQG dispatch was a fabrication of breathtaking scope. To begin with, the capture of the fort involved no "struggle," let alone a bloody one. Whereas the German statement accurately characterized Fort Douaumont as a "pillar" of the fortification system of Verdun, the French statement minimized it—the biggest concrete structure in the world!—as an "advanced element" in Verdun's "ancient organization." Just as there was no "struggle" to take the fort, so the assaults upon it, other than the artillery bombardments, were not "numerous," but just one. And the cost to the Germans? A skinned knee. As for French troops repulsing attempts to "throw them back," there were no French troops defending Fort Douaumont, so there were none to "repulse" German attempts to "throw them back." Even more spectacular were GQG claims that the Germans had lost 400,000 men in the five days of fighting culminating in the fall of Fort Douaumont.[6]

The lies were intended to avert panic among the French public and in the government. In fact, while the public held up quite well, the government was altogether another story. The overriding lesson of the Franco-Prussian War of 1870–1871 was that Germany's victory, decisive as it was, by no means brought an end to the French nation or did any permanent injury to the French people. That victory did, however, bring down an emperor, Napoleon III, and his government. Despite generating mountains of propaganda to the contrary, French political leaders were well aware that the survival of the nation and its people were not imperiled by the prospect of a German victory in 1914, 1915, or 1916. Their own positions as leaders of the nation most certainly were in deep jeopardy, however.

The situation within the nation's leadership was complicated by a breakdown in communications and trust between the military and the government. Joseph Galliéni—the tough old soldier who, having become a national hero for his successful defense of Paris during the First Battle of the Marne, was instantly appointed minister of war—was now terminally ill. The celebrated struggle to save Paris and to reinforce the French position at the Marne by rushing troops from the Paris garrison to the front in taxicabs had only invigorated the old man. But the toxic climate of French politics—both in the civil government and the army—physically broke him. On the verge of the Battle of Verdun, Galliéni, incorruptible, had launched an investigation stemming from Lieutenant Colonel Émile Driant's complaints that Joseph Joffre had recklessly dismantled the Verdun defenses. The investigation led to a widening breach between Joffre as the army's senior commander and Galliéni, the minister of war.

The breach became absolute, final, and irreparable with the fall of Fort Douaumont. Amid rumors that Joffre had explicitly ordered the abandonment of Verdun early in the battle, Galliéni demanded to see all of Joffre's orders. Although no written order to abandon the sector was found, Galliéni made it clear to President Raymond Poincaré that he intended to deliver a full report on Joffre's conduct of the war, Verdun included. This prospect was terrifying to the sitting government. Galliéni was a national hero, but Joffre was not merely a national hero. As "Papa Joffre," he was a military leader in whom a majority of the French people placed a peculiarly comforting faith. War between these two men, combined with the disastrous situation at Verdun and elsewhere on the Western Front, could well create a national crisis of morale that would not only result in losing the war but would also bring down the government.

None of this deterred Galliéni. During a ninety-minute cabinet discussion of February 26, he took umbrage at references to the *Battle* of Verdun. "Why speak of a battle?" Galliéni snapped. "Are there even any defenses? Why aren't there more troops there, given that you're opposed by seven army corps?" In reference to Joffre's insertion of Generals de Castelnau and Pétain, he concluded: "Why change commanders at the last minute?"[7]

On March 7, with the Battle of Verdun still raging, Galliéni would deliver his promised report to the Council of Ministers. It was scathing, unsparingly condemning Joffre's leadership not only in the matter of the defense of Verdun but in virtually every operation since August 1914. He demanded that the Ministry of War, not Joffre, be given complete control of the army and the conduct of the war henceforth. Then, pleading illness, he announced his own resignation.

Rather than let the fate of the government be determined by the culmination of this battle between Galliéni and Joffre, President Poincaré decided to find the facts that would speak the truth of the state of France's present war effort. It was an admirable endeavor, but his straightforward quest for enlightenment was met at every turn by more evasions and outright lies of the kind the army had issued following the fall of Fort Douaumont. After Galliéni's resignation, Poincaré pointedly asked Joffre's deputy, de Castelnau, for precise figures on losses. De Castelnau put German losses at nearly a quarter-million men—not the 400,000 initially reported. He said French losses amounted to 65,000 men and that published German figures on French POWs taken were grossly inflated and entirely false.

Unsatisfied, Poincaré pressed on. In response, he received an admission that French losses might actually be closer to 100,000. When he subsequently cornered de Castelnau a third time, the general produced a slip of paper from his coat pocket. Reading from it, he announced that, as of April 25, French casualties amounted to 125,000 prisoners, 16,594 killed in action, 57,142 wounded—and, oh yes, 51,000 missing, or perhaps 52,000. Stunned, Poincaré remarked on how wildly these figures differed from those reported earlier. De Castelnau responded only that the German figures on prisoners taken were actually rather plausible.[8]

When, in May, Poincaré received yet another set of figures, the president set off on some independent research and, finding that about 135,000 wounded poilus had been evacuated from Verdun, he challenged the army's count of wounded, which had risen to 74,844 by May.[9] Instead of attempting to resolve the contradiction, the generals let it stand. They thereby lost all credibility and yet they remained in command. Why? As historian John Mosier puts it, "the only man among [the political leaders] who had any real military expertise was missing, gravely ill (Galliéni)" and "the only insider secure enough in his position to speak out had been killed . . . (Driant)."[10] Thus the war would continue to be fought by generals no one trusted and who reported whatever they wished to a government too feckless to challenge them.

THE GERMAN VERSION

The capture of the fort that anchored the easternmost system of French fortifications, the fort whose very name was associated with French fortifications that had endured since the days of ancient Rome, started with a lowborn Thuringian sergeant's highly imaginative interpretation of his mission. Ordered to clear the westward field of advance of "obstacles," he saw Fort Douaumont as a very large obstacle indeed, gathered ten men, and cleared it. Sergeant Kunze had no way of knowing that his objective was manned by no more than forty-some-odd old men who had neither the desire, the ability, nor the weapons to resist him. His assault on the fort was, therefore, a heroic venture into the unknown. Yet, as the mission unfolded, it became comical in its anticlimax. No matter, Captain Haupt, a latecomer to the capture, was intent on the deed being portrayed as the great thing it—to a legitimate degree—actually was. To this end, he sent the latest comer of all, the officer who had had least to do with the capture, Cordt von Brandis, to Fifth Army headquarters to deliver a formal report on the capture of what *could* be deemed the jewel in the fortified crown of France.

Not that anyone in French high command had deemed it that. (Hardly!) And for that matter, it is, as we have seen, highly doubtful that Falkenhayn himself believed Fort Douaumont was of any exceptional importance. Yet von Brandis did not hesitate to tell his story to the Fifth Army commander, Wilhelm, Crown Prince of Germany, son of the kaiser. Since it was von Brandis who told the story, it was he who became its hero: the dashing young Prussian officer who singlehandedly took for the German Empire and the German people one of the great prizes of the Great War. Kunze, who actually assaulted the fort, broke in, rounded up the gun crew, and initiated the capture of the rest of the caretaker garrison—Kunze, who has been called "Germany's Sergeant York[11]—was

Lieutenant Cordt von Brandis (at right) claimed credit for the German capture of Fort Douaumont. He is pictured here with the commanding officer of his company, Captain Haupt (at left) and Colonel von Doen (center), the regimental commanding officer. All were decorated with—and wear—the Iron Cross, First Class. WIKIMEDIA

left out of the narrative entirely, as was Lieutenant Radtke, who followed up Kunze's work by assuming command of the culminating moments of the capture.

At the time, no one investigated von Brandis's story—not because they were too lazy or too gullible to do so, but because it was a very good story. Instead, Cordt von Brandis was awarded the nation's highest military honor, the Pour le Mérite. Once that happened, there was no changing the narrative. In war fought on an industrial scale, individual heroism—whether genuine, as in the case of Émile Driant, or elaborately embroidered, as in that of von Brandis—was pure gold and a scarce commodity. The people craved heroes. Later, Captain Haupt also received a Pour le Mérite, and it is surely no coincidence that he confirmed Cordt von Brandis's narrative.

The truth did eventually come out, during the 1930s, when the events of World War I were cast under a harsh, bitter, and cynical light throughout Germany and the rest of the world. The roles of Kunze and Radtke were revealed by independent historians, and the Weimar government, which had succeeded that of Kaiser Wilhelm II, rewarded Kunze not with a medal but with a job promotion. A police officer after the war, Kunze was jumped in rank. As for Lieutenant Radtke, the former crown prince of Germany—like his father, deposed, but unlike the former kaiser, allowed to return to Germany from Dutch exile—gifted him with an autographed photograph.

From the perspective of a century, the comical ease with which Fort Douaumont fell seems yet another dark condemnation of the absurdity of the so-called Great War. The alternative narrative, the von Brandis tale of singlehanded heroism, served Germany's immediate propaganda and public morale purposes. In the longer term, it further complicated the historical evaluation of the entire Battle of Verdun by lending credence to Falkenhayn's strategic claim that everything he did at Verdun was based on the assumption that France would bleed itself white before it would allow this front to be surrendered.

PÉTAIN STEPS IN

Henri Philippe Pétain was as contrary and as unpopular with his professional colleagues as the late Émile Driant. Where others were complacent, he was critical. Where others were fat and happy, he was trim and acerbic. Where others dedicated themselves to currying influence and climbing through the ranks, he spoke his mind, regardless of consequences. He had but three passions. One was firepower. Pétain believed in artillery—heavy artillery—and that put him on the outs in an army that preached flesh and blood and infantry while disdaining steel and high explosives. A second passion was the supreme value of the individual soldier. In the second global war that would follow this world war to end all wars, the American general George S. Patton wrote in his notebook, "The soldier is the army." Pétain would have agreed with him. This, too, made him an outsider in an army hierarchy that regarded the poilu as so much cannon fodder. While others polished the stars they had and coveted yet more, Pétain contented himself with the rank he had achieved at the outbreak of the war—colonel—and spent much of his time gratifying his third passion, the remarkably successful pursuit of the wives of his fellow officers, including those who had achieved higher rank than he. Indeed, when Joseph Joffre sent for him on the night of February 24, 1916, to take charge at Verdun, the general's messenger found the sixty-year-old bachelor in bed with (as usual) a younger woman whose identity is lost to history.

Unlike many other French officers, Pétain advanced strictly on his military merit. Entering World War I as a colonel, he was a brigadier general by the end of the war's first month, a general of division by the start of the First Battle of the Marne, and a corps commander by October 1914. Less than a year later, in July 1915, he had command of the entire Second Army.

Roused from bed on the night of the 24th, he reported to Joffre at Chantilly at eight in the morning on the 25th. Joffre, as usual, was calm and laconic. He had no advice to give Pétain before sending him off, telling him only that the situation was serious but not particularly alarming, and that General de Castelnau, already on the scene, would fully brief him. Although Pétain immediately left for Souilly, the frontline headquarters of the Verdun battle, it is a measure of just how poor French lines of communication and transport were that he did not meet with de Langle de Cary and de Castelnau until late in the evening of the 25th. From here, he was driven to Dugny, the headquarters of General Frédéric-Georges Herr, who told him that Fort Douaumont had been lost.

Pétain took it all in. Famed throughout the French military for his icy demeanor, an entirely unreadable exterior, it is doubtful he so much as blinked at anything Herr told him. Privately, however, he concluded that Verdun was a catastrophe—a defeat of enormous proportions. Armed

Philippe Pétain (center, straddling the curb) listens as General Charles Mangin speaks with Raymond Poincaré, who, when visiting the front, always wore a uniform that made him look more like a chauffeur than the president of France. WIKIMEDIA

with this conclusion, Pétain ordered his driver to take him to Souilly, a village on the road between Bar-le-Duc and Verdun that de Langle de Cary had used as a headquarters and that was now occupied by General de Castelnau. Pétain relayed to the general what he had just been told: Fort Douaumont had fallen. With this, de Castelnau withdrew a small field notebook from his coat pocket. He scrawled a simple order to the effect that Verdun must be defended at all costs *on the right bank*. He then tore out the page and handed it to Pétain.

And then Noël Édouard Marie Joseph, Vicomte de Curières de Castelnau, promptly withdrew into the sidelines. The Battle of Verdun was now Pétain's to conduct. At 11 p.m., Pétain telephoned General Balfourier, commanding what was left on the right bank of the Meuse: "*Allo! C'est moi, general Pétain.* I have taken over command." He added: "Tell your troops. Hold fast. I have confidence in you." Balfourier acknowledged the terse message, adding "Now everything is going to be all right."[12] Pétain rang off and then made the same call to General de Bazelaire, on the left bank.

Would "everything" now "be all right"? Well, at least Verdun finally had a commander.

The next morning, Pétain reiterated to both Balfourier and Bazelaire that *both* banks of the Meuse were to be held—held along lines he himself would lay out shortly. He added to Balfourier that three entire army corps were on their way and would bring the strength of the French army at Verdun to parity with—even superiority to—the Germans, at least in terms of manpower, if not firepower.

Had Philippe Pétain been any other senior French commander, he would have followed up this information and these instructions with the customary exhortations to attack and to fight to the last man. Being very different from those others, however, he did no such thing. Instead, he set out planning not an attack but a defense, and not just any defense, but a thoroughly organized defense in depth. It was based on his understanding that the Germans were advancing so far so fast and yet with *comparatively* few men (for Falkenhayn wanted a *cheap* victory, after all) that they were putting their infantry out of range of all but their heaviest artillery. In short, their success was forcing them to outrun their greatest strength and advantage: their firepower. This gap, this severance of infantry from artillery, would not last long, Pétain reasoned, but while it did last, the victorious Germans might just be compelled to bleed *themselves* white.

CHAPTER 13

"Now Everything Is Going to Be All Right"

There had emerged a leader who taught his army to distinguish the real from the imaginary and the possible from the impossible. On the day when a choice had to be made between ruin and reason, Pétain received promotion.
—CHARLES DE GAULLE, *FRANCE AND HER ARMY*, 1938[1]

AFTER ASSUMING COMMAND AND TELEPHONING THE GENERALS ON THE right and left banks of the Meuse, a cold, exhausted Philippe Pétain sent his aide, Captain Bernard Serrigny, to find him a bed. Because the tiny headquarters at Souilly had none, Serrigny commandeered the nearby house of an attorney. Unfortunately, the bedroom was ice cold, so, after he wolfed down some cold beans left over from the orderlies' mess, Pétain, bundled in his greatcoat, curled up on an armchair in the dining room sometime after midnight on February 26. The sixty-year-old general awoke some hours later burning with fever.

A doctor was quietly summoned. His diagnosis was pneumonia, *double* pneumonia. To those who had called him in, the physician confided that, given the general's age, the disease could well prove fatal. The men thanked the doctor, swore him to absolute secrecy, and sent him on his way. Guards were posted around the house to keep word of the general's condition from leaking out. Although five days of bombardment had failed to finish off the French armies at Verdun, the news that the commander sent to save them was critically ill might just bring about the collapse. Even though absolute bed rest for a week—probably more—was prescribed, Pétain insisted on working, relying on Serrigny and his other personal aides to act as his eyes and ears.

THE OPTION OF DEFENSE

"My center is yielding. My right is retreating. Situation excellent. I am attacking."[2] The quotation was the beau geste moment of Ferdinand Foch as he led the French Ninth Army at the First Battle of the Marne. Philippe Pétain was far too acerbic and cynical to make such an utterance as he assumed overall command of the Verdun front on the night of February 25, 1916. Besides, if anything, Pétain was the anti-Foch. Foch became the ideal to which every other French general aspired, the very embodiment of élan vital. Pétain, in contrast, did not see attaque à outrance as the answer in every situation. Like Erich von Falkenhayn, he understood the value of defense.

In a situation every bit as dire as that which Foch had faced at the Marne, it was a fresh approach to defense, not attack, that Pétain seized upon. Had he wished to echo Foch, he might have written, "My front line has yielded. The right bank has retreated. Situation excellent. I am defending in depth." And it would have been more than a handsome gesture. In a strange way, the situation really *was* excellent—for the defensive solution Pétain proposed. The Germans had indeed moved so far and so fast that their infantry had substantially outrun their heavy artillery—the very asset that had enabled the advance. It would take precious time for the heavy guns to be repositioned. During that delay, the Germans having advanced onto the right bank territory Joffre and de Langle de Cary had presented to them, were now within range of the French artillery positioned on the *left* bank of the Meuse. In fact, these guns bore directly on Fort Douaumont, now occupied by the Germans.

Pétain recognized that, though flushed with victory, the Germans were, in fact, highly vulnerable. Perhaps it was this realization that hastened his recovery from pneumonia. Or perhaps it was sheer willpower. In any case, he may even have intuited that Falkenhayn and Knobelsdorf had absolutely no plan ready for the situation as it had unfolded. So much should have been apparent by the magnitude of the task that now lay before the German commanders. They were obliged to advance their heaviest artillery—and that was not easy. Pétain may well have surmised that the German commanders assumed that their French counterparts would invariably behave in the manner of Foch, sacrificing all available lives to recapture lost territory. If this was the case, how could the Germans have planned for the French evacuation and consequent sudden collapse of the entire right bank?

Doubtless German high command was congratulating itself on its triumph, but Pétain saw that triumph as a trap.

When your prey is in a cage, there is no need to give chase. What is needed is precisely what French military doctrine persistently refused to create: defense in depth. With the Germans overextended, now was the time to create truly deadly defensive lines, with strongpoints of fire that interlocked all across the entire front.

Pétain realized that the basis of something like this already existed—in fact, had existed since the late nineteenth century, when the much-reviled Séré de Rivières system of fortifications was completed. Pétain proposed to establish his defense in depth along the line of these fortifications. He put into motion the rearming and remanning of the forts. This required, first and foremost, resurrecting the badly battered French logistics and transportation network. The existing principal west–east roadway and railway were within range of German heavy artillery and so had been effectively interdicted. Pétain ordered construction of a bypass, but work on this major roadway would take many weeks. So he turned to widening the road that ran from Bar-le-Duc in the southwestern corner of the sector to the city of Verdun. Although it had been widened somewhat in 1915, it was still little more than a country lane with a narrow-gauge railway parallel to it. Because of its narrow gauge, the railway was of limited utility. A great deal of time would be wasted in transferring cargo from standard-gauge trains arriving from the west at Bar-le-Duc to the narrow-gauge trains. Moreover, those tracks were limited as to the loads they could handle. The better solution was to improve and widen the country lane to allow efficient two-way truck traffic. Ultimately, this roadway—which became universally known as the Voie Sacrée, in wry homage to the ancient "Sacred Way" between Athens and Eleusis along which those celebrating the Eleusinian Mysteries processed—would accommodate

At the height of its use, one truck passed every fourteen seconds along the *Voie Sacrée.* AUTHOR'S COLLECTION

the two-way passage of 3,900 trucks every twenty-four hours. On the shoulders of the road, columns of reinforcements would march into battle continuously, some 200,000 men before the battle ended.

First to travel the road were trucks bringing building supplies to restore the forts, the guns with which to arm them, and the ammunition to feed the guns. As for the new defensive line, it was to run from Avocourt in the west, pass just south of Côte 304 and through the forested high ground of another hill, Le Mort Homme, cross the Meuse, and turn southward to the village of Thiaumont, from which it would continue south and then east to Fort Vaux, which was southeast of the fallen Fort Douaumont. From Fort Vaux, the line was to continue to the city of Verdun. Pétain laid out a second line behind this one. It would run through Forts de Choisel, Belleville, Saint-Michel, Rozelier, and Belrupt, which were collectively dubbed the *forts du Panic* because the prospect of their suffering attack was an occasion for genuine panic. The third line—the last ditch—was planned through Forts de Chana, La Chaume, Regret, Landrecourt, and then east to Forts Dugny, de Haudainville, Saint-Symphorien, and Génicourt.

In his ambitious defensive plan, Pétain addressed two enemies at Verdun. There were the Germans, of course. By shifting radically to a strategy of defense in depth, he succeeded in confounding Falkenhayn completely. Whether or not we believe that the German commander really set out to create the conditions that would bleed France white, everything he did in the first six days of the Battle of Verdun was based on his repeatedly validated assumption that French generals could be relied upon to attack at all costs. The soldiers might be killed or they might break and run. But the generals could be counted to attack over and over again.

Now a new French commander suddenly invalidated an assumption that had held true since 1914. And that brings up the second enemy. In doing what he was doing at Verdun, Philippe Pétain was also fighting prevailing French military doctrine. In addition to the Germans, he was fighting the French.

THE OPTION OF ATTRITION

He was fighting Joseph Joffre—or, rather, everything Joffre seemed to stand for. And yet it was Joffre who had promoted him so rapidly beginning in 1914. Pétain came of age in a French military that was haunted by and obsessed with the defeat of 1870–1871. The conclusion both his elders and contemporaries had reached was that Germany had won by demonstrating the folly of relying on fortifications; therefore, in the future, best to shun fortifications and instead embrace all-out infantry attack. Pétain, in contrast, looked at the Franco-Prussian War and concluded that German heavy artillery had won the war; therefore, France should develop heavy artillery. The trouble was that nobody among the rising French military leadership wanted to hear this, even after the Russo-Japanese War of 1905 demonstrated even more spectacularly the war-winning effect of superior firepower and the virtues of strong defenses.

Although Pétain's advocacy of unpopular ideas retarded his promotion up the ranks during the years before World War I, he was given a place as an instructor at the École de Guerre. Perhaps his superiors believed that teaching in company with the likes of Ferdinand Foch and other advocates of attaque à outrance would cast him into the shadows where he belonged. Indeed, his dry and dispassionate manner became legendary at the École, and while the majority of students fell under the spell of the fiery Foch and like-minded company, Pétain not only succeeded in winning over a small coterie of converts (most notably a young Charles de Gaulle) but also kept his minority point of view very much alive.

On the eve of World War I, in the spring of 1914, Pétain was given command of a brigade. Because he did not receive the promotion to brigadier general that should have gone with this assignment, Colonel Pétain purchased a villa to which he intended to retire. But his performance in command of his brigade at the Battle of Guise (August 29, 1914) earned him the long-delayed promotion, and it was none other than Joffre who made way for his continuing meteoric rise by cashiering one incumbent general after another—commanders who had never made waves, who had obediently cleaved to the doctrine of attack, but had nothing but combat casualties to show for it.

There is much for which Joffre should be criticized but, to his great credit, in the end, he put performance over his own doctrinal orthodoxy. As a result, Pétain was given more and more responsibility. In almost every new position of command, he compiled a record that put the majority of French generals to shame. The single exception came in one of his offensive operations in the Champagne during the fall of 1915. Acting on his faith in firepower, he prolonged an artillery preparation to the point of entirely sacrificing the element of surprise prior to launching his infantry. This resulted in very heavy casualties. But—and this is where Pétain separated himself from his colleagues—recognizing his failure, Pétain refused to double down on it. He broke off the assault rather than continue what was a useless effusion of blood.

From our perspective, the perspective of a hundred years, Pétain's approach seems obvious proof of the invaluable quality his student Charles de Gaulle described: his ability "to distinguish the real from the imaginary and the possible from the impossible."[3] Yet it was an ability that carried with it a significant danger.

Pétain admitted that it was "always prejudicial to cede ground to the enemy," thus seeming to echo the prevailing French doctrine that banned the surrender of territory and demanded that lost territory be instantly recovered, regardless of cost. Yet, he continued, the "inconveniences" resulting from yielding land were as nothing compared to "those which could result at a given moment from the capture by the enemy of three or four battalions, with a loss, by consequence, of several thousands of men."[4] Again, this seems to be common sense. In fact, American students of war might relate it to the position of no less a titan than Ulysses S. Grant, a position that, in 1863–1865, so many viewed as heretical. The Union commander rejected the acquisition of territory as the way to victory. Wars are won, he insisted, not by taking land but by killing the opposing army, even if that meant passing up or even yielding some real estate in the process.

So what was the danger in Pétain's approach to war, which was, if anything, even more heretical than Grant's? The same historical perspective that allows us to see the common sense in Pétain's embrace of defense also forces us to recognize the possibility that, in the new direction he took at Verdun, Pétain revealed those qualities in his personality that resulted in the moral catastrophe of surrender in 1940, when he led the Vichy collaboration with Nazi Germany. Bernard Serrigny, Pétain's trusted aide at Verdun, would, years later, famously attempt to dissuade the old man, already prime minister of the Vichy government, from engaging in ever closer collaboration with the Nazis. "You think too much about the French and not enough about France," he scolded.[5] To abandon the ethos of attack risked opening the door to demoralization, quite possibly on a national scale.

But Pétain was willing to take that risk. Thus Joffre ended up putting in place the one man whose record of results argued against all of his own assumptions about war. In place of offense there would now be defense. In place of attack there would now be attrition.

Of course, by 1916, attrition was hardly a radical idea. Joseph Joffre himself had come to embrace it. His problem, however, was that, even in his advocacy of attrition, he stubbornly refused to let go his embrace of infantry attack. Joffre clung to the man-for-man exchange of casualties as an appropriate instrument of attrition, reasoning that, because Britain and France combined had more men to lose, they would wear down Germany—eventually. Pétain, in sharp contrast, was not wedded to infantry. For him, the proper instrument of attrition was not flesh but iron, not infantry but artillery. "One does not fight with men against materiel," Pétain frequently declared.[6] The first half-dozen days of Verdun made clear that the Germans already knew this. France would have to catch up and overtake them.

THE FRENCH GUNS SPEAK—AT LAST

While Pétain still lay sick in bed, his aides informed him that before de Castelnau had turned over command, he ordered, in orthodox French army fashion, that Fort Douaumont be immediately retaken. The first attempt at this, unsurprisingly, ended in bloody failure. From his sickbed, Pétain issued an immediate order countermanding de Castelnau's order and canceling any future attempts to retake the fort. He sent a message to all of his commanders, directing them to "conserve" their strength but promising that "the counter-offensive will follow."[7]

What he did put into immediate action was the artillery. With the Germans on the right bank, Pétain ordered what he termed "artillery *offensives*" against them there. They were the only offensives he conducted at this moment. He worked closely with his artillery commanders to position the guns for coordinated crossfire, and he hit the exposed German infantry—still out of range of its own heavy artillery—hard, especially in and around Fort Douaumont. In contrast to the usual French practice of frontal barrage, Pétain positioned his guns on the left-bank heights for crossfire so that he could deliver a flanking barrage.

Soon, the general forsook his bed for regular tours of the artillery emplacements. His question to the battery commanders was always the same: "What have your batteries been doing?" And he told them to fire, to keep firing. "Leave the other details till later," he ordered.[8]

The barrages had two effects, one on the Germans and one on the French. On the Germans, the effect was a dramatic increase in casualties combined with demoralizing shock. The troops and their commanders had never seen anything like this from the French—not at Verdun, certainly, and, really, not on any other battlefield either. On the French soldiers at Verdun, the sound of their own guns was something very like music. At last, they were making the *Germans* suffer. At last, it was the *enemy* doing the dying. As for the infantry, the bulk of which was being held back from battle for the moment, there was the blessed feeling of no longer bearing the burden of battle alone.

THE SACRED WAY

De Gaulle wrote that Pétain could "distinguish the real from the imaginary and the possible from the impossible." Even as he redeployed his artillery for efficiency and then spurred it to continuous fire, Pétain paid close attention to the road that had been among his very first concerns, the Sacred Way, the route between Verdun and Bar-le-Duc, the transfer point for everything that came from the west.

Pétain's intention was to treat it as an artery—not just figuratively, but as literally as possible: a vessel that would never stop flowing. To do this, he worked with his engineers to keep traffic moving in both directions, continuously. Along the road, he established six major camps, staffed with mechanics and equipped with workshops. Broken-down trucks were to be pushed off the road until a crew from one of the encampments could repair it in the field or have it towed to a workshop.

The engineers estimated that operations at the Verdun front required two thousand tons of supplies to be delivered every 24 hours. The French army had entered the war in 1914 with exactly 170 *camions*—trucks. By February 1916, the number had risen significantly, and 700 were available to the forces in and around Verdun. Running continuously, these 700 could deliver 1,250 tons daily. Inspired by the "miracle of the taxis," that most colorful feature of the First Battle of the Marne, Pétain's engineers commandeered civilian trucks from all over the country, soon assembling a massive fleet of 3,500—a quantity sufficient to bring in the required two thousand tons and then some.

The vehicles were primitive. Their tires were solid rubber. The vehicles were hazardous enough when the road was frozen hard, but when a thaw hit on February 28, trucks sank up to their tire tops in a foot and a half of thick mud. General Pétain ordered his engineers to take whatever action and whatever resources they needed to "fix" the problem. And so they rounded up every Territorial in the Verdun sector, lined up those aging soldiers all along the Sacred Way, supplied them with mountains of gravel, and handed out shovels. They were instructed to throw gravel down under the wheels of the trucks as they passed. Incredibly, the desperate system worked.

"FRANCE HAS HER EYES ON YOU"

Among his prewar students at the École de Guerre, Philippe Pétain had a reputation as a dispassionate teacher with a delivery as precise as it was dry. Among fellow officers, he was regarded as a supreme cynic, icy and remote. But upon soldiers—the poilus and the noncoms and the junior officers who commanded them in the field—he exercised a kind of magic.

It was a magic based not on illusion but reality. He really did care deeply for the soldiers of the armies he commanded, and he took every opportunity to show them that he cared. Whatever he told them, they believed it because, coming from him, they knew it was worthy of belief. His very first Order of the Day closed with the exhortation, "France has her eyes on you."[9] And they believed that was true. And so it was.

All along the newly formed lines, before Pétain's arrival, the first line was nonexistent, wiped out, and the second and third bulged, sagged, and, in many places, were broken entirely. With the general's arrival, all of the lines stiffened. Men who had looked like defeated derelicts of February 25 now had the appearance of soldiers in an army. The effect of this transformation on the Germans was anything but magical. German records noted February 27 as the first day in the Battle of Verdun that "brought German arms no success anywhere."[10]

On the very hour he had assumed command, Pétain promised that three corps of reinforcements were on their way. Now they were indeed arriving. One of them, XX Corps, had already taken up positions on the right bank of the Meuse. On that bank, fighting broke out around the village of Douaumont under the very guns of the fort named after it. The Twenty-Fourth Brandenburg Regiment, whose soldiers had taken the fort so easily, now spent most of the week that began with February 27, a Sunday, fighting in and around the village. Possession of it changed

Captain Charles de Gaulle. CHARLES DE GAULLE BIRTHPLACE AND MUSEUM, LILLE, FRANCE

hands more than once, with the Brandenbergers suffering their heaviest casualties since the beginning of the Battle of Verdun.

French regiments poured in. They suffered, too. Among them was the Thirty-Third, which Pétain himself had once commanded. As he reviewed

213

the casualty lists—for Pétain reviewed them all and carefully—he recognized among the names that of an officer he recalled as exceptionally earnest and brave. A student of his at the École, this young man had been very eager to join his regiment. It was Captain Charles de Gaulle, who was now a German prisoner of war.

The fight for Douaumont village did not finally go to the French. On March 4, the remaining members of the Thirty-Third Regiment were killed, captured, or managed somehow to withdraw. When a French commander on the scene ordered (in the expected knee-jerk fashion) a desperate counterattack to retake the village, Pétain sent a runner to him. Withdraw, Pétain ordered. Let go of the village of Douaumont—for a time, anyway. He felt confident that the Battle of Verdun would continue, but—this time—it would continue without the momentum of cheap victory driving the enemy.

CHAPTER 14

Reversals of Fortune

An awful word, Verdun. Numerous people, still young and filled with hope, had to lay down their lives here . . . their Mortal remains decomposing somewhere, in between trenches, in mass graves, at cemeteries.
—LETTER OF A GERMAN SOLDIER TO HIS PARENTS[1]

EXCEPT FOR THE FIGHT OVER THE VILLAGE OF DOUAUMONT, PHILIPPE Pétain did not rise to the bait the German Fifth Army presented. The new French commander resolutely refrained from ordering offensive action against the German positions on the east bank, the right bank, of the River Meuse. This meant that the Germans had few targets to strike at the end of February and the first few days of March. Their advance infantry had outrun the heavy artillery on which it relied for support. This meant that it could not force a major attack across the Meuse onto the western, left, bank. For the most part, positions here were out of heavy artillery range.

Why didn't the Germans hasten to reposition their artillery to avoid losing valuable momentum against a French army that had been punched back on its heels?

Most historians—at least those from the Allied nations—put the blame on Falkenhayn and his notorious parsimony with troops and other resources. In contrast to French high command, Falkenhayn was not eager to trade human lives for mere territory. Unfriendly historians did not call this attitude humane, but overly cautious and perhaps timid. But this does not answer the question of why he failed to reposition his artillery. Some have suggested a certain incompetence; others, a lack of strategic vision. More than likely, however, the real problem was the great gulf between planning a battle on a two-dimensional tabletop map and actually fighting one in a three-dimensional landscape. As it turned out, neither the French commanders nor the German had much appreciation for the physical realities of the topography of the Woëvre. West of the Verdun front, the road net was poorly developed over this difficult, boggy terrain. Hence the peril of the French soldiers on this front, connected to the rest of France by the single umbilical that was the Voie Sacrée. But the very challenges that imperiled the French now likewise brought the German offensive to a crawl. The same sudden late-February thaw that had moved Pétain's engineers to dragoon every Territorial troop within miles to line up along the mud soup that was the Sacred Way to shovel gravel under the solid tires of thousands of trundling *camions* also sucked at the high boots of the German infantry and mired the wheel of the army's heavy-artillery carriages. The problem moving the heavy guns was compounded by the need to position them on the heights. This meant a slog uphill—in the mud.

DEAD HORSES

Pétain used the enforced lull in the fighting to reoccupy the right bank, not for immediate offensive operations but to dig in defensively and establish French artillery in well-coordinated crossfire positions. This not only imperiled the German infantry, it also exposed its lumbering artillery, in slow transit, to murderous French fire. From across the Meuse, French heavy naval guns emplaced on the left bank fired relentlessly against the columns transporting Germany's artillery.

World War I was the infancy of both aviation and horseless vehicular transportation. The German army was equipped with tractors to pull heavy artillery, but these proved no match for the mud of Verdun. Instead, the gun carriages were hitched to teams of horses. It required ten horses to move just one *medium* field gun of 210 mm and even more to move anything heavier. The animals now fell under French fire, and, on one day alone, seven thousand of them were shelled to death. On a front accustomed to horror, it must have been a particularly gruesome spectacle. The German expressionist painter Franz Marc, who had taken pride in

216

Horses, both for reconnaissance work and as pack animals, played a major role at the Battle of Verdun. Here, French troops ford a river in the sector. WIKIMEDIA

painting camouflage nets for the heaviest guns, had written about the early days of the battle, remarking on the "rage and force of the German attack" and concluding that he did not "for one minute doubt . . . the fall of Verdun" to Germany. The only regret he expressed in those first days, when the initiative lay wholly with Germany, was for "the poor horses."[2] At that time, the horses were French. Now it was the German steeds that fell—as, by the way, did Franz Marc, the victim of a French artillery bombardment on March 3.

It was not just the unexpected thaw that had brought the German juggernaut to a muddy stagger; it was also the sudden doctrinal and strategic shift General Pétain had brought to the Verdun field of battle. He fought far more like the Germans than he did like any other French general. Everything Falkenhayn and the crown prince had planned was planned according to their conception of a French general—a stereotype they had been engaging in battle since July 1914. But against *this* French general, who fought more like a German one, their plans were practically meaningless and certainly dysfunctional. The German generals were stuck in an unlooked-for strategic quagmire as glutinous as the water-logged Woëvre earth that clutched at the feet and wheels of the German army.

The plan had been to force the French off of the right bank—in the certain knowledge that they, blindly obedient to French military doctrine, would sacrifice everything to retake the territory they had lost. Instead, under General de Langle de Cary, the French evacuated much of the right bank without so much as a fight. Next, under Pétain, they did not launch an offensive to retake it. Yet the Germans had positioned everything in anticipation of just such an offensive. Both the topography of the right bank as well as the (original) disposition of French troops on it were perfectly suited to the flanking attacks the Germans favored. Unlike French commanders, the Germans disdained frontal attacks as far too costly. Falkenhayn in particular conceived the Verdun operation as an opportunity for a cheap victory. But the failure of the French to launch a counteroffensive meant that, on the right bank, the Germans had nothing to flank.

This did, of course, leave the left bank. True, the German heavy artillery was out of range, but even so, many of the French left-bank positions had yet to be reinforced. A German infantry attack across the Meuse was not out of the question. The problem was that it had not been planned for. Whereas the disposition of French troops on the right bank was such that flanks were exposed because the French lines were not straight, on the left bank, the lines were remarkably straight and therefore much more difficult to get around for a flanking attack, let alone a full envelopment. If the French were to be attacked on the left bank, a frontal assault was pretty much the only available option. While waiting for the cannons to be moved, on the last day of February, Erich von Falkenhayn met with Crown Prince Wilhelm and General Schmidt von Knobelsdorf to formulate a new plan.

TO RECOVER AN OPPORTUNITY LOST

It was almost certainly a very tense meeting. As February came to a close, the French army at Verdun was in deep trouble. Yet—stunningly—so was the German army. That force had begun the battle on so triumphal a note that the losses it now sustained were simply outrageous in German eyes—despite the gains that had been made against the French. At the beginning of the battle and to the consternation of Crown Prince Wilhelm, Falkenhayn had retained direct control of the units that would serve as sources of reinforcements. He promised Wilhelm that he would release them as necessary, but when the crown prince called for them, Falkenhayn dribbled out men as a miser, when asked to pony up marks, might ruefully dispense pfennigs instead. Again, some historians believe that this was in keeping with Falkenhayn's plan to let the French bleed themselves white against the Germans rather than devote massive numbers of troops in an attempt to actually break through at Verdun. Others ascribe the generalissimo's pusillanimity not to any plan but to his flawed nature—which was either overcautious or tempered by a degree of humanity that disdained what he saw as the needless effusion of blood.

Who can discover this man's true motive? All that matters is that, in the end, the Germans managed to snatch defeat from the jaws of victory. Since the end of World War I, most historians have agreed that Germany lost its chance to win the war—at least, win it decisively and quickly—when the Schlieffen Plan collapsed at the First Battle of the Marne in September 1914. Many also believe that a second opportunity at a breakthrough leading to victory was lost at Verdun at the end of February 1916, because General von Falkenhayn failed to give free rein to the Fifth Army under Crown Prince Wilhelm.

And so the commanders met. They met to discuss the ongoing status of the campaign in Verdun and the next move for the Fifth Army. Cast in its most positive light, they met to devise a means of recovering lost opportunity. Yet the only really good news Falkenhayn could bring to the discussion was the success of Germany's U-boat campaign against Allied shipping. It was putting the pinch on both Britain and France. For an advocate of attrition, which is above all what Falkenhayn was, this came as a most hopeful development—maybe even as a vindication of his conservative policy at Verdun.

For his part, the crown prince, we can well imagine, chafed at having been forced—both by Falkenhayn's orders and his refusal to release sufficient numbers of reserves—to limit his offensive to the right bank of the Meuse. For now, his men on the right bank were being pounded by French artillery firing from the left. Yet when Falkenhayn asked him about the prospects for the offensive going forward, Crown Prince Wilhelm did not hesitate to respond that the offensive against Verdun should continue. He warned that it would be more costly than originally contemplated, but he believed it held the potential for a major victory of the kind that was proving elusive along the rest of the Western Front.

Wilhelm did have three conditions for continuing the campaign. First, he could no longer be restricted merely to relieving the main attack on the right bank of the Meuse. He needed full permission to attack on the left bank as well. Second, to achieve success in his assault on the left bank, Wilhelm demanded access to adequate reinforcements. Third, Wilhelm told Falkenhayn that he needed the authority to end the campaign if and when German losses began to exceed that of the enemy—that is, when the *German* instrument of attrition began to wear down more rapidly than the *French*. This condition suggests that pessimism and doubt were beginning to inflict the usually enthusiastic Wilhelm, or perhaps it was a growing realism concerning the effectiveness of attrition.

Just as the historical record is ambiguous as to whether the so-called Christmas Memorandum was actually written before the Battle of Verdun or was fabricated after the war, so that same record fails to specify precisely what Falkenhayn actually agreed to when he met with the Fifth Army commanders. That the crown prince and von Knobelsdorf left the meeting and immediately prepared to assault the left bank implies that Falkenhayn did make satisfactory promises and did give the left-bank campaign his required blessing.

PÉTAIN'S IMPROVISATION

An entire army corps—the VI Reserve—was made available to the Fifth Army, and March 6 was set as D-day for the German assault on the left bank. While this attack was in progress, another, simultaneous offensive, was to step off on March 7 against Fort Vaux on the right bank. As the left-bank attack was intended (first and foremost) to neutralize the French artillery wreaking havoc from the rear, so the right-bank attack

Fort Vaux—scene of one of Verdun's most tenacious and heroic stands.
WIKIMEDIA

was intended to silence the guns on and near Fort Vaux, which was about a mile and a half southeast of the fallen Fort Douaumont. These guns were enfilading—firing into the flank—of the Fifth Army on the right bank. No attacking general ever wants to leave an enemy force at his rear, and so destroying or capturing Fort Vaux, on the right bank, was seen as essential to the success of the attack against the left bank.

What the crown prince—and, presumably, Erich von Falkenhayn—saw as a chance to recover lost opportunity, General Pétain regarded as *his* opportunity to reverse the fortunes of war and turn them against Germany. By refusing to play the typecast role of the French general—by not blindly counterattacking on the right bank, where the Germans were in

221

position to envelop any counterattacking force—Pétain left the German Fifth Army only two options. Either attack the French on the left bank—or withdraw from the Verdun sector entirely.

In telling Falkenhayn that attacking the left bank would come with added costs, Crown Prince Wilhelm demonstrated his understanding that conditions on the left bank were indeed different from those on the right. His brother, Rupprecht, Prince of Bavaria, fighting on another front, observed in his diary that the left bank of the Meuse was finally going to be attacked, pessimistically adding that it should have been attacked to begin with because "now the moment of surprise is lost."[3] He did not know how right he was. It was not merely that the German element of surprise was long gone, but that Pétain had actually manipulated Wilhelm into attacking him west of the Meuse.

Generals speak of "good ground" and "bad ground" for a battle. The right bank of the Meuse River was good ground for the kind of battle the German army of 1916 wanted to fight. The rugged landscape, riven by gullies, topped by steep ridges, and sown thickly with tracts of forest, was tailor-made for small-unit infiltration. In combination with massive artillery bombardment, infiltration had proved devastating in the first few days of battle. In contrast, the left bank of the Meuse, while far from flat, is less extreme. The heights are rolling hills rather than precipitous ridges, and the forests, while abundant, are more spread out. Overall, the countryside is far more open and therefore presents "bad ground" for the tactics of infiltration. An assault here would have to be of the kind the Germans disdained. It would need to be frontal rather than flanking, and it would need to be executed massively rather than by small units. In short, it would have to resemble the kind of attack that Joffre had tried over and over in Artois and the Champagne and that Falkenhayn had defended so successfully against, exacting terrible losses from the French.

As Pétain had reformed them, the French lines on the left bank began, in the north, just opposite the village of Brabant, which was on the right bank of the Meuse. From here, the French front line turned southwest toward Forges and then turned again, northwest, around Béthincourt. A little less than a mile almost due south of this village was an elevated patch of forest called Le Mort Homme: "the forest of the dead man." The wooded rise had borne this portentous name, it seems, forever. At least, no one knew—and no one knows—its origin. After many hundreds of years, the name was about to acquire an acutely poignant significance.

A mile, give or take, to the southwest of Le Mort Homme was a nameless hill designated on military maps only as Côte 304—Hill 304, meaning a hill 304 meters high, or about 900 feet in elevation. While this seems a most precise designation, it is in fact misleading. To begin with, the hill was actually just 294 meters high; more importantly, it rose from surrounding land that itself rose 280 meters above sea level.[4] This was typical of the high ground on the left bank. When the Germans attacked Côte 304, they would not be scaling a steep rise but a more gradual slope. Depending on how effectively the position was defended, this would either make the attack easier—a faster climb—or more difficult: exposing the attackers to more defensive fire from more directions for a longer time. Given the German preference for infiltration by small units, the openness of the left bank made it less of a battlefield and more of a killing field. On the rugged right bank, the attackers—German infiltrators—had the advantage. On the more open left bank, the advantage was clearly with the defenders. The gently rising high ground made it relatively easy to position artillery and provided added range and fine visibility. At the same time, it exposed any attack to defensive fire.

Although Pétain established strong positions both on Le Mort Homme and Côte 304, the principal French forts in this portion of the front were nearly three miles southeast of Le Mort Homme, in another forested ridge, called Le Bois Bourrus. Now, it should be noted that, while French forts were equipped with artillery—such as the 155-mm guns that had been mounted in the turret of Fort Douaumont—their primary function was not as artillery platforms but as hardened defensive positions for infantry. The actual artillery batteries were placed behind the forts, which served to provide defensive fire cover for the batteries.

Under Pétain's direction, the pattern of French artillery fire was thoroughly rationalized. No longer would artillery be a disdainful afterthought. For Pétain, it was a top priority. The batteries behind Le Bois Bourrus faced north and were intended to cover the left bank; however, Pétain coordinated this position with batteries and artillery spotters on

Le Mort Homme. When necessary, they could direct their own fire as well as that of Le Bois Bourrus to the right bank.

In Pétain's defense-in-depth system, the main forts were the third—rearmost—line of defense. The artillery and infantry positions on the high ground that was anchored by Le Mort Homme and Côte 304 were the second line. The first line of defense was in front of this ridge and ran through the villages of Forges, Malancourt, and Béthincourt. While Pétain had certainly improved French defenses, he did not have enough men to create true depth. Along nearly nine miles of exposed front, he deployed two divisions plus two brigades. He held one division in reserve. Pétain gave his armies a fighting chance at Verdun, but he could not work a miracle. He was deploying for the purposes of defense army units that had been trained and equipped for attack—to the almost complete neglect of defense. It was an improvisation that stunned the Germans. But, like most improvisations, it was far from perfect.

Assault on the Left Bank

Immediately after meeting with Falkenhayn, the Fifth Army commanders ordered the attack on the left bank. True, the element of surprise was gone—and so the crown prince assembled his forces without even trying to conceal them. Most boldly, his engineers began constructing to the north of French lines, on the *left* bank, Stollen—the same type of covered concrete advance positions that had been built prior to the February 21 assault on the right bank.

Pétain, who was still convalescing from double pneumonia and was thus forced to spend part of each day in bed at his Souilly headquarters, pored over a continual stream of reports. Based on what his observers were seeing—endless columns of German troop transports, the excavation activity to the north—he believed an attack on the left bank was imminent. When, day after day, no attack came, however, Pétain virtually scolded the Germans, grumbling that they "don't know their business."[5] Not that he lay idle. He ordered General de Bazelaire to accelerate all efforts to reinforce defenses throughout the left bank, especially in the north, and he directed unremitting artillery barrages against the German engineers preparing for the attack—whenever it might come.

Come it did, heralded on March 5 by the usual preparatory barrage. The targets of this fire were throughout the left bank, but the principal aim of the crown prince was to neutralize the most deadly French batteries positioned behind the forts. These guns were taking a toll on his forces on the right bank, and he was well aware that they would be used with even more deadly effect against his men when they crossed over to the left.

The preparatory barrage of March 5 was very different from that of February 21. To begin with, the front of March 5 was more compact than that of February 21, so the barrage was concentrated on a smaller area, making it that much more intense. Second, whereas the initial barrage of the battle had been directed primarily against French infantry, the March 5 barrage was focused on the artillery *behind* what was the third line of French defense. The barrage, for the most part, sailed over French infantry deployed in the front line. With their deep respect for firepower, the German commanders saw the greater threat as French artillery rather than French infantry. By destroying as much of the artillery as possible, the Germans not only intended to preserve the lives of *their* infantry, but also to deprive *French* infantry of artillery support, thereby isolating the French front line and rendering it more vulnerable to the German infantry attack on the next day.

By ten o'clock on the morning of March 6, the Bois Bourrus ridge and the batteries behind it had been pounded into one vast landscape of craters. The German infantry advanced in conjunction with a creeping artillery barrage that, this time, was aimed squarely at the frontline French defenders. Despite all of Pétain's defensive improvements, the Germans advanced with startling speed. General Hans von Zwehl unveiled a secret weapon—an armored train mounting heavy artillery that suddenly pulled into position to give the advancing infantry close support that the French could do nothing to neutralize—at least not until the massive smoke plume emanating from the heavily burdened locomotive gave away its position and brought down artillery fire from the surviving guns of the Bois Bourrus. By that time, however, von Zwehl's men were already behind the French first line. Operating in concert with another unit, the Twenty-Second Reserve, von Zwehl enveloped a portion of the French

German troops scale Le Mort Homme during one of numerous attempts to take this key high ground. Note the flamethrower at roughly the center of the top photograph and towards the left in the bottom one. These soldiers still wear the traditional *Pickelhaube* "spiked" helmet. Made of leather or even stiff paper, they were being replaced by the steel "coal scuttle" helmet during 1916. Both types were worn during the long Verdun battle.

line in a pincer movement, trapping them where the Meuse bends at the village of Régnieville.

With the front line cracked wide, the Germans ended March 6 in possession of Régnieville, Forges, and a part of the Côte de l'Oie (Goose Hill, or Ridge). This put the Germans in position to advance against Le Mort Homme, the key French stronghold. On March 7, the Fifth Army unleashed a fresh barrage, more intense than that of the previous day. This was followed by an advance toward Le Mort Homme. By this time, however, French commanders had learned a great deal from the Germans. They did not blindly attempt to retake lost ground. Instead, they promptly answered each German attack with a counterattack, and in this way, they held the frontal assault against Dead Man's Wood first to a crawl, and then they stopped it. By the afternoon of March 7, however, the Germans introduced a second component to the frontal assault—a flanking maneuver from the northeast targeting Le Bois des Corbeaux. If they could take this patch of woods, the Germans would be in position to envelop Le Mort Homme, attacking from the front *and* flank. The *two* sides, German and French, now traded artillery barrages, so that the left bank erupted into great geysers of exploding shells. But, when it came to artillery, the Germans still possessed an overwhelming advantage, and, in due course, Le Bois des Corbeaux fell to the *Bosch.*

THE FOG OF WAR

While the left bank was in total eruption—though generally favoring the German advance—action on the right bank took a stunning turn. German forces closed in on Fort Vaux, taking up positions on the outskirts of the village of that name and fighting to possess it. In a seesaw battle, the village proper changed hands (it was reported) at least thirteen times before finally falling to the Germans. Once in possession of Vaux village, the German troops assaulted nearby Fort Vaux, their assigned objective.

The fights in the village and against the fort were productive of two things: extreme violence and utter confusion. Thanks to the latter, a report was dispatched from the front to the divisional commander, General Hans Karl Moritz von Guretzky-Cornitz, that *Fort* Vaux had been taken. Guretzky-Cornitz saw no reason to doubt the report and so immediately

German troops outside of Fort Vaux. WIKIMEDIA

reported the great news to Imperial Army Headquarters, which, in turn, alerted the press and prompted Kaiser Wilhelm II to confer the Pour le Mérite upon General von Guretzky-Cornitz, who, in the meantime, had already dispatched a substantial detachment to occupy the fort. Even as Guretzky-Cornitz was accepting his decoration, the soldiers he had sent were being mowed down by totally unexpected artillery and machine-gun fire from a Fort Vaux still very much in French hands.

Now it was Joseph Joffre's turn to rejoice prematurely. Without consulting General Pétain in the matter, he transmitted an Order of the Day message directly to the French Second Army. Interpreting the German blunder—the confusion of the name of the village with the name of the fort, which resulted in sending a substantial contingent of men to their deaths—as a triumph of French arms, he congratulated the soldiers of the Second Army. He promised that they were now among "those of whom it will be said—'they barred the way to Verdun!'"[6] Next, having given all credit to the Second Army, Joffre apparently thought better of it and clawed back at least some of that credit for himself, reporting to the National Defense Council of the French cabinet that, as they could now plainly see, *he* never had any intention of abandoning the right bank of the Meuse.

A HEROIC REPRIEVE

Joffre's rejoicing was entirely for the wrong reason. He had no French victory to celebrate. He did, however, have a German blunder to be happy about. The German reversal on the right bank put that operation out of synch with the very real progress the Germans were making on the left bank—albeit at a cost that, despite the crown prince's warning, General von Falkenhayn found terribly disturbing.

As for the French, even Pétain could not permit the Bois des Corbeaux to remain in German hands. Le Mort Homme, to the flank of which the Bois offered access, was far too important to lose. The Bois des Corbeaux, therefore, had to be retaken—and retaken pretty much at all costs. General de Bazelaire accordingly ordered a lieutenant colonel named Macker to recapture the woods with his elite regiment.

Macker had a reputation as a regimental commander steeped in the neo-Napoleonic school of élan vital. A fellow officer described how Macker, after working "out all the movements" of the operation early on the morning of March 8, the day appointed for the counterattack, "then went to array himself appropriately for the great occasion. Being without shaving water, he emptied the remains of a bottle of wine into his mess-tin and dipped his brush into the wine to soap himself. He finally appeared before his men clean and sleek, and so self-possessed that even the most faint-hearted among them found himself reassured and confident of victory."[7]

Macker mustered the battalions of his regiment in three tightly formed waves. Taking up a position at the head of the second wave, "he looked at his watch, lit a cigar, instructed the officer leading the first line not to hurry, because of the distance to be covered, and on the stroke of seven o'clock raised his cane as the signal to start. The chaplain at his post gave them all his blessing. The colonel, stick in hand and cigar between his teeth, led the second wave" on the four-hundred-yard march to the

Bois des Corbeaux.[8] The more they were fired upon by artillery—exploding in the deadly shrapnel of antipersonnel rounds—and machine guns, the more tightly they held their parade formation. At one hundred yards from the perimeter of the woods, Macker ordered his men to fix bayonets. His next order was to charge the woods.

The entire spectacle had all the theatrical makings of a French reenactment of the British charge in the Crimean War that doomed the Light Brigade. Yet, as it turned out, the Germans had arrogantly failed to reinforce their advance. Once the French regiment was inside the wood, the understrength German contingent occupying it was stunned by their audacity as well as by their sheer number. As luck would have it, one of the first to fall in the charge was the German commander, and so, suddenly leaderless, the outnumbered Germans hurriedly fled the woods. Surprise, inferiority of numbers, and absence of command were ample reason for the ignominious withdrawal, but we should not underestimate the "moral effect" of a bayonet attack. In a war that seemed capable of innovating a limitless array of industrial age horrors—high explosives, poison gases, aerial bombardment, machine guns, and on and on—the primitive blade at the end of a heavy rifle wielded at intimate range by a snarling enemy was one horror to which no one seemed to grow accustomed. Throughout World War I, soldiers who had withstood assault by every other weapon and weapon system were often terrified into instant submission or flight by the glint of a bayonet.

With the Bois des Corbeaux once again in French hands, Le Mort Homme was given a reprieve. The Fifth Army despaired, one German chronicler describing the left-bank assault as "utterly collapsed" and calling it a "tragedy."[9] So ended March 8, 1916. But tomorrow would be another day.

CHAPTER 15

Fight for a Dead Man

The war will end at Verdun.
—KAISER WILHELM II, ADDRESS OF APRIL 1 1916[1]

THE GERMAN FLIGHT FROM BOIS DES CORBEAUX AT THE POINT OF Lieutenant Colonel Macker's bayonets was a significant setback, since Le Mort Homme—the Dead Man's Woods—was quite possibly the keystone of the French position on the left bank of the River Meuse. The Germans regrouped on March 9 for a fresh assault on Le Mort Homme, this time through the largely ruined village of Béthincourt to the northwest.

Once again, Macker's regiment stood in the way. It now occupied Bois des Corbeaux, the Forest of Crows. As one of Macker's officers recalled, the German counterattack "developed from the direction of Forges," northeast of Béthincourt, at about six o'clock in the evening of the 9th.[2] The Frenchmen managed to break up the assault with machine gun and rifle fire, even taking fifty German prisoners. On the morning of March 10, the French regiment was reinforced by two additional companies and, thus augmented, ventured out to attack Cumières Wood, due south of their position and just to the east of Le Mort Homme. It was important to seize control of this ground because the Germans could easily use it to attack Le Mort Homme from its eastern flank. Alas, in this endeavor, Lieutenant Colonel Macker was killed by machine-gun fire, along with two other regimental officers. He "fell without uttering a sound."[3]

The demise of the valiant colonel heralded a general assault that evening, beginning at eight. An entire German division swept into Bois des Corbeaux, and "the wood was soon alive with the Boches. Our attenuated

numbers were speedily overborne, and we had lost our commanding officer, though his spirit was still with us. We only gave ground slowly, foot
by foot, and from time to time we went forward and drove them back for
a space." The beleaguered regiment sent up flares as a signal to commence
an artillery barrage in front of the defenders. "But owing to the thickness
of the wood our flares could not be seen by the artillery," so no fire was
forthcoming. The dwindling members of Macker's regiment gradually
withdrew, consoling themselves with the knowledge that, "in their swift
attacks the German infantry suffered terrible losses which prevented any
swift advance, and though we lost our reconquered wood we prevented
the enemy from debouching from it."[4]

Before March 10 dawned, the German assault had taken or retaken
not only Bois des Corbeaux but also Cumières (which changed hands
repeatedly), and then the Côte de l'Oie. Macker's regiment bore the brunt
of most of these assaults. By the time Côte de l'Oie was lost, the French
regiment was almost completely without officers and, on the morning of
the 10th, withdrew from the area, leaving Le Mort Homme to fend for
itself.

SQUALOR

An entire German division had been sent to overwhelm a single depleted
French regiment. By the end of March 10, it had accomplished its mission, but at a cost that was both shocking and profoundly disheartening
to the Germans. With the French having been driven out from around Le
Mort Homme, the Germans on the left bank did not rush to attack this
objective but waited until reinforcements arrived.

March 14 swept winter aside with startling speed. The day was brilliant, the air—though suffused with the acrid scent of cordite and decom-
position—was balmy with the promise of an early spring. The Germans
opened up on Le Mort Homme with an artillery barrage, saturating both
the heights and the area surrounding it. What had been a network of
French trenches was now a growing collection of shell holes. The French
defenders fought from these, falling back from one shell hole to the next.
German attackers, having killed or driven out the French owners of each
shell hole, took possession of each as if it were a palace of great worth.

The advance toward Le Mort Homme was a spectacle of relentless squalor. Men fought fiercely to possess each hole, and the miserable condition of the defenders and the attackers grew increasingly equal as a blood-drenched state of entropy settled over the northwestern portion of the left-bank front in the Fortified Region of Verdun.

On a map, the German commanders could chart the course of their progress. By the close of March 14, they were in possession of the entire eastern end of the French first line. Yet instead of yielding, the French line beat back the German push to take Le Mort Homme itself. How could this be? The maps showed the German advance. The maps showed the inevitability of German victory. But the attrition was staggering. In the relentless fight for Dead Man's Woods, it was the *German* army that was bleeding itself white.

Still, the crown prince and his commanders persisted. Just as, thanks to the arrival of Pétain, the French had learned to fight a murderous defense, so the Germans had become accustomed to something approaching attaque à outrance. And they did not quit.

On March 16, the attackers dragged forward through the spring mud more of their artillery. They used it to deliver a barrage over a broader front, and then they assaulted Le Mort Homme yet again. Yet again, the assault was repulsed. Over the next five days, the Germans kept returning to their objective. The Dead Man: It had never been a particularly attractive ridge, but it was now rotten with craters, eaten away as if by some supernatural mutation of elemental forces. Le Mort Homme was ugly and desolate, yet the Germans persisted in attacking it so that they might possess it, at all costs, a battered and ruined Holy Grail. To each new attempt, on each new day, they added more firepower, always widening the barrage in an effort to keep the defenders at a distance.

By March 21, the unremitting German shellfire had eliminated the utility of Le Mort Homme as a position for artillery spotters, let alone as a platform for artillery. There would be no dishonor in suspending the fight here and turning to other objectives. But the Fifth Army commanders were not so inclined. It is as if they had caught the infection from Joffre and his subordinates, always willing to double down on the most elusive and costly of objectives. The great irony, of course, is that Pétain emulated the earlier habits of the Germans. He made the most of defensive firepower. While avoiding futile assaults—the *métier* of the French disciples of Colonel de Grandmaison—he insisted on taking defensive stands sufficiently stubborn to invite the German attackers to break themselves upon them.

The cost to both sides was astronomical. As the end of March approached, 89,000 poilus had been killed, along with 81,607 *Boches*, on the left bank, where combat was focused on the now-ruined Le Mort Homme. While the German instrument of attrition was being ground away somewhat more gradually than the French, a certain gloomy panic decanted through the German ranks, replacing the exhilarating elixir of conquest that had flowed freely during February. The left bank *was* a very different environment from the right. Open to begin with—and therefore unsuited to the tactics of infiltration that were the Germans' strong suit—the landscape of the left bank was now so battered that it had been beaten into a certain uniformity of appearance. Shell holes provided cover for defenders, whereas attackers had to move *en masse* across great swaths of leveled landscape. There, artillery, machine guns, and rifle fire cut them down like sheaves of wheat.

The Germans still enjoyed a major advantage in artillery firepower, but the infantry weapon that had created such terror in the early days of the battle, the portable flamethrower, was now quite often an instrument of fiery suicide. The fuel tanks the soldiers wielding the flamethrowers wore on their backs made them conspicuous targets. A bullet piercing a tank would, at the very least, transform the man attached to it into a human torch. More often than not, a direct hit on a tank resulted in an explosion that took out not only the man with the flamethrower but anyone near him as well. If, however, the man and not the tank was struck by a bullet, depending on the range of the assailant and the weapon used—rifle or machine gun—the force of the incoming round often spun the wounded man around, so that an entire line of his companions in arms was swept by flame.

CÔTE 304

Battered as Le Mort Homme was, French artillery spotters and even French artillerymen were able to salvage some usable ground on that now all but shapeless mound. Yet it became clear to the Fifth Army commanders that French fire from nearby Côte 304—Hill 304—was taking a severe toll on any attempt to finally capture Le Mort Homme. For this reason, even as they continued to throw one assault after the other against Le Mort Homme, the Germans decided to turn their attention simultaneously to Côte 304. Pétain had deployed his artillery, meager as it was, for maximum leverage. Crossfire abounded. To take Le Mort Homme, Côte 304 had to be taken, but the guns that had been returned to Le Mort Homme presented a grave danger to any unit attempting to take Côte 304.

It was a conundrum, but the attackers had to start somewhere, and Côte 304 was their choice. They mounted their assault from a position between the villages of Malancourt and Avocourt, well to the west of the main battlespace. This was particularly dangerous ground for the Germans, since it was firmly held by the French and heavily fortified. But, the crown prince and von Knobelsdorf decided, establishing a base of attack here was worth the risk and the losses. If possessing Côte 304 was necessary to possessing Le Mort Homme, which was, in turn, necessary to possessing the left bank of the Meuse in the Fortified Region of Verdun, possessing the line between Malancourt and Avocourt was necessary to get at Côte 304. The logic of this blood-soaked puzzle seemed to dictate a highly hazardous course. There was really no choice.

The Fifth Army commanders selected the crack Eleventh Bavarian Division to make the assault. Deep behind the French forward lines, the Bavarians excavated Stollen and began undermining—tunneling under—French defenses. The mines would be packed with explosive charges and remotely detonated. The objective was to bury the French defenders in their own trenches. Mining was covert work, yet the French were pretty generally aware of it, and they continually bombarded the engineers constructing the Stollen as well as those excavating the mines. The bombardment took a heavy toll. No matter, the Bavarians persisted—even after several of their mines failed to detonate.

In the end, it was the human factor, not tunnels and explosive charges, that made the difference. The Bois d'Avocourt was a wooded tract between Avocourt and Malancourt. It was held by the French Twenty-Ninth

Division, a unit that had been absorbing punishment since the very beginning of operations in and around Verdun. Morale had long ago vanished. An alarming number of men deserted daily, deliberately drifting into the hands of the Germans, to whom they revealed much about quick passages through a landscape thickly sown with barbed wire and other obstacles. Armed with such extraordinarily detailed intelligence and presented with a rare opportunity to once again exercise the tactics of infiltration, the Bavarians attacked on March 20, handily eviscerating the Twenty-Ninth Division at Avocourt and capturing an entire French brigade—nearly three thousand troops—at a single blow.

It was a French disaster and, even worse, a disgrace. Strangely enough, however, it created more outrage than panic among the left-bank defenders. The French gunners responded with a furious bombardment of the German-occupied Bois d'Avocourt, and when, on March 22, the Bavarians attempted a breakout toward Côte 304, French machine guns opened up from every conceivable angle, slaughtering the attackers by the battalion. Nevertheless, by March 28, the Germans had advanced to the western slope of Côte 304, and the French line in this area was folded back on itself. Still, the French continued to fight. On March 29, they rushed men into the Bois d'Avocourt, determined to repair the breached line at this point. Lieutenant Colonel Henri de Malleray, who had gained fame before the war as a writer on military subjects, led the assault and succeeded in retaking a portion of the occupied woods before machine-gun fire severed both of his legs from his torso, leaving him mortally wounded and helpless. That very evening, his young son, a second lieutenant, was on his way to the woods when he ran into his father's commanding officer. The youngster, having learned that his father had retaken a piece of Bois d'Avocourt but unaware of the horrific wound that had by this time killed him, asked the colonel if he was pleased with his father. The battle-hardened officer found no words except to exclaim, "Ah! Mon pauvre petit!"[5] (Ah! My poor boy!).

Once again, on a map and by the numbers, the Germans were unmistakably gaining—not nearly as fast and as far as at the beginning of the battle, but they were gaining ground at the expense of the French, and they were killing more of the French than the French were killing them. But that was just it. The French *were* killing them, a lot of them. What is more, the battle was wearing down the attackers, even those who had escaped death or injury. They were tired. Despite being told of the progress they were making, they were becoming demoralized. Disturbing reports were reaching the top echelons of German command: Men were doing the unthinkable in a German army. They were refusing orders to advance. They were ignoring orders to attack. The small-unit approach that had served the Germans so well early in the battle began to work against them now. Although overall German losses were, at this point, still less than those on the French side, entire small units—companies, platoons, squads, combat teams—were often wiped out. To survivors in these units, it appeared that the entire German army was being decimated.

Still, the Germans inched forward. The village of Malancourt fell on March 31. On April 5, Haucourt was in German hands, followed on the 8th by Béthincourt—or the rubble that was left of it. Mindful of the German losses, which were grievous, and the French, substantially heavier, Kaiser Wilhelm II declared that, whereas the Franco-Prussian War had been decided at Paris, the current war would be decided at Verdun.

It was the ultimate absurdity, but it sounded like the ultimate truth. The French had disdained Verdun, had stripped its forts of guns and garrisons. The Germans? Well, Falkenhayn had seen it as an opportunity for a cheap victory. Now *both* sides spoke of Verdun as the most important tract of real estate on the planet—certainly the most important in this "Great War." The more it was reduced to ruin, the more valuable it appeared.

By early April, the Germans decided to attack Côte 304 and Le Mort Homme simultaneously. On April 4, two German divisions attained control of the top of Le Mort Homme for the first time, and by April 9, the Germans had also taken the crest of Côte 304.

Attaining this high ground should have meant the collapse of the French left bank. Yet the French second and third lines held. The very day after the Germans had taken Côte 304, Pétain issued to his armies an Order of the Day that began, "The 9th of April was a glorious day for our forces" and concluded with a paraphrase of Joan of Arc: *"Courage! On les aura!"* (Courage! We will get them!).[6]

Volcano

Despite the fact that the Germans were atop Le Mort Homme, it smoldered like a volcano, and nobody really knew who was in control of it. In fact, it became a suffocating stage on which portions of the two opposing armies blindly contested. Possession of the top was entirely fluid. What seemed most solid was the pall of heavy smoke that would neither drift off nor blow away. Germans might be driven off by French, and French by Germans, but the dense cloud seemed destined to possess the battered hill forever.

The French were exhausted, the German soldiers dispirited. Yet the German commanders kept attacking, fueled by reports of their own successes. In the end, both sides claimed April 9 as a high point on the road toward victory. The French counted German corpses and rejoiced. The Germans held the top of Le Mort Homme.

But then the rains came, torrential spring rains that brought a halt to the fighting atop and around Le Mort Homme for nearly the next two weeks. Sickness brought on by exposure outstripped bullets and exploding shells as causes of death—though by the end of April, the French opened fire on the German positions atop Le Mort Homme, firing from positions that included Côte 304. In response, on May 3, more than five hundred German cannon directed their fire along a tight front about a mile wide that included Côte 304. Instead of assaulting this position yet again with infantry, the Germans decided simply to blast the French off the heights with heavy artillery. In fact, they were not so much blown off the hill as they were buried alive in fresh shell craters.

The German fire destroyed French machine-gun emplacements on Côte 304, cut off supplies of food as well as ammunition, and prevented both reinforcement and evacuation of the wounded. The high ground in any battle is typically associated with mastery of the tactical situation. In the case of the bombarded French on Côte 304, the heights were the embodiment of chaos.

At last, the Germans breached the chaos by finally launching an infantry assault. Even with the French position atop the hill greatly compromised, it took the Germans several days of bloody fighting to attain the summit. Once there, the fighting in this small area unfolded intensely over three days. At last, however, Côte 304 was captured, and the French fire against German-held Le Mort Homme was extinguished.

Now the German guns zeroed in on Le Mort Homme, an "intense barrage," Crown Prince Wilhelm wrote in his memoirs, that "was at once a magnificent and awe-inspiring sight." As "Mort Homme flamed like a volcano," the very "air and earth alike trembled at the shock of thousands of bursting shells."[7] This was followed by the infantry attack. At first, Wilhelm's chief of staff, observing from Bois de Consenvoye, frantically telephoned headquarters to report the apparent failure of the attack as troops fell back. "I was able to correct him," Wilhelm wrote. "What he had seen were the crowds of [French] prisoners!"[8] Astoundingly, considering the extent of the artillery and infantry assault and the absence of fire from Côte 304, it would require nearly a month—the rest of May—for the Germans to take the whole of Le Mort Homme.

Nivelle Takes Command

Throughout April, Erich von Falkenhayn was unimpressed with the slow progress of the Fifth Army. Yes, the French were dwindling. Yes, meter by meter, they were yielding territory on the left bank. But the cost was far beyond anything he had imagined.

During this same month, Joseph Joffre was having second thoughts about Philippe Pétain. He could not deny that Pétain had saved the Verdun sector from instant collapse, but it seemed to Joffre that he had saved it only to deliver it into an agonizing process of attrition. Joffre was therefore ready to try something else. Or rather, he was ready to go back to his old ways. He wanted a general who would return to the offensive, to attaque à outrance.

The problem for Joffre was that Pétain had been *his* choice to take the place of de Langle de Cary. These days, Joffre was fending off a lot of criticism of his habit of choosing officers only to replace them a short time later. He conceded that his critics even had a point. Anointing and then replacing commanders was indeed hard on morale and courted defeatism. The solution, Joffre decided, was to *replace* Pétain by *promoting* him. Doing so would not only ratify his own sagacity in having chosen Pétain in the first place, it would allow him to replace him without drawing criticism. After all, if you promote an officer from one position to another, you need to put somebody else in the original position.

Although Pétain was directing the entire Battle of Verdun, he was officially commander of nothing more or less than the Second Army. Joffre bumped him up to command of the Central Group of Armies, which included the Second, Third, Fourth, and Fifth Armies. To command Second Army in Pétain's place, Joffre chose General Robert Nivelle, who, in the conduct of war in the Fortified Region of Verdun, would nominally report to Pétain but actually answer directly to the GQG.

Pétain understood perfectly what was going on—not that he could do anything about it. Nivelle was his antithesis, the ultimate advocate of offense as Pétain was the ultimate champion of defense. Nivelle believed with his whole soul in all-out-attack. If there was anything Pétain could take comfort in, it was that Nivelle did, in one respect, differ significantly from other French officers of the Grandmaison persuasion. Unlike them, he never disdained artillery. Trained as an artillery officer, he believed fervently in firepower. As historian John Mosier put it, Nivelle "realized that howitzers were preferable to bayonets."[9]

Born of a French father and an English mother, Nivelle was raised a Protestant, which proved a boon to his rise in the military. The French army of the late nineteenth century was rife with suspicion of ultra-Catholic officers. Educated at the École Polytechnique, he entered the army in 1878, served in the artillery in Algeria, Tunisia, and in China—during the Boxer Rebellion (1898–1901)—and by the eve of World War I was an artillery colonel of high reputation.

At fifty-seven in 1913, he was also younger than most of his fellow senior officers, who were already in their sixties. Besides, he looked and acted younger than a man even in late middle age. He was dashing, vigorous, brimming with energy, and yet possessed of an eminently Gallic savoir faire and aplomb that instantly inspired confidence in anyone with whom he came into contact. He spoke well and with precision—the same precision with which he handled artillery. His use of artillery in countering one German attack after another was given much credit for the French victory at the First Battle of the Marne in September 1914. Even in the Alsace, during the disastrous Battle of the Frontiers in August–September 1914, and at the inconclusive First Battle of the Aisne that followed the First Marne, it was Nivelle's performance as an artillerist that gave the French something to recall with admiration. His assignment to command of the Second Army at Verdun, which took effect on May 1, 1916, was accompanied by a promotion to the rank of *general de division.*

THE RETURN TO FORT DOUAUMONT

Surprisingly, Robert Nivelle did not turn his immediate attention to the left bank, where the fight for Le Mort Homme seemed to be in its terminal yet interminable final stage. Instead, he listened eagerly to the plan of General Charles Emmanuel Marie Mangin, commander of the Fifth Division of the Second Army.

A relative youngster at just fifty in 1916, Mangin had been born in Sarrebourg, in the Moselle region of Lorraine. He was just five years old when the Prussian victory in the 1870–1871 war carved up his homeland, and he came of age with a vengeful passion for the profession of arms. Failing on his first try to gain entrance to the French military academy of Saint-Cyr, he enlisted in the Seventy-Seventh Infantry Regiment in 1885, reapplied to the academy the following year, and was enrolled. He fought in all the French colonial hotspots, including Sudan, Mali, and French North Africa. After serving in the Fashoda Expedition on the White Nile in 1898, he commanded a battalion in Tonkin (today the northernmost province of Vietnam) during 1901–1904 and then participated in the occupation of Senegal from 1906 to 1908.

Mangin's experience in colonial warfare shaped his concept of battle, which was primal and brutal, and it also gave him a profound respect for the African colonial soldier. In 1910, he published a book titled *La force noire*—The Black Force—in which he argued that the French Colonial Forces would become an indispensable asset in what everyone believed was the great European war that was bound to come.

The face of Charles Mangin was marked by the ferocity of his colonial career. To modern eyes, he bears an uncanny resemblance to Joseph Stalin, a broad, thin-lipped mouth set in perpetual half-grimace beneath a thick black moustache. He came into World War I believing absolutely

General Charles Mangin; his men nicknamed him "The Butcher"—and not to honor his prowess in the killing of Germans. WIKIMEDIA

Members of the Forty-Third Battalion of Senegalese *Tirailleurs* hold a banner inscribed with their victory in retaking Fort Douaumont. WIKIMEDIA

in attaque à outrance and in the "savage" sovereign effectiveness of the North African *Tirailleur* in any attack.

Tirailleurs—"shooters" or, more precisely, skirmishing shooters—were recruited from the French colonial population beginning in the 1840s and proved highly effective. Mangin used them to great effect in the Battle of Charleroi (August 21–23, 1914), which nevertheless ended in defeat. Mangin's ferocity stood in stark contrast to his colleagues, who had accepted the wisdom of retreat in that battle. He was both admired—by the likes of Joseph Joffre—and despised, chiefly by the very men under his command, who called him "The Butcher." His response to this assessment was encapsulated in a pronouncement that became infamous: *"Quoi qu'on fasse, on perd beaucoup de monde"* (Whatever you do, you lose a lot of men).[10]

What Mangin proposed to Nivelle was to act on an idea he had first suggested in the closing days of April. It was to recapture Fort Douaumont. This objective was right out of old school French doctrine: Number one, yield no ground. Number two, immediately recover whatever ground

243

you have yielded. He told Nivelle that the operation would require no less than four full infantry divisions supported by artillery—this in the midst of a desperate and losing struggle for the left bank. What could possibly have moved Nivelle to listen to him seriously?

As a proponent of both attaque à outrance and firepower, Nivelle was a rare hybrid among French officers, who, more typically, were either champions of infantry in extreme attack (the majority) or firepower in the service of defense in depth (Pétain's position—a minority view). Nivelle seems to have believed that his guns could physically break through Fort Douaumont and that a heavy infantry follow-up would thereby overwhelm the dazed and exposed defenders.

If this was indeed the case, it was a peculiar delusion, given the recent history of Fort Douaumont. It had been captured by a German sergeant, three junior officers, and a portion of a Pionier company. Their success was due to the fact that the fort had been all but totally abandoned by the French. Forty-odd overage Territorials, unarmed, were not terribly difficult to overpower. As to the condition of the fort, even after suffering continual bombardment by heavy German guns, it was mostly intact—sufficiently so to serve the German occupiers as a forward base. In fact, the effect of the German and then French artillery bombardment had been to render Fort Douaumont, as an objective of infantry attack, stronger than ever before. The landscape surrounding the fort was pocked by shell craters and thus transformed into an obstacle course destined to impede any overland assault. Moreover, the fort now anchored a very strong German position. Not only had troops fanned out and moved forward from Fort Douaumont, all the territory east of it was solidly German and had been so for some time. Any infantry assault would move slowly—and be exposed to German fire on *three* sides.

"Whatever you do, you lose a lot of men." Verdun was demonstrating the truth of this maxim. But did this obligate commanders to do things—impossible things—destined to lose quite so many men?

After taking command, Nivelle authorized the Mangin assault. By way of preparation, he launched an artfully orchestrated artillery barrage and, on May 22, sent elements of the Fifth and Thirty-Sixth Divisions to storm Fort Douaumont.

At first, the assault went remarkably well. Thanks to the barrage and to vigorous antiaircraft gunnery, which took down six German observation balloons, the occupiers of the fort did not see the approach of the French. In consequence, the first wave was on top of the fort within eleven minutes of commencing the assault.

It did not matter. Despite all the disdain the French high command had heaped upon the very idea of concrete fortifications, the triumphant force that now swarmed over the carapace of Fort Douaumont could find no way to penetrate it. They were effectively marooned on a concrete island. The German defenders picked them off, one by one, using rifle fire alone. The process took a day and a half. By May 23, the attackers were either dead or prisoners of war.

THE CHANGING CALCULUS OF ATTRITION

Even Charles Mangin was dissuaded from attempting another assault on Fort Douaumont. As for Robert Nivelle, he rapidly shifted course—back to the defense-in-depth ethos of his predecessor. By this time, however, the end of May, the Germans had managed to capture all of Le Mort Homme as well as the nearby village and wood of Cumières. For his part, Crown Prince Wilhelm believed that the left bank was about to collapse. All he had to do is hold on and wait.

Indeed, the French commanders had plenty to worry about. The left bank was in general retreat. The right bank was imperiled—potentially by an incalculable mass of German manpower still east of the Verdun sector. From the moment the Battle of Verdun began, Joseph Joffre had been appealing to his British colleagues to contribute to an offensive on the Somme, northwest of Meuse. Now a battle on the Somme had new urgency. Joffre saw it as a means of taking pressure off Verdun, a sector undeniably undergoing collapse.

On the German side, as of the end of May 1916, if Crown Prince Wilhelm felt some sense of achievement, Erich von Falkenhayn was far from flushed with triumph. Verdun was supposed to have been a cheap victory. If the German army managed to break through, fine. But the point of operations here was that, even if the army *failed* to break through, Germany would still win by the mere fact of inexorably wearing away the French army. The reality was different. By the end of May, with Germany in possession of the Dead Man, Falkenhayn counted up his losses. It now seemed to him quite possible that Germany's losses at Verdun had climbed above those of France. The instrument of attrition appeared to be wearing down faster than its object.

CHAPTER 16

"They Shall Not Pass!"

"Whatever you do, you lose a lot of men."
—GENERAL CHARLES MANGIN[1]

THE DESOLATION THAT WAS THE FORTIFIED REGION OF VERDUN IN spring 1916 was concentrated along both banks of the Meuse River. To those fighting there, it must have seemed the entire universe. Everything else—home, farm, factory—was a distant memory, maybe a dream. There was, however, a world beyond the Meuse, and, in this *world* war, what happened in that wider world mattered.

In contrast to the frozen lines of the Western Front, the Eastern Front was all about movement. The armies of Russian czar Nicholas II were the biggest of any combatant. The total numbers mobilized were some 12 million, compared with (at their height) 8.4 million for France, 8.9 million for Great Britain, 5.6 million for Italy, and 4.3 million for the late entry on the Allied side, the United States. Between 1914 and 1918, Germany mobilized 12 million, Austria-Hungary 7.8 million, and Turkey 1.2 million. The Allies took comfort in the immensity of the Russian army, referring to it as the "Russian steamroller," and yet its performance ranged consistently from disappointing to disastrous. In the great Battle of Tannenberg, fought during just four days, from August 26 to August 30, 1914, Russia lost 170,000 killed, wounded, or captured out of the 230,000 men of its Second Army.

The exception to this dismal record was achieved by General Alexei A. Brusilov, a rarity among the czar's high commanders in that he was not only courageous but highly skilled. On June 4, 1916, he moved against the Austro-German line in two places. He did so in a series of maneuvers that were not only well planned and well executed but were not preceded by any of the usual preliminaries: the massing of troops or the use of artillery preparation. Thus surprise was total, complete, and devastating, and he managed to rout virtually the entire Austrian Fourth Army, with the Seventh soon following it into perdition. Seventy thousand prisoners fell to Brusilov's Offensive, which penetrated deeply into Galicia and the Hapsburg Empire, igniting panic not only in Vienna but in Berlin as well. Immediately, four German divisions were transferred from the Western Front to the Eastern, where the Germans planned an offensive for July. For the Germans, this gave a sudden urgency to bringing the Battle of Verdun to a successful conclusion. After taking Le Mort Homme, Crown Prince Wilhelm had shifted back to the aggressively defensive posture that served the Fifth Army so well early in the Verdun battle. His intention was to create the conditions in which the French, badly weakened on the left bank, would have no choice but to relinquish it. Urgency gave Wilhelm reason to return to the offensive.

FROM LEFT TO RIGHT

In shifting back to the offensive, Crown Prince Wilhelm also shifted from the left to the right bank of the Meuse. Satisfied that Le Mort Home and Côte 304 were firmly in German hands and that, therefore, the left bank was neutered if not utterly neutralized and completely won, Wilhelm redoubled efforts to capture the remaining French forts on the right bank. The most important of these were Forts Vaux and Souville, both south of Fort Douaumont.

By no means had the Germans been inactive on the right bank. Early in March, they were beginning efforts to isolate and cut off the two forts, but it was not until the impetus of the Brusilov Offensive that they opened up an artillery bombardment of Fort Vaux on June 2.

It was the smallest of all the forts associated with Verdun—less than a quarter of the size of Fort Douaumont. The only guns it had been equipped with were French 75s. Those that could be removed had been, during the high command's general gutting of all forts in the Verdun sector. Fort Vaux was left with a turret that mounted a permanently installed

On June 12, 1916, German artillery opened up on a trench west of Fort Douaumont, instantly burying Three Company, 137th Infantry Regiment. The men were forgotten until after the war, when French teams exploring the battlefield discovered bayonets affixed to rusty rifle barrels, protruding from the ground. Upon excavation, a corpse was found with each rifle and bayonet. Seventy men were buried alive here. The story of the "Tranchée des Baionettes" ("Bayonet Trench") captured the world's imagination. WIKIMEDIA

A German soldier takes aim from behind a ridge near Fort Vaux. Note the dead poilu (his nationality evident from his "Adrian" helmet) to his left. IMPERIAL WAR MUSEUM

75, but the turret had been destroyed by a German 420-mm shell shortly after the fall of Fort Douaumont. So, in June 1916, Fort Vaux had nothing bigger than a machine gun.

But, in contrast to Fort Douaumont at the time of its fall, Fort Vaux was fully garrisoned when the Germans attacked it on June 2. It also had been fitted with a heavy reinforced concrete top, which survived even the 420-mm shell impacts that had wrecked the turret. Much of the fort's superstructure had been gnawed away by the big guns, whose shells fell at the rate of 1,500 to 2,000 an hour during the height of the preparatory barrage. Nevertheless, the internal corridors and stations were intact and sheltered the garrison, which was commanded by Major Sylvain-Eugene Raynal.

Raynal had not begun the war as a garrison commander. Far from that tame duty, he was in charge of a regiment of Algerian Tirailleurs—the fierce elite colonials in whom General Mangin put so much stock. Wounded by machine-gun fire in September 1914 and then even more severely injured by an artillery shell impact on his command post four months later, he spent ten months in a hospital before he was released, barely able to hobble. He should have been discharged but, at his request, he was retained by the army and assigned to garrison duty, which was considered an alternative to a frontline command. That is how he found himself commanding a desperate stand in June.

After pounding the fort with artillery, German infantry held it under siege, periodically storming it, only to be repulsed each time. On June 3, attackers penetrated the wall and entered the tunnels leading to the main barracks. Raynal and his men had set up sandbag barricades from behind which they fought the invading Germans, taking a heavy toll on the attackers. With the electricity cut off, much of the claustrophobic "battlefield" was pitch black, pierced by flashlights, hand-carried battle lanterns, and even candles. It was also incredibly crowded. Not only did Raynal have his assigned complement of 250 garrison troops, he was also sheltering an additional 350 poilus who had sought refuge from exposed combat outside. Many of these men were wounded. As the enemy entered the tunnels and corridors, firing as they walked or crawled, the Frenchmen made a slow fighting retreat, withdrawing foot by foot, piling more sandbag barricades as the Germans made their gradual gains. Bullets ricocheted, and men—on both sides—died. The smell of decomposing bodies overwhelmed the choking fumes of cordite.

On June 4, the invaders suddenly withdrew from the tunnels and corridors. There was blessed silence, but, soon enough, black smoke began billowing through the darkness. A cry of "Gas! Gas!" But it was neither gas nor a false alarm. It was the product of flamethrowers, whose nozzles a team of German Pioniere had thrust into whatever apertures in the battered fort's structure they could find. Their intention was to smoke out the remains of Raynal's garrison. A Lieutenant Girard ran into one densely smoke-filled corridor to recover a precious machine gun that had been abandoned in the initial panic of what was believed to be a gas attack. He recovered the weapon before passing out from near-asphyxiation. It served now as the garrison's principal defense. At length, the flamethrowers ran

"The Last of Fort Vaux: The Gallant Commander's Farewell to the Wounded," an illustration created for the London-based *Graphic* "by Paul Thiriat, our special artist with the French forces, from material supplied by one of the heroic defenders." AUTHOR'S COLLECTION.

out of fuel, and Raynal ordered all vents to be opened. A second attempt at smoking out the garrison was tried elsewhere in the fort. This time, the defenders were able to sweep the Pioniere with the machine gun before they could begin their attack in earnest.

Periodically throughout the siege, Raynal released carrier pigeons—he had four of them from a signal unit that had sheltered in the fort—in futile attempts to call for relief. After the flamethrower assault, he scrawled another message: "We are still holding. But . . . relief is imperative. Communicate with us by Morse-blinker from Souville, which does not reply to our calls." Then he added, "This is my last pigeon."[2]

By the night of the June 4 flamethrower assault, the water collected and stored in cisterns was all but exhausted. Thirst became a problem more pressing than flamethrowers and machine-gun fire. A rainstorm on June 5 partially replenished their supply, but it was not much. On the night of June 5, a relief column materialized, only to be cut down by a German artillery barrage. Without hope of rescue and with water once again running out, Raynal distributed the last of the available supply—a half pint per man—and attempted to signal Fort Souville in Morse code using a blinker lamp. There was no reply. During June 6, the biggest excitement was an outburst of madness from a lieutenant, who suddenly threatened to end all their collective misery by detonating a stockpile of hand grenades. That night, the remnant of the garrison sought relief from their thirst by licking the slime off the corridor and tunnel walls.

Early on the morning of June 7, Major Raynal sent out an officer and two men with a white flag. A Lieutenant Werner Müller, commanding a machine-gun battery, was the first to see the emissaries. He beckoned to them. The officer handed Müller a letter addressed "To the Commander of the German Forces Attacking Fort Vaux." Müller handed the letter to his captain, and the two German officers followed the surrender party into one of the fort's tunnels. A pair of sooty and malodorous poilus snapped to attention and escorted the officers to Major Raynal. A set of surrender terms was quickly written, the major signed them, and, in handing back the document, also presented the German captain with a garishly ornamented bronze key of the type a proud village mayor might present to some visiting hero. It was the key to Fort Vaux.

Of the 600 men who had been crammed into Fort Vaux, 163 were killed during the siege, and 191 more were wounded. Two hundred forty-six—together with Major Raynal's pet cocker spaniel—presented themselves as prisoners of war. The toll on the 5,200 German attackers was a staggering 2,740 killed and wounded, among which were sixty-four officers. In the end, it was thirst—not the more than five thousand soldiers of the German army—that had conquered the little fort. Before he joined his men for transportation to a prisoner-of-war camp—they would spend the next two and a half years there, until released on November 11, 1918—Major Raynal was led to the headquarters of Crown Prince Wilhelm. He greeted the major and presented him with a sword captured earlier from a French officer. It was a sign of profound respect—and one of those peculiar chivalric gestures that periodically marked a war of bestial brutality conducted on a vast industrial scale in places of darkest squalor.

OBSESSION

The eyes of the world, it was repeatedly said throughout the entire Battle of Verdun, were on this patch of Europe. But throughout their weeklong ordeal, Raynal and his men felt they were entirely alone, cut off from everyone except those who wanted to kill them. They were aware of troop activity outside, but they had no way of knowing that no less a figure than General Robert Nivelle repeatedly ordered attacks intended to rescue the small heroic garrison. Between June 2 and June 6, he sent in five missions. All were slaughtered, virtually to a man.

This did not stop Nivelle. The cost of rescuing mere men might be too great but that of aiding heroes was beyond price. When the fifth mission, which consisted of four companies of infantry—heavily burdened, oddly enough, with useless scaling ladders, as if assigned to take a medieval castle—failed on June 6, Nivelle organized another to be sent in on June 8. It was much larger. Of brigade strength, it was no ordinary brigade. Nivelle designated it a "Brigade de Marche," and it was composed of elite units gathered from all over the Verdun sector. As it was being assembled on June 6, Nivelle convened a council of war with some twenty of his generals, all of whom, it seems, had had enough. They objected vociferously to the idea of sacrificing this so-called Brigade de Marche, which was to be drawn not from the right bank but from the extremely imperiled left.

Nivelle would hear none of it. The more unanimous and strenuous the objections, the firmer he stood. On June 7 came the news that Fort Vaux had surrendered. If Nivelle's subordinates breathed a sigh of relief that the insane expedition of the Brigade de Marche was now rendered moot, they soon found that the jeopardy remained. Nivelle scoffed at the "news" as just another German deception—a pure hoax intended to demoralize the French troops. With that, Nivelle affirmed that the mission would go forward, and he personally addressed two regiments of North African colonials who had been hand-picked for service in the special brigade. He congratulated the men on having been selected "for the finest mission that any French unit can have, that of going to the aid of comrades in arms who are valiantly performing their duty under tragic circumstances."[3]

Few events in the Verdun saga—a battle whose sheer futility, built on a combination of industrial-scale warfare, outmoded doctrine, and contradictory motives, seemed to epitomize World War I itself—were more sadistically absurd than Nivelle's insistence on sacrificing a specially assembled elite brigade to save a comparative handful of other French soldiers, soldiers now reported to have surrendered. And yet the mission was pushed forward through a driving rainstorm that rendered the terrain "so slippery," according to one sergeant major, "and so difficult . . . that one marches as much on one's knees as one's feet."[4]

The ordeal of merely marching under severe weather conditions was made that much more terrible by the fact that the colonials had been continuously engaged on the front and were drained. Reportedly, one African soldier committed suicide rather than set out that morning. In any event, only one of the two colonial regiments—they were Moroccans—made it as far as the vicinity of Fort Vaux, where, in the blinding rain, they ran headlong into a German attack bound for Fort Tavannes, just south of Fort Vaux. The other colonial regiment, the Second Zouaves, never even left their point of departure. The German artillery, which was to clear the way for the attack on Fort Tavannes, was turned on them instead. A barrage of 210-mm howitzer fire virtually annihilated the Zouaves.

French artillery was doing much the same against the German attack bound for Fort Tavannes, however. Those who survived the barrage did battle with the Moroccans outside of Fort Vaux. As their commander later reported, they attacked one another, withdrew, then attacked again. In the meantime, the Germans occupying what was left of Fort Vaux evacuated. When the Moroccans ventured in to occupy the fort, the Germans attacked from the outside, and the Moroccans withdrew. In the end, both the Germans and the Moroccans, substantially diminished in number, turned away from Fort Vaux entirely. "The Vaux garrison has capitulated," the colonial commander reported. "Nothing is left in the attacking battalions but debris."[5] It was a strange note. The "debris" that had been Fort Vaux was now conflated with the "debris" that had been the "battalions" assigned to recapture the fort. Ruin, of things and of people, was universal.

Philippe Pétain's "promotion" to commander of the French central army group had left Robert Nivelle in charge of the Second Army. Protocol as well as the implied will of Joseph Joffre dictated that the actions of that army were entirely Nivelle's prerogative. But Pétain was unquestionably his senior and, at the risk of offending Joffre and even humiliating Nivelle in the eyes of his subordinates, Pétain intervened after this failed and futile attack with what seemed a commonsense order: There would be no new attempts to retake Fort Vaux, abandoned now by both armies.

Green Cross

The fall of Fort Vaux and the ground it had defended did not bring about a major breakthrough on the right bank, but it did encourage the local German commanders, who decided that the right bank, like the left, was now ripe for the taking at last.

Neither the French nor the Germans had shown themselves averse to trying—over and over again—tactics that had failed over and over again. On June 22, however, the Germans added a new element to the usual preparatory artillery barrage. It had started the day before as the customary storm of high-explosive shells. The objective of the attack was obvious to the French. Fort Souville, southwest of Fort Vaux and northwest of Fort de Tavannes, fronted artillery that swept the two main ridges running to the Meuse. The system of forts throughout the right bank of the Verdun sector was essentially oriented with respect to these two natural obstacles. The idea was that the forts would catch any advancing army, hemmed in by the ridges, in an artillery crossfire. With Forts Douaumont, Vaux, and Tavannes neutralized or in German hands, Fort Souville was almost all that stood between the principal German lines and the city of Verdun. Take Fort de Tavannes, Verdun would fall, and the right bank would surely crumble.

Clearly, this is what the Germans now aimed to do. General Schmidt von Knobelsdorf assembled thirty thousand men, spearheaded by an Alpine Corps, composed of quite probably the best infantry troops in the entire German army. That was one advantage he had. The other was that the entire attack could be concentrated on a narrow front just three miles broad. Never a particularly sanguine commander, Knobelsdorf, on this occasion, struck his subordinates as unusually buoyant. True, he had good troops and a favorably compact front. But fine advantages had proved disappointing time and time again—just witness the staggering cost of the battle on the left bank.

It was on the evening of June 22 that the true source of Knobelsdorf's rare optimism became apparent. During the run-up to the battle, German troops marching up to the line passed ammo dumps stacked and stacked with highly unusual shells. Or, rather, they were shells decorated unusually. Each bore a bright acid-green cross boldly painted on the casing. What did this mean? Oh, it was secret. But if it was secret, why paint such a bold mark? Oh, that was secret, too. But rumors buzzed throughout the ranks. This "secret" would break Verdun wide open.

Near Fort Souville, Lieutenant Marcel Bechu, a staff officer of the French 130th Division, was settling down to dinner with his chief, the division's commanding general. "And what is so rare as a day in June?" the popular nineteenth-century American poet James Russell Lowell asked. Many might answer an *evening* in that month. So it may have seemed to Bechu, savoring relief from the region's customarily dreadful raw weather and the usual hell of ceaseless combat. Even the day's shelling had ceased.

But the silence made it all that much easier to hear the strange, very strange, sound that suddenly rose up from the east. Bechu described it as "multitudinous soft whistlings, following each other without cessation, as if thousands and thousands of birds cleaving the air in dizzy flight were fleeing over our heads." It was, he wrote, "novel and incomprehensible."[6] Within moments, a sergeant threw open the door of the shelter in which Bechu was dining with his general. He had not knocked, and he did not salute, but simply blurted out the news that thousands of shells were passing overhead—yet without bursting. The general calmly suggested they all go outside to have a look.

Bechu described a "pungent, sickening odour of putrefaction compounded with the mustiness of stale vinegar"[7] emanating from the nearby Ravine des Vignes. He heard voices—shouting, choked—warning of *Gas! Gas!* But what first struck Bechu most forcibly was the behavior of the artillery pack horses. They were frenzied, everywhere breaking from their tethers and running throughout the battery heedlessly, aimlessly, while foaming at the mouth.

For most of the men, this was their first exposure to gas. Even those who had experienced it, had never experienced it on this scale—for the simple reason that it never had been used before on this scale, in such a massive and sustained barrage. Moreover, it was a new chemical agent. Very soon, the Allies would learn that it was phosgene, or diphosgene, which the Germans called "Green Cross Gas." Generically known as carbonyl dichloride, in high concentrations, it attacked anything that lived—from horses, to people, to the very leaves on the trees, which withered and died on contact with it. In high concentrations, it had the smell of putrefaction, but in lower concentrations—for instance, at the periphery of a barrage—it smelled either like musty hay or new-mown hay or even green corn. It killed people and animals by damaging the proteins in the alveoli lining the lungs, so that the CO^2–O^2 exchange essential to life was disrupted if not blocked entirely. Victims suffocated. Some recovered. Some died. Some suffered disability for the rest of their lives.

Phosgene would prove to be the most lethal among the chemical agents unleashed in World War I, responsible for about 85,000 of the 100,000 deaths due to chemical warfare. In its debut at Verdun, phosgene directly resulted in 1,600 French casualties. More immediately, however, it created universal panic and utter chaos, which were rapidly amplified as it became apparent that the gas masks the French employed at this point in the war were almost useless against the new agent. Troops donned their masks quickly, only to find themselves coughing, retching, and vomiting into them. When they tore off their masks in a reflexive effort to breathe, they were doomed.

Unlike some of the earlier agents, phosgene was effective even in relatively low concentrations. As the gas drifted to the rear areas of the front, it dissipated sufficiently to be virtually odorless. Soldiers either did not don their masks or, thinking it was safe to do so, they removed them. Slowly, insidiously, they would become woozy, nauseated, and short of breath. Some lived, some died. Medics who treated troops exposed to the brunt of the attack often became contaminated and, clutching their throats, collapsed on top of their patients. Chaplains fell unconscious while administering absolution. To officers with a knowledge of history, the scene recalled a medieval plague.

Tactically, the phosgene barrage was effective far beyond the roughly 1,600 casualties it directly caused. The Germans had concentrated the Green Cross barrage on the French artillery positions. At this point in

An aerial reconnaissance pilot snapped this view of Fort Froideterre, one of the forts associated with Fort Douaumont on the right bank of the Meuse. MINISTÉRE DE LA DEFENSE

the Battle of Verdun, although the Germans still unquestionably enjoyed superiority of firepower, the disparity that had prevailed in February was now not nearly so great. When one side commenced an artillery preparation prior to an infantry attack, the other side fired its artillery against the enemy artillery. The result was an artillery duel that was almost always mutually destructive. Neither side gained a decisive advantage through artillery alone. Due to Green Cross, however, the French artillery was unable to respond to the German barrage. The French gunners were dead, disabled, or fled. The Green Cross barrage ended, and the barrage of conventional high-explosive shells commenced—battering the French lines with relative impunity throughout the rest of the night of the 22nd.

At five o'clock on the morning of June 23, the German infantry advanced, almost unopposed by the badly disrupted French artillery. As the main thrust of the infantry attack hit between the French 129th and 130th Divisions, the absence of French fire was of great consequence. Not only were more German soldiers surviving to reach the French lines, the French defenders were demoralized by the failure of artillery support. Infantry had become accustomed to the sound of artillery at their backs. Without it, they felt themselves cut loose and left to fend for themselves. Panic and despair quickly set in. Poilus in the forward posts simply fled. German units reported to their commanders that the front of the front line had been abandoned. Fort Thiaumont (really, an ouvrage, or rudimentary fort) about a mile and a half west of Fort Vaux was quickly overrun, and the ouvrage atop Côte de Froideterre, a mile southwest of Fort Thiaumont, was enveloped. At the same time, the Ravine des Vignes, adjacent to Fort Souville, which contained an underground command post that served four French units, was besieged.

The complex was nicknamed "Quatre Cheminées" because of the four ventilator pipes that protruded up through the earth. Troops from the Bavarian units that had led the attack now dropped hand grenades down these cheminées in an effort to force the occupants out.

To the left of the Bavarian assault between the French 129th and 130th Divisions, the German Alpine Corps attacked the village of Fleury, which occupied a central position south of Fort Douaumont, west of Fort Vaux, and midway between Forts Thiaumont and Souville.

At about nine in the morning, the French artillery finally awakened. While the artillery positioned on relatively low ground close to the front line was utterly neutralized by the Green Cross barrage, the guns and gunners located on the heights were relatively untouched by the gas, which, heavier than air, clung to the ground, the trenches, and the shell holes. Still, in the space of just four hours, between five and nine that morning, the Germans had gained more than a mile of territory—a huge advance by Western Front standards. But now the French artillery rained down on Fleury. Then French infantry units engaged the Germans in the rubble-choked streets of the village. It was, alas, too little too late. Fleury was in the German grasp by early evening. Another nearby village, Chapelle Saint-Fine, was also overrun. It was at this most desperate point that General Robert Nivelle issued his Order of the Day, which was

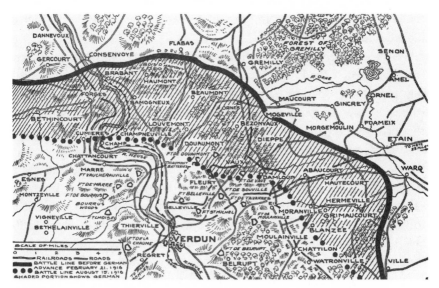

This simple map shows the menace to the city of Verdun as of August 15, 1916, which marked the greatest extent of the German advance during the battle. The heavy line marks the battle line of February 21, 1916. The dotted line marks the battle line of August 15. The shaded area is the territory gained by Germany between these dates. WIKIMEDIA

made famous by it concluding sentence: *Ils ne passeront pas!* (They shall not pass!).

Opportunity Lost

With Fort Souville hemmed in if not surrounded, the German infantry attack came perilously close to the fort itself, which was the nerve center of the French right bank. Moreover, located just three miles from the town of Verdun, it was regarded as the last French bastion east of the Meuse.

In an atmosphere of desperation, General Nivelle put the fate of the area centered on Fort Souville in the hands of the man they called "The Butcher," Charles Mangin. Predictably, Mangin called for an immediate all-out counterattack. For once, it was precisely the right order at the right time. Chapelle Saint-Fine was very thinly held, and Mangin's counterattack very quickly retook it. This, it turned out, was sufficient to bring the German advance grinding to a halt—on the very threshold of what looked to be a decisive victory.

Attacking across a narrow front allowed the Germans to concentrate forces and pierce the French line. Yet it left the German forces with nothing more than a narrow salient. Because Falkenhayn had not allocated sufficient reserves to allow the Fifth Army to exploit the breakthrough that had been achieved, the salient was left vulnerable not only to *infantry* attack but, even more, to French *artillery* fire from three sides—west, north, and south. The Germans needed three things to enable them to exploit the breach they had made. They needed reserves to hold the salient. (They weren't getting any.) They needed more Green Cross shells to further disrupt the French defenses. (No more gas shells were available.) Most of all, they needed water. As the winter and spring just ended were among the coldest and bitterest in recent memory, late June brought some of the hottest days anyone in the region had ever experienced. The attackers, parched, were spent. Worse, as more French artillery came on line, French gunners opened up a bombardment *behind* the salient, cutting it off from the German rear. Alarmed, Schmidt von Knobelsdorf gave the command on June 25 to suspend the attack. The order amounted to an admission that yet another opportunity to break through and end the Battle of Verdun had flown in and flown out again.

CHAPTER 17

A Regular Hell

"The battles there exhausted our forces like an open wound. . . . The battlefield was a regular hell and regarded as such by the troops."
—PAUL VON HINDENBURG,
ON FIRST TOURING THE VERDUN SECTOR[1]

"THEY SHALL NOT PASS!" IT WAS SO STRIKING A RESOLVE, SO DEFIANT, SO admired, that it was widely misattributed to Philippe Pétain, especially by soldiers and their families, who bore no affection for Robert Nivelle. It was also recycled for use on propaganda posters later in the war, was translated by Romanian soldiers fighting against the Germans at Mărășești in September 1917, by the Turks at the Dardanelles ("The Dardanelles are not passed"), and, between the world wars, by the Communists during the Spanish Civil War (*"No Pasarán"*), by British anti-fascists protesting the British Union of Fascists in London's East End in 1936, and by a number of Central American revolutionaries up through the 1980s. In the run-up to World War II, *Ils ne passeront pas* was even inscribed on the insignia of units assigned to garrison the infamous Maginot Line.

It is nevertheless a peculiarly ambiguous imperative. Pétain's earlier words of encouragement, paraphrasing Joan of Arc, were far more straightforwardly aggressive: *"Courage! On les aura!"* (Courage! We will get them!).[2] Yet Pétain was the advocate of defense over offense. No wonder "They shall not pass" seemed more suited to him than to Nivelle, the champion of attaque à outrance. It is about resistance, dogged and desperate resistance, not offensive initiative. It is, to be sure, a declaration of defiance, but the defiance of those who hang on by their fingernails, not those who wield a sword they believe mightier than that of their enemy.

THE FORT SOUVILLE DECISION

On June 25, 1916, when Schmidt von Knobelsdorf called a halt to the German advance on the right bank of the Meuse, the French were indeed hanging on, and just barely. Their left bank positions were badly mauled and imminently imperiled. On the right bank, they clung to the heights of the river, a thin line, a final line, a line defended by the oldest and feeblest of the Séré de Rivières system of forts, and held by an army much reduced in strength following one attack after another and one futile riposte after another. Fort (or Ouvrage) Thiaumont was lost. Fleury, mostly destroyed, was held by the Germans, as were the woods adjacent to the villages of Vaux and Chapitre.

The French had been on the receiving end of a slow, systematic nibbling away of their defensive positions. It was a process overseen by General Karl Bruno von Mudra, a magnificently mustachioed Prussian commander who had been instrumental in blocking the French in the Argonne by chewing away at them throughout 1914–1915. Decorated with the Pour le Mérite for this sustained campaign of attrition, he was put in command of an assault group on the right bank of the Meuse. He took a toll. In fact, tactically viewed, every German offensive at Verdun since February 21, 1916, had succeeded—at least as measured by the dwindling amount of real estate the French army owned in the sector. French personnel losses mounted, too—killed, wounded, and captured in the sector surpassing 185,000 by June.

But the thing is, German losses at Verdun climbed beyond 200,000 during this same period. The string of German tactical gains had come at a great cost, what one might well judge to be a pyrrhic cost. Joseph Joffre was mindful of the French losses, but even more mindful of the German ones. Back during December 6–8, 1915, he had met with the commander of the British Expeditionary Forces (BEF), General Sir Douglas Haig, at GQG in Chantilly.

Together, Joffre and Haig agreed on a grand Allied strategy by which simultaneous offensives by the Russians on the Eastern Front, the Italians

The Grand Quartier Général (GQG) commandeered the entire Hôtel du Grand Condé as its headquarters. Built in 1908, the remodeled hotel survives today in Chantilly. WIKIMEDIA

on the Italian Front (against Austria-Hungary), and the combined French and British forces on the Western Front were to overwhelm the Central Powers. Initially, Haig proposed dividing the British and French efforts. The BEF would conduct an offensive in Flanders with the objective of reducing the German army there as well as depriving the Germans of access to the Belgian coast, from which they were operating U-boats against Allied—especially British—shipping. Joffre agreed to this in December 1915 and reiterated his agreement in January 1916, but then, in February 1916, he pushed for a combined Anglo-French offensive at the Somme River, the place at which the BEF and French army made contact. Almost immediately after this combined offensive had been decided on, Falkenhayn moved against Verdun, and Joffre was immediately forced to divert to Verdun divisions intended for the Somme. For this reason, Somme operations were scaled back from a massive offensive designed to win the war to a strictly limited offensive intended to relieve pressure on the French at Verdun.

The city of Verdun—after weeks of artillery bombardment. NEW ZEALAND HISTORY NET

The Battle of the Somme began on July 1 and quickly forced the Germans to transfer some of their heavy artillery from Verdun to the Somme front, along with some infantry divisions. This exacerbated a drain on German troops that had been triggered by the unexpected Russian success of the Brusilov Offensive on the Eastern Front. Together, the demands of the Somme and the Brusilov Offensive had the effect of making an already conservative and even parsimonious Erich von Falkenhayn simultaneously more cautious and more desperate at Verdun. He, Crown Prince Wilhelm, and an increasingly anxious Schmidt von Knobelsdorf agreed that the next move on the right bank had to be against Fort Souville.

By the end of June, Fort Souville was the French nerve center of the beleaguered right bank of Meuse. Knocking it out would deliver a crippling blow to the French. Occupying it would deliver to the Germans the commanding heights that overlooked the city of Verdun, whose fall would surely mean the end of the French hold on this portion of the front.

Moreover, Fleury, which the Germans had captured on June 23, was now the object of repeated French counteroffensives mounted at the behest of Charles Mangin. As a result, the village changed hands over and over again—a total of sixteen times by August 17. Fighting for Fleury came at great cost to the Germans. Taking Fort Souville would, the German commanders believed, put an end to this struggle by delivering the village into German hands once and for all.

By the second week in July, the Germans had laid in a new stockpile of the Green Cross gas shells that had been so effective in the attack of June 21. On July 9, therefore, the preparatory barrage began with a spectacular bombardment using some sixty thousand of the gas shells, all concentrated on French artillery positions. What the Germans had not reckoned on was the French army having developed, manufactured, and distributed the new M2 gas mask, which was far more effective against phosgene (and other agents) than the masks in use just a few weeks earlier. The French were expecting a phosgene barrage, the new masks were at the ready, and, as a result, the Green Cross assault, massive though it

Fort de Souville was an important French command post on the right bank of the Meuse. Unremitting artillery fire made it look like a relic of the Stone Age.
WIKIMEDIA

was, had very little effect on the French artillery. Nevertheless, the Germans followed the gas barrage with an even more massive conventional high-explosive barrage that lobbed a total of more than 300,000 shells against Fort Souville as well as the approaches to it. At least five hundred of those impacts were from naval guns modified for land use, which delivered mammoth 360-mm rounds.

After two full days of bombardment, three German infantry divisions advanced against the fort. They quickly fell victim to their own unwieldy numbers and the devastation wrought by the intensive bombardment of a very concentrated area. Progress over the rugged moonscape was tortuous, and when a large number of German infantry became bottlenecked along the approach to the fort, French artillery—relatively unaffected by the gas barrage—poured the wrath of Verdun's weary defenders down upon them. Those who escaped the high explosives did not necessarily escape with their lives. Sixty French machine gunners emerged from the bowels of Fort Souville with their weapons at the ready. Under fire, they clambered atop the rubble of the fort's superstructure, set up their machine guns, and mercilessly raked the survivors.

A fight for the top of the battered fort ensued, and on July 12, thirty German infantrymen from the 140th Regiment attained the summit of the fort, saw below them the grim vista of the Verdun battlefield and the partially ruined city of Verdun itself. What a position! But, within minutes, the men were forced off by a strong French counterattack that killed some, made prisoners of others, and sent a few running for their lives.

Falkenhayn now ordered Crown Prince Wilhelm to break off the offensive and return to a defensive posture. The brief lull that followed this command was an irresistible lure to General Mangin, who never experienced a silence without wanting to fill it with fire and blood. His men had pushed the Germans off of Fort Souville and, in fact, had sent most of them back to their positions of July 10. Encouraged by this result, Mangin, on July 15—the day after Bastille Day—ordered the Thirty-Seventh Division to make a new counterattack, this time against Fleury—which was once again in German hands, fiercely held by members of the elite Alpine Corps. It proved a disaster for the outnumbered French, bringing

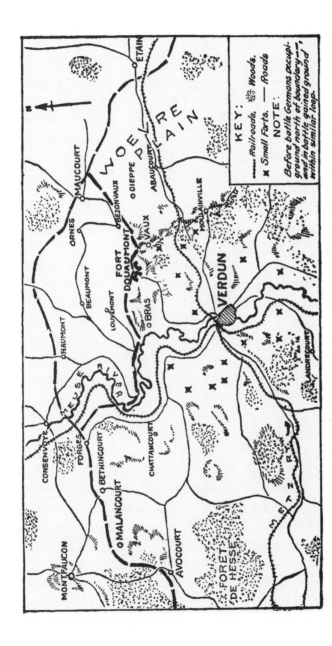

Prior to the start of the Battle of Verdun on February 21, 1916, the Germans occupied the ground north of the dashed boundary line. In battle, they gained the territory within the dashed loop—territory mostly relinquished during the fighting of October–December 1916. WIKIMEDIA

total French casualties for the period of February 21 to July 15 to 275,000, 25,000 more than the German losses, which had risen to 250,000.

As Falkenhayn had ordered an end to the German offensive, so Philippe Pétain, again risking the ire of Joseph Joffre, ordered Nivelle and Mangin to cease all further attacks—except in cases where preparation was absolutely adequate. In effect, both commanders, German and French, had ordered an end to the Battle of Verdun—a battle that had lost much for both sides and gained nothing for either, save, perhaps, for the privilege of France to claim "They did not pass."

ENDLESS BATTLE

Erich von Falkenhayn was chief of the German General Staff. He ordered an end to the German offensive at Verdun. Philippe Pétain, commander of Army Group Center—fifty-two divisions in or near the Verdun sector—unconditionally ordered an end to the French offensive at Verdun.

And yet the Battle of Verdun continued.

On August 1, Schmidt von Knobelsdorf ordered a new surprise attack against Fort Souville. It advanced less than three thousand feet toward its objective before it was discovered. General Mangin then launched his customary series of counterattacks, one after the other, for the next two weeks. They managed to gnaw back a very small slice of the three thousand feet the Germans had taken.

General Nivelle approved of Mangin's operations, and Pétain did nothing to stop them because they were not attacks (which he forbade) but counterattacks (which could not be forbidden). The case was different among the Germans. Crown Prince Wilhelm, tired of seeing his Fifth Army worn away to achieve so little, had welcomed Falkenhayn's order to end the Verdun offensive. By mid-August, however, it became apparent to him that his own chief-of-staff, Schmidt von Knobelsdorf, had not given up on taking Verdun. The August 1 attack toward Fort Souville was material proof of that. Worse, on August 15, while the Fifth Army was engaged in resisting one of Mangin's counterattacks, Knobelsdorf—minus his superior, the crown prince—met with Falkenhayn. He argued that, because the French were in the midst of transferring troops from Verdun to the Somme, now was the perfect time to mount

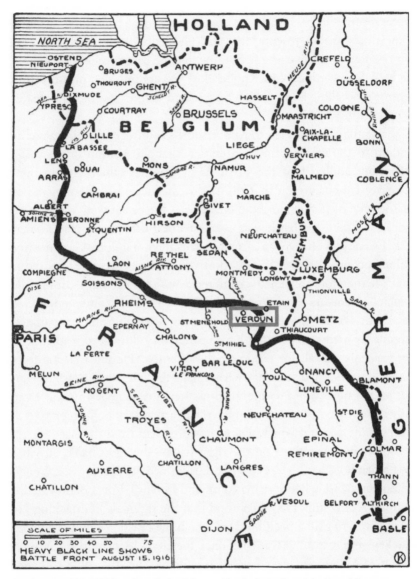

On August 15, 1916, when Schmidt von Knobelsdorf met (minus his commanding officer, Crown Prince Wilhelm) with Erich von Falkenhayn, the Western Front battle line looked like this. This "big picture" view shows that Verdun was a French salient bulging into German-occupied France. WIKIMEDIA

a new offensive at Verdun—and to do so before the onset of fall and winter. From the perspective of the passage of one hundred years, the irony is inescapable. Joseph Joffre had pleaded with the British to commence a joint offensive on the Somme in large part to relieve pressure on the French at Verdun. Now Knobelsdorf was arguing that pressure at the Somme was calling away French forces from Verdun and thereby creating an opportunity there.

Falkenhayn responded to Knobelsdorf's counsel by sending a memorandum to the crown prince reiterating that the Verdun offensive had ended, but adding that the Fifth Army was nevertheless to maintain an aggressive posture on that front. This was necessary, he argued, both for the sake of *discouraging* the enemy and for *encouraging* the German people. In short, the battle was over, but the Fifth Army was to behave as if it were still on. Duly alarmed by this memorandum, Crown Prince Wilhelm concluded that Knobelsdorf was planning an attack behind his back. He therefore convened a conference with his left-bank commander, General Hermann von François, and his right-bank commander, General Ewald von Lochow. With the French position on the left bank still hanging by a thread (it must have been a very durable thread indeed), von François was all for resuming the offensive. He felt that his forces controlled the left bank—or at least held the whip hand over it—and that to quit now would be a fatal admission of weakness. This was essentially the same position as Falkenhayn had articulated in his memo to the Fifth Army. General von Lochow, however, had lived through the cost of conducting operations on the right bank—the right bank, on which the French hold had *seemed* so weak. His immediate predecessor, General Bruno von Mudra, had lost his command in April. Von Lochow had no desire to follow him. He understood that the rationale of attacking Fort Souville was to gain a position from which the city of Verdun itself could be taken. The reasoning was that, once the city fell, the entire sector was certain to follow. But, von Lochow countered, he had come to believe that taking Fort Souville would have precisely the same effect as taking Fort Vaux had. It would only incite further French counterattacks, and that would mean more fighting and more casualties without any tangible gain. His recommendation was simply to consolidate the present German positions, which, after all, represented considerable progress from their February starting points.

Wilhelm reported to Falkenhayn that his army's two principal commanders were diametrically divided on what to do next at Verdun. Falkenhayn responded by advising the crown prince that the decision would not be his—Wilhelm's—to make but would be determined by the echelon above him, namely Army Group Command. Instead of taking this as an affront or, even worse, a vote of no-confidence, Wilhelm wrote in his postwar memoirs that he "was secretly glad to be freed from a weight of responsibility that had become intolerable."[3] He also resolved to get rid of Schmidt von Knobelsdorf. Doing this was beyond his power but not that of his father, the kaiser. And so he wrote to him immediately.

The cover of the most recent translation of *Memoirs of the Crown Prince of Germany*[4] features a photographic portrait of Wilhelm III lovingly admiring his young son, whose arm rests upon his seated father's leg as the crown prince places his hand upon that arm. Both father and son smile, looking at one another and not at the camera. No such photograph exists of Wilhelm III and his father, the kaiser. Indeed, Wilhelm II's August 23 order transferring Schmidt von Knobelsdorf to the Russian front and command of an army corps may have been the first and was perhaps only time the kaiser acceded to his son's advice and request.

The new chief-of-staff of the Fifth Army was General Walther Freiherr von Lüttwitz, with whom the crown prince would get on famously. In stark contrast to Knobelsdorf, von Lüttwitz recognized Verdun for the eater of men and materiel that it had become, agreed with the crown prince that any thought of a breakthrough was now a delusion, and worked with him to minimize the ongoing drain of resources in this sector.

In the meantime, however, on the veritable eve of Knobelsdorf's departure for the east, with German forces disengaging at Verdun, Mangin's counterattacks finally began to have dramatic effect. On August 18, the French retook Fleury. This took pressure off of Fort Souville, which, in turn, seemed to signal the safety of the town of Verdun—or what was left of it. Crown Prince Wilhelm saw this development as inevitable. It was the price of preserving the Fifth Army from further futile bloodletting. In

Berlin, however, it was taken as damning evidence of the failure of Erich von Falkenhayn.

For many months, Theobald von Bethmann-Hollweg, chancellor of Germany, had been urging Kaiser Wilhelm II to dump Falkenhayn. It had been an uphill battle, since Falkenhayn was firmly fixed in the kaiser's firmament as a favorite star. But Bethmann-Hollweg persisted. He had ample reason. No man in the German government—not even the kaiser himself—bore more direct responsibility for committing Germany to war than the chancellor. When the Austrian archduke and heir apparent Franz Ferdinand was assassinated in Sarajevo on June 28, 1914, Bethmann-Hollweg encouraged the Austrian government to make war on Serbia (as the alleged instigator of the assassination), assuring Austria's foreign minister Count Leopold Berchtold that the kaiser would lead Germany in full alliance. He even covertly doctored a message from Britain's foreign secretary, Sir Edward Grey, who suggested mediation between Austria and the Serbs. Grey's message concluded that "the key to the situation lies in Berlin . . . if Berlin seriously wants peace, it will prevent Vienna from following a foolhardy policy."[5] Bethmann-Hollweg deleted the closing sentence from the version he handed to Wilhelm II. When war became inevitable and his deception was revealed, Bethmann-Hollweg met with the kaiser and offered to resign. Wilhelm II flatly refused the offer. He would not let Bethmann-Hollweg off so easily. "You've made this stew," the Kaiser snarled at him, "now you're going to eat it!"[6]

Two years into the stew he had made, Bethmann-Hollweg figured it would be much more palatable if the war were being won and not lost. Falkenhayn, he long believed, was not committed to absolute victory. Now that the news coming out of Verdun was suddenly peppered with French triumphs, Bethmann-Hollweg was ready to press his case against Falkenhayn all the harder. When a development on the Eastern Front materialized on August 27 in the form of the news that Rumania was entering the war on the side of the Allies, Bethmann-Hollweg pounced. Not only had Falkenhayn failed at Verdun, he told the kaiser, he had promised that Rumania could not possibly enter the war before the harvests had been gathered at the end of September. He, Erich von

Falkenhayn, had allowed the imperial government to be taken by surprise as Rumania was joining the Allies before August even ended.

On August 28, 1916, Kaiser Wilhelm II summoned Field Marshal Paul von Hindenburg, hero of the Eastern Front, to an audience. He appointed him chief of the German General Staff, effective August 29, whereupon Erich von Falkenhayn had no choice but to tender his resignation.

No Escape

Field Marshal von Hindenburg, together with his Eastern Front second-in-command Erich Ludendorff, immediately toured the Verdun front.

After the war, Hindenburg wrote:

> *I found myself compelled by the general situation to ask His Majesty the Emperor to order the offensive at Verdun to be broken off. The battles there exhausted our forces like an open wound. Moreover, it was obvious that in any case the enterprise had become hopeless, and that for us to persevere with it would cost us greater losses than those we were able to inflict on the enemy.*
>
> *Our forward zone was at all points exposed to the flanking fire of superior hostile artillery. Our communications with the battle-line were extremely difficult. The battlefield was a regular hell and regarded as such by the troops.*[7]

Hindenburg and Ludendorff ordered all attacks to cease immediately. By this time, French counterattacks had not only recovered Fleury but also much of the territory that had been yielded to German hands in July and August. The new German chief of the General Staff ordered an end to attacks, not a withdrawal from Verdun. So when the French line advanced on September 3, the Germans counterattacked on September 4–5 but failed to push the French back. The endless battle seemed at last to be moving toward an end—and one that the French could count as a victory after all. To the French, the horror of Verdun looked to be approaching blessed, honorable, maybe even triumphant, relief.

Kaiser Wilhelm II (center) confers with his two new Western Front commanders, Paul von Hindenburg (left) and his military partner, Erich Ludendorff (right). WIKIMEDIA

But at Verdun, squalid death was never far from any prospect of triumph, and no place on that miserable field of battle was more squalid than the Tavannes Tunnel. It was a narrow, single-track railway tunnel that was part of the rail line running from Verdun to Metz. The tunnel ran for some 3,800 feet through the Meuse Hills, and during the Battle of Verdun, because of its proximity to Fort Souville, it was commandeered to serve the French forces as a subterranean barracks, shelter, supply warehouse, and aid station, as well as a concealed trench communicating with Fort Souville. Capable of housing or sheltering as many as four thousand men, the tunnel also contained a number of important forward command posts.

Yet it was a relentlessly miserable, eternally nocturnal place, fouled by the ever-present stench of urine and excrement—since an acute shortage of even makeshift latrine facilities meant that some four thousand poilus relieved themselves continually in odd corners of the structure. In July,

276

when the German offensive pressed hardest on Fort Souville and vicinity, the Tavannes Tunnel was often filled beyond its four-thousand-man capacity. The divisional commander, who was forced to spend considerable time in the tunnel during this period, could no longer stand conditions there. He ordered the entire facility to be cleaned—but those cleaning efforts served only to stir up the filth and so were quickly abandoned for fear of spreading infection.

Despite the Dantesque horrors of the Tavannes Tunnel, troops who were under incessant shelling took substantial comfort in (as a Lieutenant Pierre Chaine put it) "having a mountain above one's head."[8]

On September 4, during the night following the first day of German counterattacks aimed at retaking Fleury, a fire broke out in a part of the tunnel used to store signal rockets. Very quickly, the exploding rockets ignited a nearby grenade dump. The exploding grenades quickly touched off a store of gasoline used to run the lighting generator. This, in its turn, ignited yet more hand grenades.

By this time, the men of Verdun had seen no end of explosions. But, remarkably enough, these were something entirely new. Artillery shells for the most part made their impact out of doors. The men in the tunnel were trapped in an explosive inferno contained in a subterranean vault housing thousands. The force of the explosions hurled both living men and dead bodies through the tunnel and against the walls and ceiling and floor. Body parts shot through the concrete tube like artillery shells. Fire was everywhere. The heat of combustion drew in air from the outside with hurricane force, creating what in the wider world would be called a firestorm, but in the confines of Tavannes was a monster blow torch fed by a seemingly limitless supply of fuel. Those who somehow found their way outside quickly discovered that they had escaped into the middle of an ongoing German artillery barrage.

By the time the grenades had all blown up, the hurricane-force winds died down, and the sources of fuel were exhausted, more than five hundred brittle, charred-black remains were tallied. They were added to the running total of killed, missing, and wounded at the start of September in the Fortified Region of Verdun: 315,000 French, 281,000 Germans.

CHAPTER 18

"The First Offensive Battle of Verdun"

It would be only too easy to produce the impression that all these sacri-fices had been incurred in vain.
—PAUL VON HINDENBURG, *OUT OF MY LIFE*[1]

THE RATIONALE OF A WAR OF ATTRITION IS THAT BOTH SIDES WILL BE worn down, but the victor will be worn down less than the vanquished. There is, however, an alternative end to attrition. One side may simply quit before the other does. By the end of August, Philippe Pétain was beginning to hope that Germany, at Verdun, was nearing the verge of quitting. For this reason, as he saw it, this was not the time to engage in one improperly prepared attack after another. Resolved to adequately prepare for a final offensive push that really would be final, his orders to Robert Nivelle and, through him, Charles Mangin, were to refrain from attacks for the present. Whereas those two generals wanted to attack repeatedly and to the uttermost, Pétain wanted to conserve Second Army resources for a single meaningful attack to be made at just the right time. He could not, however, prevent Mangin from *responding* to German attacks with French counterattacks. Realizing this, Mangin made it his practice to define virtually every attack he undertook as a counterattack. The question was: Would Mangin's willingness to spend men and mate-riel so prodigally leave Pétain anything to work with when it finally came time for the offensive he contemplated?

Based on Paul von Hindenburg's postwar memoirs, Pétain read the German attitude with remarkable accuracy. "When I look back now," Hin-denburg wrote, "I do not hesitate to say that on purely military grounds it would have been far better for us to have improved our situation at Verdun by the voluntary evacuation of the ground we had captured." In other words, Hindenburg had come to believe that merely calling off attacks was not a sufficient response. If a place had become a "regular hell," why remain there at all?[2]

It turns out that this was not a rhetorical question. There was a pressing reason to remain. Hindenburg wrote that, at the time, he could not simply evacuate:

> *To a large extent the flower of our best fighting troops had been sacrificed in the enterprise. The public at home still anticipated a glorious issue to the offensive.*
>
> *It would be only too easy to produce the impression that all these sacrifices had been incurred in vain. Such an impression I was anxious to avoid in the existing state of public opinion, nervous enough as it already was.*[3]

For a hundred years now, historians have argued about the "importance" of Verdun. Did the French *really* consider it sacred ground? Did Falkenhayn *really* believe the French would bleed themselves white rather than lose Verdun? Was Verdun, in actual fact, a backdoor into France, a truly strategic crossroads? In short, was it *really* worth the sacrifice?

It turns out, the answer depends on what one means by "really"? If that word refers to some inherent value to the Verdun sector, more than one answer is possible. To allow a massive breach of the Séré de Rivières system of forts by relinquishing Verdun might well have been a strategic loss from which France could not have recovered. This aside, was Verdun somehow "sacred" to the French people? Various figures, French as well as German, asserted this in 1916, but there is no empirical evidence that it was actually the case. If, however, we discard the idea of *inherent* value for *perceived* value, the sacrifice becomes more understandable—if not absolutely justifiable. The tragic irony is that the perception of the value of Verdun was created ex post facto or, more accurately, *during* the fact. It was a self-fulfilling function of the price paid for Verdun. Verdun *had* to be worth the sacrifice made to possess it because so much had been—and was being—sacrificed to possess it. The more that was lost at Verdun, the more valuable Verdun appeared to seem or was made to seem. Its inherent worth, militarily, politically, spiritually, became increasingly difficult to assess.

It was the fact of sacrifices made that prevented Hindenburg from voluntarily evacuating Verdun. The fact of sacrifice also prevented men like Nivelle and Mangin from refraining from nearly compulsive offensive attacks. As Hindenburg explained after the war, "We were disappointed in our hopes that with the breaking-off of our offensive at Verdun the enemy would more or less confine himself to purely trench warfare there," which, presumably, would have created a relatively low level of casualties acceptable to both sides.[4]

"Purely trench warfare" would have made Verdun no different from any other place on the Western Front. The war might have proceeded in the manner of business as usual. But, no. For the reason that *they* had sacrificed so much, the French wanted more than business as usual. "At the end of October," Hindenburg wrote, "the French opened a largely-conceived and boldly-executed counter-attack on the eastern bank of the Meuse, and overran our lines."[5]

1ÈRE BATAILLE OFFENSIVE DE VERDUN

The new German commanders wanted to leave Verdun because of the sacrifices they had already made there, but, precisely because of those sacrifices, they could not leave. The alternative to leaving, as they saw it, was to create conditions conducive to a kind of holding action, a relatively low-level trench war. The French, however, would not allow this—because of the sacrifices *they* had already made at Verdun.

What Pétain himself designated as *1ère Bataille Offensive de Verdun* (First Offensive Battle of Verdun) began on October 19. Its objective was to recapture Fort Douaumont, the anchor of the Verdun system of fortifications, which the policies of Joseph Joffre and the rest of the French high command had essentially discarded even before the Battle of Verdun had begun.

What would an offensive from Pétain, champion of defense in depth, look like? The first clue was in the designation itself. Pétain did not conceive of his operation to reclaim Fort Douaumont as a mere "offensive" but as something bigger and more consequential, a "battle." Pétain had banned attacks unless they were fully prepared. The First Offensive Battle of Verdun was meticulously prepared. It was ambitious, requiring an advance of more than 1.2 miles—an epic distance on the stalemated Western Front. When he was first assigned to Verdun, Pétain had introduced the practice of rotating soldiers out of the front line every two weeks. It was unprecedented in the French army, and his predecessor, Fernand de Langle de Cary, was an adherent of the standard French practice of keeping troops at the front indefinitely—a policy General Nivelle resumed once he replaced Pétain as commander of the Second Army. Prior to the offensive, Pétain completely replaced seven of the twenty-two divisions concentrated in the Verdun sector. He wanted the freshest troops possible. In addition, he emulated the combined-arms organization that had worked so well for the Germans early in the Verdun battle. He therefore radically reorganized all of the infantry platoons at Verdun. Not only did they contain riflemen but they also included designated grenadiers and machine gunners, all tightly integrated in the same platoon under the same noncoms and officers.

For this *offensive* battle, Pétain was also determined to work with both Robert Nivelle and Charles Mangin, not in opposition to them. As he saw it, his strength was in planning, preparation, and imposing leadership discipline to prevent a premature attack with inadequate resources. At times, his role would be to restrain his two subordinates but, even more important, he intended to exploit their strengths and inclinations to the utmost. While Pétain was responsible for the overall plan, Nivelle would work out the tactical details. Pétain especially relied on Nivelle's skill as a master artillerist. There would be a preliminary barrage—a massive one, for which Pétain ensured a French artillery presence that, for the first time at Verdun, would be superior to what the Germans had.

Just as critical to the success of the offensive would be the use of Nivelle's expertise in managing the "creeping barrage." The creeping—or moving—barrage was not entirely an innovation of World War I. The idea of precisely registering (aiming) and timing an artillery barrage to accompany an infantry attack was introduced in the Second ("Great")

Boer War of 1899–1902, albeit only in conjunction with relatively limited attacks by small infantry units. In World War I, the tactic was coordinated with very large-scale attacks. While most military historians cite the Battle of the Somme as the occasion on which the creeping barrage reached the height of its development, it was Nivelle at Verdun who dared to bring an intense barrage as close to the advancing infantry as possible.

What Nivelle planned was actually a "double creeping barrage." The infantry would be ordered to advance precisely 100 yards in precisely four minutes, which would put them 75 yards behind a barrage from the 75-mm field guns and 150 yards behind a barrage from the heavier artillery—hence the "double" barrage. To achieve this precision, Nivelle took steps to ensure reliable communication between infantry and artillery commanders. In preparation for the offensive, he sent engineer units to excavate trenches, six feet deep, in which they laid telephone cable. The cable was covered over with earth to protect it from shell impacts. The work was a major utility construction task, but it was essential to providing what Nivelle sought to achieve: artillery fire capable of breaking through enemy defenses so that infantry could exploit breaches immediately, before the enemy could bring up fresh troops to plug holes created by a preliminary barrage. Nivelle was so confident of the level of precise coordination that could be achieved between artillery and infantry that, when it came time to actually execute the attack, he reduced the distance between the troops and the falling shells.

Pétain oversaw the planning of an attack on a front he believed would be sufficiently wide to facilitate an adequate follow-up. Unlike some of his fellow commanders, he was not in awe of the German war machine. He recognized that the great German offensive of June 23 had been seriously flawed. The attack had been made on a front too narrow to adequately exploit. Pétain was determined not merely to emulate the enemy but to do better than they had. He committed a full three divisions to the first line of the attack, with three more to follow, and he held another two in reserve. Pétain also pulled in artillery from all over the Western Front, 650 guns in all, of which about half could be classed as heavy artillery. Among these were two 400-mm "railroad guns"—"super-heavy" artillery pieces transportable only by rail and firing mammoth one-ton shells. Because

Late in the Battle of Verdun, the French brought in two large naval guns modified to operate from railroad cars. The original of this photograph was hand colored, suggesting that the guns were objects of pride among French artillerists. AUTHOR'S COLLECTION.

the Germans had been forced to transfer a substantial number of their big guns to the Somme, the French now enjoyed an artillery advantage: 650 versus perhaps 500 German guns. As for ammunition, Pétain had started stockpiling it since the beginning of October. Restored rail lines running to Verdun had brought in some fifteen thousand tons of shells.

Where did Charles Mangin, the irrepressible "Butcher," fit into this tactical picture? Pétain and Nivelle agreed that his ferocity was best suited to the point of greatest contact, the capture of Fort Douaumont itself. Field command was therefore assigned to one of his direct subordinates, Arthur Guyot d'Asnières de Salins, who commanded the Thirty-Eighth Division, which consisted primarily of the African colonial troops in which Mangin so fervently believed. The early experience with the French Colonial Forces at Verdun had been disappointing, even disastrous. Mangin and others recognized that this was not due to any racial or cultural inferiority—as many others suggested—but was the result of a deficiency in training. In North Africa, the colonials had proved themselves able warriors time and time again, but they had never been exposed to combat on the unrelenting industrial scale of the European Western Front. Pétain therefore ordered the creation of a full-scale model of the proposed battlefield—complete with a representation of Fort Douaumont—at Stainville, near the Bar-le-Duc depot on the southwestern periphery of the Verdun front. Here, the Thirty-Eighth Division was thoroughly rehearsed in a specific mission to retake a specific fort. This time, they would not be thrown into combat unprepared.

Pétain recognized another deficiency in earlier attempts to recapture specific objectives. Not only were attacks inadequately prepared, very little provision had been made for follow-through after the initial assault. It was one thing to storm and take an objective, but quite another to hold onto it once taken. In the past, shortage of supplies and provisions, most immediately water, often prevented even a victorious force from holding what it had conquered. The great lesson of the siege of Fort Vaux was that the French garrison had been defeated not by force of arms but for want of water. Pétain recruited a French engineer who had been responsible for supplying fresh water to crews excavating the Panama Canal. He assigned him the task of devising a quick, dependable means of watering troops in the field and under fire. The engineer created a system of highly portable canvas pipes capable of conveying a flow of water across even thoroughly shelled ground.

OCTOBER 19–25

The battle began on October 19 with an artillery barrage, which was monitored by observers in tethered observation balloons known as *saucisses*, "sausages," because of their elongated shape.

French observation planes also circled overhead to assist in directing fire by direct radio ("wireless") connection. Due in large measure to aerial observation, the artillery spotting was remarkably accurate, almost certainly more consistently accurate than ever before in any war. Most of the heaviest fire was concentrated on German-occupied Fort Douaumont, and by October 21, heavy artillery impacts had destroyed the fort's observation turret. Throughout the ongoing bombardment of October 22, the principal structure of the fort stood up well, sheltering the garrison inside.

A French tethered observation balloon, called a *saucisse* ("sausage"), is transported to a launch site at the Verdun front. HTTP://LOUIS.GENEVIEVE.FREE.FR

Shortly before noon on October 23, however, one of the one-ton 400-mm shells fired from the railroad guns penetrated the reinforced concrete carapace of the main fort building. The biggest shells were typically fitted with time-delay fuses rather than percussion fuses. They were designed to penetrate structures and then detonate after penetration. This is what happened on the 23rd. Having crashed into the fort's interior, the shell exploded, sending an earthquake-like shockwave throughout the main building. This was followed by multiple detonations in the field hospital with the fort and the barracks as more 400-mm shells penetrated.

Fort Douaumont's commandant, Major Rosendahl, had his hands full merely trying to contain the chaos and panic now prevailing within "Uncle Douaumont" after these first impacts. Late on the same day, the sixth 400-mm shell to penetrate to the interior of the main building crashed into the Pioneer Depot, where signal rockets, hand grenades, and small arms ammunition were stored. A terrific explosion—the combination of the shell's high-explosive charge and the cooking off of the stored munitions—tore through the corridors of the fort, sending thick asphyxiating fumes throughout the entire structure and threatening to spread fire to a dump of unused French shells that had been captured along with the fort. Overwhelmed, Rosendahl saw no hope and immediately ordered the abandonment of the fort, save for a squad that bravely volunteered to remain behind to fight the fire—mostly in the hope of buying time for the others to get clear. Just how they were to fight the fire was unclear, however, since the fort's water supply had been cut off and all available water used up. There were stores of bottled French mineral water, and it was to these that the firefighters now resorted.

But what awaited those who managed to escape the inferno spreading within Fort Douaumont? Outside, the artillery bombardment was unrelenting, and it now included poison gas shells precisely targeted on the tunnel portals to the outside. Nevertheless, on the night of October 23, most of the surviving garrison managed to escape and withdraw. The fort was soon empty, even the firefighters having at last withdrawn as the fires, miraculously, burned themselves out. By this time, the French bombardment elsewhere on the front—continuous for three days and more intensive than anything the Germans had yet experienced at Verdun—suddenly stopped late in the afternoon of October 22. To the Germans, the meaning of this cessation could not have been clearer. The infantry attack was about to commence. The order went up and down the line of German artillery: Commence the counterbarrage, which was aimed at the ground on which the French were surely *about* to advance—for the secret to killing attacking infantry was to aim not where it was, but where it will be.

The problem was that the French infantry did not materialize. There was no advance. The lifting of the preparatory barrage was a ruse by the wily Nivelle intended to lure the well-camouflaged German artillery to fire, thereby revealing its position. French artillery spotters quickly called in their muzzle-flash observations, the French gunners relaid their cannon accordingly, and then they unleashed intensive counterbattery fire precisely targeting the German artillery and destroying a significant portion of it. The pounding continued through the morning of October 24. Then it stopped. Up to this point, French artillery had fired 855,264 shells

Fort Douaumont late in the 1916 battle, after artillery pounding by the Germans and then by the French. WIKIMEDIA

in preparation for the offensive to retake Fort Douaumont. Of this number, 532,926 were 75-mm shells. The rest were 155-mm, 370-mm, and 400-mm shells—each of the latter weighing one ton.

At 11:40, through a thick late-morning fog on October 24, the men of the Thirty-Eighth, 133rd, and Seventy-Fourth divisions attacked. They moved out even more closely than originally planned behind the creeping field-artillery barrage—a mere fifty-five yards, traversing that same distance in two minutes. The creeping heavy artillery barrage was 160 yards ahead of the infantry, effectively forcing both the German field artillerymen and machine gunners to stay under cover.

The German defenders had not been prepared for a creeping barrage—not on such a scale. As for the artillery preparation that had preceded it, Hindenburg later recalled that the "rate of fire of the [French] artillery and trench-Mortars [had been increased] to the extreme limit of capacity of material and men," so that when the infantry attack began, accompanied by the creeping barrage, it was very inadequately countered by "physically exhausted and morally shaken defenders."[6] Throughout the summer, the village of Fleury had changed hands no fewer than sixteen times, Fort (or Ouvrage) Thiaumont had remained stubbornly in German hands. Now both fell within minutes. A French listening post, which had tapped into German telephone communication, heard a frenzied commander report that he had only a single man left, the others having fled. The intensive barrage had cut off most of the Germans in the vicinity of Fort Douaumont and the smaller forts associated with it. In consequence, the defenders were thirsty, hungry, and, as Hindenburg later wrote, exhausted physically and shaken morally.

The French Thirty-Eighth Division, with its colonial troops—including the elite regiment of Moroccans who had earlier performed so poorly in an attack to retake Fort Vaux—headed straight for Fort Douaumont. A battalion of the Moroccans was tasked with making the first direct assault on the smoldering heap that was all that remained of the battered prize. Expecting the worse, they met with only sporadic resistance and swarmed over the rubble in search of an entrance. Finding it, they ventured in and soon discovered a bedraggled contingent of just twenty-nine Germans, who quickly raised their hands in surrender. They were under the command of a Captain Prollius, who had wandered into the fort the day before with four officers and twenty-five men. Finding the place empty, he had sent a runner to request reinforcements to defend the fort. No German commander answered the plea, and so Prollius and his little band were left to fend for themselves. Their surrender was a kind of poetic justice, a reprise of the surrender of the French skeleton crew that had manned Fort Douaumont when it fell to the Germans on February 25.

THE FOLLOW-UP

By October 25, the French offensive had rounded up some six thousand German prisoners. A significant amount of German-occupied real estate was reclaimed, including—in addition to the still-usable ruins of Fort Douaumont—Fort Thiaumont (together with nearby Thiaumont Farm), the village of Douaumont, and the northern end of Caillette Wood. The Germans' Damloup artillery battery was captured, along with some fifteen pieces of heavy Krupp artillery. Although Vaux pond was retaken, the attempt to regain the ruins of Fort Vaux itself failed. It seems that the German garrison clung as tenaciously to this as the French garrison had. French heavy artillery pounded Fort Vaux for a week, but only after a 220-mm shell ignited an internal explosion on November 2 did the surviving members of the German garrison evacuate. In the end, a single company of poilus reclaimed what was left of the small fort without firing a shot. Three days later, on November 5, the French army had returned to the front line of February 24.

Thus it was *status quo antebellum* after nine months of continuous combat and some 300,000 killed on both sides. During December 9–17, Charles Mangin led a new right-bank offensive that had been planned by General Nivelle. The first six days were an intensive artillery preparation in which 827 French guns lobbed 1,169,000 shells against remaining German positions east of the recovered French front line. On December 15, four infantry divisions advanced—another four being held in reserve—against five German divisions, which were supported by 533 guns. Two-thirds of the German infantry was in direct contact with the attackers, while a third was held as a reserve. Whereas the French divisions were close to full strength, their German counterparts were badly understrength, each with less than half the usual complement of seven thousand men.

Once again, Nivelle designed a closely calibrated creeping barrage to accompany the infantry assault. The field-gun component of the creeping barrage was directed against the German first line, but the heavier guns, firing 150 yards in advance of the infantry, were deliberately registered on the second line and were intended to cut off avenues of retreat and reinforcement. The Germans suffered a heavy defeat, in which 13,500 of the 21,000 troops in the five engaged divisions became casualties. They were, for the most part, victims of the heavy artillery that French high command had scorned before and even during the early days of the Battle of Verdun. Most of the casualties were prisoners of war, who were captured while sheltering themselves from the creeping barrages of the French. Infantry functioned mainly to round them up.

The December offensive pushed the closest German point to the heavily damaged city of Verdun back nearly five miles. The French quickly repaired the 155-mm turret of Fort Douaumont and garrisoned the facility. One hundred fifteen pieces of German artillery were captured, along with 11,387 prisoners, who were consigned to crude quarters as a bitter winter settled in. When a prisoner delegation of German officers complained to Charles Mangin about the rude accommodations they had been assigned, the general replied with an elaborate show of courtesy: "We do regret it, gentlemen, but then we did not expect so many of you."[7] It was a paraphrase of Frederick the Great's riposte to his prisoners following his victory at the 1757 Battle of Rossbach during the Seven Years' War: "But, gentlemen, I did not expect you so soon, in so great number." The German officers, now captive, would have recognized the allusion, which must have savored of pungent bitterness.

EPILOGUE

There is no question that the performance of the French army at Verdun improved after Philippe Pétain took command on February 25. Also, without doubt, when Pétain, Robert Nivelle, and Charles Mangin stopped operating at cross purposes and instead collaboratively pooled their divergent talents in October, the results were even more impressive. But it is no less true that France was able to claim the Battle of Verdun as a victory largely because the new German commanders in the sector, Paul von Hindenburg and Erich Ludendorff, could not bring themselves to "voluntarily evacuate" the battlefield. Instead, they attempted to fight a holding action against an enemy that, thirsting for vengeance, fought fiercely to win.

The victory the French claimed on December 20, 1916, was, in fact, limited to the right bank of the Meuse River. On the left bank—the west bank—German troops still held Côte 304 and Le Mort Homme as well as numerous other places. In addition, on the east bank, they also clung to Côte Talou and the village of Beaumont. It was not until August 11, 1917, that a *2ème Bataille Offensive de Verdun* (Second Offensive Battle of Verdun) was launched with the object of reclaiming this stolen real estate.

The French committed four entire army corps to the offensive, which began on August 11 with an artillery preparation that used some three thousand guns. By this time, France had built, bought, or captured an enormous arsenal of artillery. "*Le feu tue*," Pétain declared: "Firepower kills."[1] When he first said it, it was an utterance that defied prevailing French military doctrine. Now the former disdain for firepower seemed a distant, if profoundly embarrassing, memory—gone, gone with Joseph Joffre, whom Prime Minister Aristide Briand, in a bid to save his job, unceremoniously kicked upstairs. Appointing Joffre "general-in-chief of the French armies" and "technical adviser" to the government as well as "consultative member" of the War Committee, Briand replaced him with Robert Nivelle as "Commander-in-Chief of the Armies of the North and

Northeast." That was on December 13, 1916. Within days, it was clear to Joffre that the appointment had come without any actual power. On the verge of angrily resigning, Joffre was suddenly promoted to marshal of France on the day after Christmas. Now, though still without real power, he could not possibly resign. To do so would be incredibly unpatriotic.

After nine days of a massive barrage of some three million rounds, a million of which were heavy shells, the infantry assault stepped off on August 20. In just four days, the French retook Bois d'Avocourt, Le Mort Homme, and Bois des Corbeaux, as well as the three tunnels—named Bismarck, Kronprinz, and Gallwitz—the Germans had run beneath Le Mort Homme and Côte 304 to connect their front lines with the left-bank rear. On the right bank, objectives left in German hands in December 1916 were retaken, including the Bois de Talou, Champneuville, Côte 344, a piece of Bois des Fosses, and all of Bois le Chaume and Mormont Farm. On August 25, Côte 304, and the towns of Samogneux and Régnieville, all on the left bank, were recovered, and on August 26, the right-bank village of Beaumont was placed under attack. By the end of the offensive, the French had taken 9,500 prisoners, thirty pieces of artillery, about a hundred trench mortars, and 242 machine guns.

To this day, there is no universal agreement on precisely how many soldiers fought at Verdun and how many were killed, wounded, or captured there. The current most widely accepted estimates are that 1.14 million French soldiers and 1.25 million German soldiers fought at Verdun. Casualty figures range from 315,000 to more than 540,000 for the French, of which 156,000 to 162,000 were likely killed. Among the Germans, the casualty figures vary from a low of just over 280,000 to a high of 434,000, including approximately 143,000 killed. Nearly 300,000 French and German soldiers are still classified as missing, and in 1932, French president Albert Lebrun dedicated the Douaumont Ossuary, which contains the unidentified skeletal remains of an estimated 130,000 combatants.

All of these numbers, vague as they are, assume a battle that began on February 21, 1916, and ended on December 20 of that year. Recent historians such as John Mosier[2] have argued that this battle was only the most

famous of several *Battles* of Verdun, the precise number of which is inde-
terminate but which may fairly be said to span virtually the entire war.
Indeed, the fact that fighting took place in the vicinity of Verdun prior to
February 21, 1916, and that the French victory declared on December 20,
1916, was confined to objectives on the right bank of the Meuse and was
followed by more fighting in the sector, suggests that recognizing but one
Battle of Verdun is more convenient fiction than historically defensible
fact. Doing so turns the saga of Verdun into a tale whose narrative arc is a
journey from disastrous French military errors to a triumphal resurgence
of French arms. To convert this narrative into an even more inspiring story
of national redemption, it is necessary to interpret Verdun in accordance
with the spin contemporary French propagandists and those sympathetic
with their views promoted during and after the battle itself. In their view,
Verdun was a place sacred to France. When Germany menaced Verdun,
it menaced France, her people, and her very soul. Conversely, when the
errors of French arms were redeemed by the triumph of French arms, the
French nation, people, and soul were saved.

This larger narrative fits the interpretation of the entire war as it was
delivered to the American people by President Woodrow Wilson: a cru-
sade to make the world safe for democracy and thus a war to end all wars.
In the century that has passed since the 1916 battle, many have dissented
from this view, but it was persuasive in April 1917 when President Wilson,
who eked out reelection in 1916 on the slogan "He kept us out of war,"
secured from Congress a declaration of war against the Central Powers.

Looking back on Verdun from today's perspective, the battle or battles seem to epitomize the war from start to finish—as a mass immolation that saved no one, settled nothing, and that, far from ending all wars,
created the very global conditions that made another world war almost
inevitable. For Wilson and for a majority of Americans in 1917, however,
Verdun was not a futile bloodletting but proof of France's determination to win at all costs and the likelihood that, without help, it would be
defeated nevertheless. The unparalleled barbarity of Verdun, a product of
the Old World, convinced the American president that only the principal
nation of the New World could finally alter the grim course of human
destiny. We are waiting, still.

ENDNOTES

Prologue

1 Jonathan Olley, "The Forbidden Forest," *Orion Magazine* (March 11, 2009), https://orionmagazine.org/article/the-forbidden-forest/.
2 George Seldes, *You Can't Print That! The Truth behind the News, 1918–1928* (Garden City, NY: Payson and Clarke, 1929), 24–37.
3 "Pyrrhus," in *Plutarch's Lives,* Project Gutenberg, www.gutenberg.org/files/674/674.txt.

Chapter 1

1 Frank H. Simonds, "The Battle for Verdun as France Saw It," *American Review of Reviews* 53 (1916): 566–67.
2 John Mosier, *Verdun: The Lost History of the Most Important Battle of World War I, 1914–1918* (New York: NAL Caliber, 2013), 331.
3 Micheal Clodfelter, *Warfare and Armed Conflicts: A Statistical Reference to Casualty and Other Figures, 1500–2000* (Jefferson, NC: McFarland, 2002), 444.
4 Information Division, U. S. Army Garrison, Verdun, "Battlefields of Verdun 1914–1918" (September 1962), 13.
5 Mosier, *Verdun: The Lost History,* 1.
6 Alistair Horne, *The Price of Glory: Verdun 1916* (1962; new edition, New York: Penguin, 1993), 1.
7 Simonds, "The Battle for Verdun as France Saw It," 566–67; Mosier, *Verdun: The Lost History,* 331.
8 William Philpott, *War of Attrition: Fighting the First World War* (New York: Overlook Press, 2014), 26.
9 For a discussion of the so-called Schlieffen myth, see Terence Zuber, *The Real German War Plan 1904–14* (New York: History Press, 2010).
10 Horne, *The Price of Glory,* 11.
11 Quoted in Alan Axelrod, *Miracle at Belleau Wood: The Birth of the Modern U. S. Marine Corps* (Guilford, CT: Lyons Press, 2007), xiii.
12 Mosier, *Verdun: The Lost History,* 12.
13 Mosier, *Verdun: The Lost History,* 13.
14 Mosier, *Verdun: The Lost History,* 169.
15 Horne, *The Price of Glory,* 42.
16 Horne, *The Price of Glory,* 50.
17 Simonds, 566.
18 The memoir, Erich von Falkenhayn, *Die Oberste Heersleitung 1914–1916 in ihren wichstigen Entschliessungen,* appeared in English translation as *General*

Headquarters, 1914–1916, and Its Critical Decisions (London: Hutchinson, 1919). Falkenhayn's rationalization of his decision to attack Verdun is well summarized in an unsigned review of the English edition published in the *Spectator,* December 27, 1919, 15, http://archive.spectator.co.uk/article/27th-december-1919/15/general-von-falkenhayns-memoirs-general-von-falken.

19 Erich von Falkenhayn, "Verdun," *Militär-Wochenblatt, Zeitschrift für die deutsche Wehrmacht* 104, no. 6 (July 12, 1919): 98–107.

20 Erich von Falkenhayn, "Christmas Memorandum" (December 1915), in *General Headquarters,* 176ff (emphasis added).

21 See Paul Jankowski, *Verdun: The Longest Battle of the Great War* (New York: Oxford University Press, 2013), 28, and Robert T. Foley, "A New Form of Warfare? Erich von Falkenhayn's Plan for Victory in 1916," www.academia.edu/4955145/_A_New_Form_of_Warfare_Erich_von_Falkenhayns_Plan_for_Victory_1916. As Foley (and others) point out, the writers of Germany's official postwar history of the Great War were never able to locate the Christmas Memorandum.

22 Barbara Tuchman, *The Guns of August* (1962; reprint ed., New York: Presidio Press, 1994).

23 Library of America, "How Barbara Tuchman's *The Guns of August* Influenced Decision Making during the Cuban Missile Crisis," *Reader's Almanac: The Official Blog of the Library of America,* http://blog.loa.org/2012/03/how-barbara-tuchmans-guns-of-august.html.

24 A. J. P. Taylor, *The First World War: An Illustrated History* (London: Hamish Hamilton, 1963), 94.

Chapter 2

1 Philpott, *War of Attrition,* 185.

2 William Manchester, *The Arms of Krupp 1587–1968* (Boston: Little, Brown, 1968), 121, 120.

3 "Artillery," in Spencer C. Tucker, ed., *The European Powers in the First World War: An Encyclopedia* (New York: Garland, 1996), 70–71.

4 "Artillery," *The European Powers,* 71.

5 "Artillery," *The European Powers,* 71.

6 Hogg quoted in "Artillery," *The European Powers,* 70.

7 Arthur F. Hurst, *Medical Diseases of the War* (London: Edward Arnold, 1918), chap. 21.

8 Horne, *The Price of Glory,* 285.

9 Horne, *The Price of Glory,* 286.

10 Horne, *The Price of Glory,* 286.

11 "Flamethrowers," in Tucker, ed., *The European Powers,* 255.

12 Horne, *The Price of Glory,* 13.

13 "Submarines," in Tucker, *The European Powers,* 664–66.

14 "Submarine Warfare, Central Powers," in Tucker, *The European Powers,* 671.

15 Philpott, *War of Attrition,* 180.

16 Kathleen Burk, *Britain, America and the Sinews of War, 1914–1918* (London: George Allen & Unwin, 1985), 5.
17 Charles Inman Bernard, *Paris War Days* (Boston: Little, Brown, 1914), 79–80.
18 Mosier, *Verdun: The Lost History*, 20
19 Mosier, *Verdun: The Lost History*, 21.
20 Alan Axelrod, *Political History of America's Wars* (Washington, D.C.: CQ Press, 2007), 358.

Chapter 3
1 Alfred Joubaire, quoted in Malcolm Brown, *Verdun 1916* (Stroud, UK: History Press, 2003), 55.
2 Joubaire, quoted in Brown, *Verdun 1916*, 55.
3 Joubaire, quoted in Brown, *Verdun 1916*, 56.
4 Jelle Peters, "Germany Had Already Lost World War I before It Began," *Jelle Peters: The Official Site*, http://jellepeters .com/16-new/56-germany-had-already-lost-world-war-i-before-it-began.
5 H. G. Wells, *War and the Future: Italy, France, and Britain at War* (London: Cassell, 1917), 16.
6 Mosier, *Verdun: The Lost History*, 198.
7 Horne, *The Price of Glory*, 30.
8 "Character Sketch of Joffre," reprinted in *Poverty Bay* (New Zealand) *Herald*, October 29, 1914, 3.
9 "Character Sketch of Joffre," 3.
10 "Character Sketch of Joffre," 3.
11 Quoted in Horne, *The Price of Glory*, 24.
12 Jankowski, *Verdun: The Longest Battle*, 53–54.

Chapter 4
1 Translated in Mosier, *Verdun: The Lost History*, 138.
2 Gabriel Bichet, *Le role des forts dans la Bataille de Verdun* (Nancy: Imprimerie Georges Thomas, 1969), 17–19, quoted in Mosier, *Verdun: The Lost History* 6.
3 Martin Samuels, *Doctrine and Dogma: German and British Infantry Tactics in the First World War* (Westport, CT: Greenwood Press, 1992), 52.
4 Heym quoted in George Herbert Perris, *The Battle of the Marne* (Boston: John Luce, 1920), 182–83.
5 Mosier, *Verdun: The Lost History*, 118.
6 Joseph Joffre's figures cited in Mosier, *Verdun: The Lost History*, 122.
7 Georges Boucheron, *L'Assaut: L'Argonne et Vauquois avec la 10e division* (Paris: Parin, 1917), 59–80, translated in Mosier, *Verdun: The Lost History*, 127–28.
8 André Pézard, *Nous autres à Vauquois* (Paris: La Renaissance du Livre, 1917), 63, translated in Mosier, *Verdun: The Lost History*, 131.
9 Translated in Mosier, *Verdun: The Lost History*, 138.

Chapter 5

1 The message of the German crown prince was acquired by French intelligence officers; it is quoted in Jankowski, *Verdun: The Longest Battle*, 53–54.
2 "Christmas Memorandum," quoted in Horne, *The Price of Glory*, 36. Emphasis added.
3 Crown Prince Wilhelm, *Memoirs of the Crown Prince of Germany* (1919; translated and reprinted, Uckfield, UK: Naval and Military Press, 2009), 177.
4 Kuhl's comments cited in Horne, *The Price of Glory*, 39.
5 Rupprecht's comments cited in Horne, *The Price of Glory*, 39.
6 Crown Prince Wilhelm, *Memoirs of the Crown Prince*, 177.
7 Horne, *The Price of Glory*, 43.

Chapter 6

1 Quoted in Jankowski, *Verdun: The Longest Battle*, 51.
2 Herr quoted in Horne, *The Price of Glory*, 51.
3 Herr to Galliéni, quoted in Horne, *The Price of Glory*, 51.
4 Joseph Simon Galliéni, *Les carnets de Galliéni* (Paris: Albin Michel, 1932), translated in Jankowski, *Verdun: The Longest Battle*, 53.
5 Joseph Joffre, letter to Galliéni, December 16 and 18, 1915, translated in Jankowski, *Verdun: The Longest Battle*, 53.
6 "Women in Print," *Evening Post* (Wellington, New Zealand), 89:70 (March 1915), 9; retrieved from http://paperspast.natlib.govt.nz/cgi-bin/paperspast?a=d&d =EP19150324.2.132.
7 Driant to Paul Deschanel, translated in Horne, *The Price of Glory*, 52.
8 Joffre to Poincaré, translated in Horne, *The Price of Glory*, 53.
9 Crown Prince Wilhelm quoted in Horne, *The Price of Glory*, 56.
10 Edward M. Strauss, trans., *Poilu: The World War I Notebooks of Corporal Louis Barthas, Barrelmaker, 1914–1918* (New Haven, CT: Yale University Press, 2014), 163.
11 Strauss, *Poilu: The World War I Notebooks*, 163.
12 Caroline Alexander, "Faces of War" (February 2007), *Smithsonian.com*, www.smithsonianmag.com/history/faces-of-war-145799854/#EBHLGA5tRmBoMC9A.99.
13 Strauss, *Poilu: The World War I Notebooks*, 43–44.
14 www.bl.uk/world-war-one/articles/the-daily-life-of-soldiers.
15 www.theguardian.com/world/2013/oct/01/france-first-world-war-soldiers -cowardice-executed-memorial; http://centenaire.org/sites/default/files/references -files/rapport_fusilles.pdf.
16 Driant, letter to his wife, translated in Horne, *The Price of Glory*, 68.
17 General Herr's battle orders, translated in Horne, *The Price of Glory*, 68.

Chapter 7

1 Émile Fayolle, *Carnets secrets de la grande guerre* (Paris: Plon, 1964), 28–29; translated in Mosier, *Verdun: The Lost History*, 241.
2 Corporal Stephane quoted in Horne, *The Price of Glory*, 71.

3   Denis Winter, *Death's Men: Soldiers of the Great War* (New York: Penguin, 1979), 115.
4   Winter, *Death's Men*, 116.
5   Winter, *Death's Men*, 118.
6   Winter, *Death's Men*, 117.
7   Horne, *The Price of Glory*, 76.

Chapter 8

1   Translated in Horne, *The Price of Glory*, 76.
2   Eyewitness remarks on the first day of the battle were collected and translated by Horne. Driant's inspirational speech is cited on p. 79.
3   Horne, *The Price of Glory*, 79.
4   Horne, *The Price of Glory*, 80.
5   Horne, *The Price of Glory*, 81.

Chapter 9

1   Translated in Horne, *The Price of Glory*, 88.
2   Translated in Horne, *The Price of Glory*, 81.
3   Translated in Horne, *The Price of Glory*, 87–88.
4   Translated in Horne, *The Price of Glory*, 88.
5   Translated in Horne, *The Price of Glory*, 89.

Chapter 10

1   Translated in Horne, *The Price of Glory*, 97.
2   Raymond Recouly, *Foch: Le Vainqueur de la Guerre* (Paris: Hachette, 1919), 121.
3   Translated in Horne, *The Price of Glory*, 97.
4   Horne, *The Price of Glory*, 98.
5   Horne, *The Price of Glory*, 98.

Chapter 11

1   Fernand Marie Albert Chaligne, *Histoire militaire de Verdun* (Paris: Charle-Lavauzelle, 1939), 167; translated in Mosier, *Verdun: The Lost History*, 252.
2   Chaligne, *Histoire militaire de Verdun*, 167.
3   John Terraine, *The Great War, 1914–1918* (New York: Macmillan, 1965), 208.
4   Mosier, *Verdun: The Lost History*, 254.
5   Mosier, *Verdun: The Lost History*, 259.

Chapter 12

1   Yves Buffetaut, *La bataille de Verdun, de l'Argonne a la Woëvre* (Tours: Éditions Heimdale, 1990), 63, cited and translated in Mosier, *Verdun: The Lost History*, 263.
2   Quoted in Horne, *The Price of Glory*, 116.

3   Robert E. Duchesneau, "The Forts of Verdun," www.oocities.org/pentagon/base/
    3495/FVerdun1a.html.
4   Buffetaut, 63, cited in Mosier, *Verdun: The Lost History,* 263.
5   Buffetaut, 63, cited in Mosier, *Verdun: The Lost History,* 263.
6   Buffetaut, 63, cited in Mosier, *Verdun: The Lost History,* 263.
7   Galliéni, *Les carnets de Galliéni,* 273, translated and cited in Mosier, *Verdun: The Lost
    History,* 269.
8   Raymond Poincaré, *Au service de la France* (Paris: Plon, 1931), 7:143, translated and
    cited in Mosier, *Verdun: The Lost History,* 270.
9   Poincaré, *Au service de la France,* 7:143, translated and cited in Mosier, *Verdun: The
    Lost History,* 270.
10 Mosier, *Verdun: The Lost History,* 271.
11 Wehrmacht-Awards.com, www.wehrmacht-awards.com/forums/showthread
    .php?t=478486.
12 Horne, *The Price of Glory,* 143–44.

Chapter 13

1   Charles de Gaulle, *France and Her Army* (1938; Charleston, SC: Nabu Press,
    2010), 32.
2   Raymond Recouly, *Foch: Le Vainqueur de la Guerre* (Paris: Hachette, 1919), 121.
3   De Gaulle, 32.
4   Pétain quoted in Horne, *The Price of Glory,* 138.
5   Quoted in John Terraine, *The Great War* (1965; reprint ed., Ware, UK: Wordsworth
    Editions, 1997), 143.
6   Pétain quoted in Michael Carver, *The Warlords* (1976; reprint ed., Barnsley, UK: Pen
    & Sword, 2005), 62.
7   Pétain quoted in Horne, *The Price of Glory,* 144–45.
8   Pétain quoted in Horne, *The Price of Glory,* 145.
9   Horne, *The Price of Glory,* 148.
10 Horne, *The Price of Glory,* 148.

Chapter 14

1   Quoted in *Grenadier Regiment 916 (NE),* https://groups.yahoo.com/neo/groups/
    Grenadier-Regiment916_NorthEast/conversations/topics/935.
2   Franz Marc quoted in Horne, *The Price of Glory,* 150.
3   Crown Prince Rupprecht quoted in Horne, *The Price of Glory,* 156.
4   Measurements cited in John Mosier, *Verdun: The Lost History,* 272.
5   Pétain quoted in Horne, *The Price of Glory,* 156–57.
6   Joffre "Order of the Day" translated in Horne, *The Price of Glory,* 160.
7   Henry Dugard, *The Battle of Verdun (February 21–May 7)* (New York: Dodd, Mead,
    1917), 188–89.
8   Dugard, *The Battle of Verdun,* 190.
9   Quoted in Horne, *The Price of Glory,* 159.

Chapter 15

1 Kaiser Wilhelm II quoted in Horne, *The Price of Glory*, 165.
2 Dugard, *The Battle of Verdun*, 191
3 Dugard, *The Battle of Verdun*, 191.
4 Dugard, *The Battle of Verdun*, 191–92.
5 Quoted in Horne, *The Price of Glory*, 164, and Dugard, *The Battle of Verdun*, 197.
6 Horne, *The Price of Glory*, 166.
7 Horne, *The Price of Glory*, 171.
8 Horne, *The Price of Glory*, 171.
9 Mosier, *Verdun: The Lost History*, 285.
10 Charles Mangin quoted in Jonathan Krause, "'Only Inaction Is Disgraceful': French Operations under Joffre, 1914–1916," in *The Greater War: Other Combatants and Other Fronts, 1914–1918*, edited by Jonathan Krause (New York: Palgrave Macmillan, 2014), 27.

Chapter 16

1 Charles Mangin quoted in Krause, "'Only Inaction Is Disgraceful,'" 27.
2 Sylvain-Eugene Raynal quoted in Horne, *The Price of Glory*, 258.
3 Robert Nivelle quoted in Horne, *The Price of Glory*, 265.
4 Quoted in Horne, *The Price of Glory*, 265.
5 Quoted in Horne, *The Price of Glory*, 266.
6 Marcel Bechu quoted in Horne, *The Price of Glory*, 285.
7 Marcel Bechu quoted in Horne, *The Price of Glory*, 286.

Chapter 17

1 Paul von Hindenburg, *Out of My Life* (1921; reprint, n.p.: Pickle Partners, 2013; Kindle ed., vol. 1, chap. 6.
2 Elizabeth Greenhalgh, *The French Army and the First World War* (London: Cambridge University Press, 2014), 143.
3 Crown Prince Wilhelm, *Memoirs of the Crown Prince*, 181.
4 Crown Prince Wilhelm, *Memoirs of the Crown Prince*.
5 Fritz Fischer, *Germany's Aims in the First World War* (New York: W. W. Norton, 1968), 76.
6 Kaiser Wilhelm II quoted in David Allen Butler, *The Burden of Guilt: How Germany Shattered the Last Days of Peace, Summer 1914* (Havertown, PA: Casemate, 2010), 103.
7 Hindenburg, *Out of My Life.*, vol. 1, chap. 6.
8 Pierre Chaine quoted in Horne, *The Price of Glory*, 306.

Chapter 18

1 Hindenburg, *Out of My Life*, vol. 1, chap. 6.
2 Hindenburg, *Out of My Life*, vol. 1, chap. 6.

3 Hindenburg, *Out of My Life*, vol. 1, chap. 6.
4 Hindenburg, *Out of My Life*, vol. 1, chap. 6.
5 Hindenburg, *Out of My Life*, vol. 1, chap. 6.
6 Hindenburg, *Out of My Life*, vol. 1, chap. 6.
7 Will Durant and Ariel Durant, *The Story of Civilization, vol. 10* (New York: Simon and Schuster, 1967), 50.

Epilogue

1 James R. Chrislip, "'Firepower Kills': The Evolution of French Infantry Tactics at Verdun," *Voces Novae: Chapman University Historical Review* 4, no. 1 (2012), http://journals.chapman.edu/ojs/index.php/VocesNovae/article/view/334/711.
2 Mosier, *Verdun: The Lost History*.

INDEX